THE REGULATORY COMPLIANCE MATRIX

Regulation of Financial Services, Information and Communication Technology, and Generally Related Matters

Guido Reinke

London – Brussels – New York
GOLD RUSH Publishing 2015

GOLD RUSH Publishing

*Government's view of the economy could be summed up in a
few short phrases:
If it moves, tax it.
If it keeps moving, regulate it.
And if it stops moving, subsidize it.*

Ronald Reagan, 40th President of the United States
(1911-2004)

PREFACE

This book is one of the few books on the market that have seriously attempted to demystify regulatory compliance. The European regulatory environment is challenging and is frequently characterised with attributes like complexity, dynamism and multiple levels of governance. Even for many professional practitioners, regulatory compliance is uncharted territory – too many people really do not know where to start and what exactly is needed to avoid the dread notice 'non-compliant'.

One reason for this uncertainty is all too simple: little or no effort has ever been made to organise comprehensively all of the laws and regulations that businesses and other organisations are obligated to comply with. The legal publications abound which focus on specific aspects such as tax law, Internet law or corporate governance; however, a publication that provides practical help for scoping and overviewing all the regulations that all organisations should watch out for is rare. What is needed most is a structured compendium of the laws, regulations and norms which are applicable to entities doing business in Europe. But in addition to norms applicable to all organisations, this guide also categorises those which apply more specifically to the Financial Services and Information and Communications Technology sectors (as well as to the IT department of companies in any sector).

This guide was not written in a day. It is based on more than 15 years of the author's own research, stakeholder participation, experience in drafting compliance guidelines for industry associations, working with regulators at European and national level, and the hands-on practice of conducting regulatory compliance audits and implementing compliance frameworks. The author has worked for the European Commission's Information Society Directorate General in Brussels, for regulated industries, and at Big Four professional services firms; and has been involved in all aspects and phases of the regulatory lifecycle – from issue emergence and policy initiation to implementation and retrospective evaluation. The approach presented in this book is anything but one-dimensional.

The author of this book is on a mission – *to contribute to better understanding of regulation and the process by which regulations are made, and to provide practitioners with useful tools to assist them with their compliance efforts.* In this sense, I hope readers will find the following publication useful for their daily work in the regulatory minefield, and effectual in making their working life easier, so that never again will the *regulatory beast* prowling about keep them awake at night.

ACKNOWLEDGEMENTS

I am grateful to all the Chief Compliance Officers, legal counsel, Chief Operating Officers, Chief Risk Officers, and senior managers who have been telling me for years how dynamic, complex and mystifying the legal and regulatory landscape that directly affects them is. I also learned that the regulators themselves rarely have *a simple answer*. But for this baffling state of affairs, there would have been little need to publish such a guide.

I would like to extend my gratitude to all my professional colleagues that I have met on the journey toward compiling this Regulatory Compliance Matrix, a precursor of which I have published previously in my book *Industry Governance and Regulatory Compliance*.

I am also thankful for the intellectual stimulation of Jerry W. Bains, whose legal background in particular helped me to understand the multi-dimensional complexity of the legal landscape. His sharp pen saved me from embarrassing typographical and grammatical errors.

Above all, I am thankful for all my friends and family who have supported and encouraged me, particularly in dark moments when I feared I was drowning in the deluge of laws and regulations. This book is dedicated to them, and to all who have supported me in my efforts to make regulation more understandable, giving me their advice, but more importantly, their encouragement and their enthusiasm.

Guido Reinke

TABLE OF CONTENTS

LIST OF FIGURES

INTRODUCTION

Many are the books that have been dedicated to this aspect or that of the myriad policy domains, to specific legal and regulatory issues, and especially to the fields of risk management and assurance, without, however, attempting comprehensiveness. Industry associations and regulatory authorities try from time to time to fill the gaps in regulatees' comprehension by publishing "how to" guides aimed at assisting them with selected regulations. What is missing is a comprehensive approach to guidance that encompasses both knowledge and practice, both a matrix index of all applicable norms (within scope) as well as tools for compliance that practitioners can put to use immediately. These tools should help organisations save money and time in the effort to raise their organisations' regulatory maturity level.

Of all the tools in this book, the Regulatory Compliance Matrix is the most important, because it solves the thorniest issue in regulatory compliance – the scoping of compliance programmes. Identifying the relevant regulations at the very beginning of a compliance programme not only avoids non-compliance, but also enables regulations to be categorised for batching and tackling as a unit, enabling significant time and costs to be saved.

This introduction Chapter sets the scene. Most of this book reads like a "regulatory directory", therefore the first order of business must be to establish a consistent understanding of how readers can apply this guide: what regulatory compliance is, what the consequences are of non-compliance, and what greater efficiency requires. Especially if you are an expert in the field, you may become fascinated by certain sections. If you jump straight to the core chapters, you could miss some important aspects to consider when leading regulatory compliance programmes.

A. What regulatory compliance is and how it is defined

Regulatory compliance is a multi-disciplinary process governing organisations' adherence to laws and regulations. These originate with supra-national or national authorities, but may in the first instance be enforced through policies, procedures and processes internal to organisations with the legal obligation to comply. Most business organisations develop compliance frameworks compounded of "tools", which may be generally accepted industry standards, frameworks (often developed by industry associations), and guidance published by regulators and other authorities. Reliance on such ready-made resources often reduces the risks of non-compliance, which include losses of money, reputation, and even legal rights, e.g. through loss of the licence to do business, leading to a complete collapse of the organisation.[1]

B. What are the costs of non-compliance?

One question which is bound to be uppermost in the minds of regulatory compliance specialists and general managers alike is *"What are the costs of non-compliance?"* or *"What happens if we do nothing?"* It sometimes happens that the cost of breaching a regulation is less than the cost of complying with it; at least, it may seem so from afar. EU Member States implement European law inconsistently, and in addition, the enforcement powers of their regulatory authorities vary. Hence both their norms and the penalties for breaching them vary. In practical terms, this means that the fines organisations may have to pay for the same breach differ widely from state to state, even under "EU law". And this does not even take account of the much wider differences in strictly domestic laws and regulations. Thus, a general answer to this question cannot be provided, nor an actual cost pre-calculated for particular cases.

It should also be noted that the penalties and sanctions imposed by national regulators change over time as well. This happens in part because public and consumer perception of the scandalousness of non-compliance changes. Other factors like pressure from lobbies and political parties may lead to regulatory changes as well. For this reason, organisations would indeed be remiss if they do not perform an annual risk assessment covering all of their key liabilities. They need to review each category presented in the Regulatory Compliance Matrix to rate their risk for "compliance failure". But, in addition to the costs that individual firms may incur, practitioners would be well advised to consider the long-term, systemic impact that their own (not just others') non-compliance may have on the whole industry. Costs which are not internalised, but assumed to be external ("somebody else's problem") may well return to the short-sighted firm in the form of a whole new (and much stricter) regulatory regime.

Provided below is in essence a "checklist" in aid of organisations trying to make such a risk assessment and weigh up the costs of non-compliance. Costs incurred by the individual organisation are listed ahead of costs systemic to the whole industry. For all regulatory categories, the costs of non-compliance can be broken down into the following domains and sub-areas[2]:

1. Financial penalties
2. Operational costs

---

1   For a detailed list of costs of non-compliance, please see following section.

2   For comparison's sake see also "The rising costs of non-compliance: From the end of a career to the end of a firm", an article by Stacey English and Susannah Hammond (2014) on Thompson Reuters Accelus.

3. Personal implications

4. Regulatory consequences

Part A: Costs for the individuals or single organisations

(1)   Financial penalties

(a)   *Fines and repayments*: Organisations that do not comply with regulations are subject to pecuniary fines. In addition, in the UK at least, the FCA (the financial regulator) has exacted restitution in the form of organisations *paying back* their customers who were charged for services not specifically consented to, such as payment protection insurance (PPI). And more and more, regulators are seen to require utilities companies to pay back customers whom they overcharged. All such repayments, restitutions and refunds are of course additional costs for organisations.

(b)   *Loss of licence and service offering*: If the firm loses its licence to undertake regulated business on a temporary or permanent basis, this means that its services must be either suspended or stopped. The actuality or just the possibility of fines may also lead to the strategic decision to abandon services under high regulatory scrutiny and thus of high risk. The risks associated with operating in these markets may outweigh the profits.

(c)   *Decrease of the firm's share price*: Of utmost importance for senior management in publicly listed companies is to create shareholder value. The board is accountable to its shareholders. If due to financial penalties, reputational loss or other factors the share price drops, this will have a direct impact on the shareholders, who may choose to disinvest (a double-whammy for the organisation).

(d)   *Reduction in competitiveness*: Acts of non-compliance entail risks of failure which are factored into regulators' assessments of the supervisory protocols that they impose on individual organisations. This is an extraordinary burden that can easily put a firm at a competitive disadvantage. On the other end of the spectrum, scandals over treating customers unfairly, and misconduct-related fines (*e.g.* for mis-selling of products), negatively impact reputation and goodwill. Organisations that cannot show compliance may not be able to avoid a negative press, which is itself a source of competitive disadvantage.

(e)   *Opportunity cost of "doing nothing (or doing less)"*: The repercussions and disruption caused by compliance failures can be enormous. Instead of concentrating on business growth, organisations in the hotseat are obliged to respond to regulators, to plan and implement compliance programmes in haste, and to get up to speed quickly to make sure that the changes work effectively. Heightened scrutiny by regulators and a negative press can lead to widespread uncertainty on all organisational levels. For example, a given financial institution may be obliged to increase liquidity or capital under the EU's Capital Requirements Directive (CRD) and Capital Requirements Regulation (CRR), which is the EU's implementation of the Basel III Accords. A higher risk index entails a higher capital requirement, tying up financial assets that might have been invested in productive enterprise.

(f)   *Loss of suppliers*: The impact of regulatory enforcement actions can damage relationships not only with investors but also suppliers. Most organisations have strict procedures "onboarding" new suppliers. Larger organisations have preferred supplier lists, but suppliers too may decline to do business with organisations that they fear may fail in the foreseeable future.

(2)   Operational costs

(g)   *Expensive, lengthy remediation or mitigation programmes to address non-compliance issues*: To revise existing controls (*remediation*) or devise new controls (*mitigation*) to compensate deficiencies in preventing or detecting control failures is not only expensive, but can also distract the organisation from focussing on its core business functions. Belated compliance requires immediate hiring of new permanent staff and contractors; training existing staff; compensating customers; plus legal costs. It is estimated that the UK banking sector has had to set aside more than £24bn for the mis-selling of payment protection insurance (PPI). The financial ombudsman has said, "[A]lthough numbers are slowly declining, it will be years before we can truly say this mis-selling scandal is over" (FT, January 2015). Uncertainty about the regulator's reaction is clearly one of the biggest worries organisations face, and lax, non-proactive compliance will only compound this uncertainty.

(h)   *Repercussions of enforced changes on business*: Enforcement actions may order businesses to suspend products or services until the non-compliance has been resolved. Complex remediation or mitigation may require overhaul of systems and controls, with the retraining of staff that that entails, and even a complete withdraw of products.

(i)   *Costs to third parties and investment in own staff*: Regulators often require that investigations into potential breaches or other non-compliance issues are conducted by independent third-parties. The FCA, the UK's financial regulator, has confirmed that in fiscal year 2013-14 (ending 31 March 2014), its Section 166 (Skilled Person) power was used in 50 cases at an estimated cost of £145.7m to the affected businesses. In total, 18 professional audit, law and consultancy firms have been appointed by FCA to perform this work (FCA: 2014). Their fees are the non-compliant organisations' loss.

(j) *Loss of licence to operate*: Regulators issue and renew licences to do business in highly regulated industries. Examples include financial services; utilities (*viz.* gas, electricity and water companies); airlines; and pharmaceutical companies. In addition, individual employees with certain job functions must either operate under their company's licence, approved by the relevant regulators, or qualify for a licence of their own. Examples of the former include company licences to deal in financial services, external audits and many utilities. Examples of the latter include financial advisors, pilots, and doctors. If an organisation or individual loses a licence due to non-compliance, they will be obligated to quit offering their services altogether.

(k) *Increasing complexity of control deficiencies*: In the past, many compliance failures were relatively easy to fix (*e.g.* a failing system control led to a data breach). Today the regulatory focus has shifted to organisational governance and conduct. In the UK an example of this evolution is called Treating Customers Fairly, a principle-based framework which penalises unethical final outcomes, not just breaches of formal legal rules. Such compliance failures are much more complex, as typically the whole organisation is involved. In addition to fixing emergent problems, long-term training and awareness programmes are needed to drive behavioural and indeed cultural changes in the whole organisation.

(3) Personal implications

(l) *Increased legal and personal liability, including dismissal, loss of licence and imprisonment:* Senior managers can now be made personally responsible for the failure of their business organisations. In 2013 for the first time ever, the UK Financial Conduct Authority sanctioned more individuals than organisations in the financial services sector. The punishments imposed on senior management are driving behaviour changes. Thus for example, the Financial Stability Board has drafted detailed descriptions of the duties of key organisational functionaries, such as CEO, chief risk officer, and internal auditor, in their "Principles for an effective risk appetite framework". Organisations are required to undertake comprehensive compliance programmes to ensure that these functionaries meet the FSB's (and others') minimum standards. Often, independent third parties must conduct these reviews, which cost hundreds of thousands of euros (or pounds). Serious offences like bribery and corruption can lead to lengthy jail sentences. A criminal conviction will make employment in highly regulated industries difficult, if not impossible. Even if the consequences are not so harsh, senior executives may be "named and shamed" or be forced to resign in consequence of an enforcement action.

(m) *Enforced staff changes (in particular to senior management)*: Non-compliance can have serious extra-legal consequences for senior management, which may include dismissals, demotions, transfers and pay cuts. Oftentimes, criminal fines and civil settlements force the resignations of senior staff under pressures both internal and external to the organisation. The organisation itself then suffers the loss of valuable experience and insights not only in the orgnisation's core business but also in the investigation and prevention of further non-compliance.

(4) Regulatory consequences

(n) *Additional expensive reporting requirements:* New regulations are almost always accompanied by new reporting requirements. This may requires not only high frequency reporting, sometimes even daily, but also high volumes of data to be provided to regulators, also often on a daily basis. This is because transaction reports may reveal market abuse and manipulation amid securities financing transactions and primary market transactions (such as issuance, allotment or subscription) in shares and bonds.

Some regulators with Europe-wide or global reach have been mandated to introduce far-reaching reporting standards. For example, the European Banking Authority (EBA) has played a key role in the implementation of CRD IV (the Capital Requirement Directive)/ CRR (the Capital Requirement Regulation) (also referred to as Basel III) framework in the EU. The EBA produced a set of Binding Technical Standards (BTS), Guidelines and reports, including reporting templates. The templates are complex and comprehensive, and demand information on thousands of items[3]. Some templates are so complex that no one person in the regulatory agency itself would be able to complete them. And then, requests for clarification are answered by nothing

---

3   CRD reporting requirements cover own funds and leverage; large exposure; net stable funding; liquidity coverage ratio; financial reporting; capital ratios and Pillar II adjustments. reductions for significant investments; balance sheet; income statement; market risk; building society liquidity; forecast data from firms; sectoral information; solo consolidated data; interest rate gap report; large exposure; IRB portfolio risk, daily flows; enhanced mismatch report; liquidity buffer quantifying securities; funding concentration; pricing data; retail, SME and large enterprises; currency analysis and prudent valuation. (Bank of England website at http://www.bankofengland.co.uk/pra/Pages/regulatorydata/formscrdfirms.aspx (January 2015) and EBA website at http://www.eba.europa.eu/regulation-and-policy/supervisory-reporting/implementing-technical-standard-on-supervisory-reporting-data-point-model- (January 2015)).

better than a centralised helpdesk. This obliges businesses to bring in, at great cost, external experts who have helped other organisations with similar reporting requirements in order to set up the reporting operation and help complete the templates.

Part B: Systemic costs for the whole industry

(1) Financial penalties

(a) *Increase of fines:* The 2009 credit crunch precipitated an unprecedented number of bankruptcies and taxpayer bailouts of well-known and (thitherto) respected companies. In hopes of re-building consumer and investor confidence, new regulations were introduced concerning corporate governance and related issues, with significant fines attached to non-compliance. In the past, when the fines were more moderate, they were sometimes perceived as nothing but "a cost of doing business". The new and much heavier fines are designed to hurt and thus to drive positive change.

(b) *Stricter and more costly licencing requirements*: For example, without a licence, organisations in highly regulated industries are unable to operate. Governments lay out specific requirements and impose costs for licenses. For example, European telecoms operators paid €109 billion in licence fees in the UMTS/IMT-2000 License Auctions for spectrum allocations. Indeed, many telecoms operators have been struggling under the financial burden, given also their infrastructure investment expenditures for 3G services, estimated to have fallen within the range of €148-224 billion by 2010 (McKinsey & Company, 2002). The licencing fees are already so high, so that any further increase in the overall burden of getting licenced would be bound to result in numerous business failures and in prohibitively high costs to new market entrants.

(c) *Decrease of shareholder value*: Although it is difficult to find clear evidence of a correlation between the burden of regulation and share prices, rumours of compliance failures and significant fines may lead to the public perception of an "unquantifiable risk" that causes a drop in share prices. In the aftermath of the 2009 credit crunch, share prices took longer to recover due to enforced restructuring by regulators (*e.g.* the splitting up of retail and wholesale banking in the UK). . For example, the share prices of the Big Four banks in the UK, and of Deutsche Bank and Commerzbank in Germany, have not recovered to the level they were before the financial crisis as at the date of this writing.

(d) *Increase of capital, liquidity and solvency requirements:* Due to severe compliance failures in the past, regulators are now enforcing a stricter regime of "capital reserves" for financial institutions. Improvements in balance sheets through an increase of provision for eventual losses do not come for free. This means that financial institutes have less capital to invest in their core business. Banks and insurance companies in particular are effected by Basel III (or Third Basel Accord) and, in Europe, by the Solvency II Directive, respectively.

(2) Operational costs

(e) *Expensive, lengthy remediation or mitigation programmes may lead to additional charges for customers:* If non-compliance costs, both penal and reputational, become excessive, this may affect the whole industry and its customer base. For example, the UK banking industry's reputation for probity was tarnished by the PPI scandal, when payment protection insurance was sold to unwitting customers "by default". As the repercussions mounted, the industry faced not only the high cost of penalties but also a loss of public trust, which may have led and might still lead to noticeably more resistance by all customers (not just those personally harmed by PPI) to the industry's marketing efforts. As deeper distrust by customers erodes their willingness to pay for any extra services, the cumulative loss of income to banks might well force them to start charging for basic services like cash withdrawals. [4]

(f) *Insufficient skilled staff availability externally or in-house*: To find compliance-and-risk staff with relevant experience has become more difficult for the industry as a whole. Added to this are higher recruiting costs to hire staff experienced and skilled enough to "keep firms out of trouble".

(3) Personal implications

(g) *Enforced reduction of bonuses*: As individuals at all management levels are held increasingly accountable for lower performance or non-compliance, bonuses may be reduced or in extreme cases eliminated. The European Banking Authority (EBA) published an opinion in 2014 that the "variable component shall not exceed 100% of the fixed component of the total remuneration (200% with shareholders' approval)" (EBA, 2014). As the EBA opinion was not in line with the employment contracts of some high-flying executives and traders, this sparked outrage in certain circles.

---

4   This is a real threat. In general, regulatory costs create a Hobson's choice: in banking, this means either cut operational costs or increase revenues by charging more for banking services. As cost cuts can are achievable only medium- or long-term, charging for services must be the first option. By long custom personal banking in the UK is free of charge: customers can withdraw money from big-bank cash machines gratis. As in many other countries, however, UK banks are reaching the point where they may have to abolish "free banking" if compliance costs continue to increase.

(4)   Regulatory consequences

(h)   *Revisionary, more far-reaching regulations*: Before 2009, the UK financial services regulator in particular took a "soft" approach to regulating the industry so as to attract more business to London. As long as the industry created revenue for the government and value for customers, "everything" was allowed which was not expressly forbidden. Only when things turned sour with the credit crunch in 2009 and stakeholders lost billions, and governments had to bail out the financial services industry to prevent a complete collapse of critical banks, were regulators forced to take a stricter approach. A plethora of new regulations were introduced, many of which had global implications, as the financial marketplace has no boundaries any more. Along with this, new guidance, standards, rulebooks, opinions and other materials were produced to assist financial institutions with implementation. New laws and various changes to existing ones, often without any clear indication whether or when these would be enacted or in what time-frame they would have to be implemented, brought about widespread uncertainty in many industry sectors.

(i)   *More scrutiny by regulatory authorities*: Nowadays, when regulators detect or even suspect non-compliance, they may impose additional and more frequent reporting requirements, which may lead to overlapping requests for information from multiple regulators. More frequent inspections – some on very short notice – are also a risk. All of this causes greater distraction for senior management from the running of paying business. When financial regulators around the globe discovered widespread benchmarks-rigging (in a widely "self-regulated" market), they started investigating the London Interbank market over its Offered Rates (LIBOR, the fundamental global interest rate benchmark), as well as foreign exchange (FX), gold, silver, oil and other benchmark rates. The FCA "along with authorities in the US and Switzerland, levied fines worth £2.7bn on six banks, including two British ones [RBS and HSBC], in what is a record financial punishment for the British regulator" (*The Telegraph*, January 2015).

(j)   *Requirement for expensive and specialised compliance skills*: Since 2010 firms have had to invest heavily in risk and compliance capacity as a result of the heavier regulation brought about by previous non-compliance. Due to the mounting workload, there is now a high demand for these skills, which cover remediation of control and conduct failures, management of regulatory changes, management of internal and external stakeholders, and monitoring and reporting. The FT has reported that a "shortage of qualified compliance staff in the banking and asset management industry has sparked a surge in salaries as groups struggle to cope with the flood of new regulations coming into force after the financial crisis" (FT, 27 October 2013). According to Astbury Marsden, in 2014 the average salary for compliance functions was £87,292 – up by 12.5% from £77,567 in 2013, – but for risk and governance functions it was £96,630 – down by 14.7% from £113,278 in 2013 (Astbury Marsden, 2014:p10). This shows that more technical staff that has a good understanding of the new regulatory regime has become more highly valued than the staff that only deals with broad risk and governance issues that existed under the old regulatory regime.

Even so basic a list as this demonstrates that it is impossible to add up a simple price tag for "non-compliance". Even if some organisations do nothing – either deliberately or because they are unaware of all the specific requirements – in the long term non-compliance will jeopardise their ability to stay in business. It is of the essence, then, to make risk assessments based on multi-dimensional criteria (as in the above list) in order to assure that senior management have all the information necessary to make *fully* informed decisions.

C. The myth: Regulation is complicated

Practitioners in the field of regulatory compliance and risk management often feel overwhelmed by the apparently bottomless complexity of the multi-level governance structures in Europe. Multi-national and large business organisations rely on the rare skills of their Risk & Compliance departments, General Counsels and external professional advice to guide them through the maze of laws and regulations, yet despite all these resources and efforts thrown up against the regulatory tsunami of multiple regulators and their enforcement agencies, costs are still getting out of control. According to the *Financial Times*, "Wall Street banks and their foreign rivals have paid out $100bn in US legal settlements since the financial crisis [started in 2009 up until 2015]" (McGregor and Stanley, 2014). Fines and repayments peaked in the UK in the fourth quarter of 2014, when the Financial Conduct Authority (FCA) exacted more than £1,164m from the financial services industry, which is more than 40% of the fines, overall, imposed by its predeccessor (the Financial Services Authority) and itself since 2002 put together.

Most small and medium-sized organisations (SMEs) are less regulated; however, due to lack of resources, they are even more confused about what to do. Changes to company law, or taxation and data privacy laws often require them to hire external advice. This uncertainty and constraint on funds that could have been invested elsewhere at greater profit are a big distraction to SMEs. The risks can be high, but often SMEs are unaware of this until they feel the impact.

Does the answer lie with professional service firms that provide legal, regulatory, tax and other advice? What they usually tell organisations is that the regulatory landscape has become so complex, dynamic and multi-level that there is no simple answer. The first big wave of regulation to hit organisations listed on the American stock exchange was the Sarbanes-Oxley Act (SOx) in 2002. Professional services advice was sought in particular by public-listed companies. A few years later, SOx had been "commoditised" and the fees dried up for professional service firms. But thanks to legislators who worked tirelessly to make sure that new regulations are passed, often long after the fact, professional services firms were able to extend their services helping organisations with yet newer governance regulations (*e.g.* the EU's Capital Requirements Regulation and Directive); complex tax liabilities (*e.g.* in the Electronic Commerce space); and new consumer rights (*e.g.* Treating Customers Fairly). Of course, there is no simple answer to this that professional service firms could provide organisations.

If practitioners working for the industry and professional service firms do not have all the answers about how to avoid compliance failures and their often dire consequences, then who does have the answer? Surely, law enforcement agencies (*a.k.a.* the independent regulatory authorities) ought to be able to provide some advice.

At the global, European and national levels various authorities do produce standards and guidance to assist business organisations; however, many of these authorities have only a very restricted outlook on what has been done by other authorities. Traditionally, regulators are more focussed on enforcing the regulations in their specific domain or jurisdiction than on trying to see the bigger regulatory picture. Although this attitude has been slowly changing in recent years and regulators are now reaching out to other regulators from independent agencies or operate on a different level of governance, no regulators yet have a full picture of the complexity and range of regulations that organisations need to comply with. Often regulators are too busy attending the committees, workshops and meetings of other authorities, which may help them with their own understanding of how their regulatory agenda fits into the wider landscape, and allow them to adjust their sometimes conflicting regulatory demands, but which still does nothing for regulatees struggling with compliance with the multitude of regulations.

As evidenced in the book *Industry Governance and Regulatory Compliance* (*q.v.*), industry plays a pro-active role "in the new consultative governance of the regulatory regime, resulting in industry's predominating influence in shaping public policies, regulations and standards, in order to achieve the business objectives of enhanced innovation, competitiveness and consumer satisfaction" (Reinke, 2009:11). Industry obviously has an interest in good regulation; however, their involvement often is confined to subject-matter expertise, and contains little *strategic* advice. As regulation is not their core business, they may be key stakeholders but are not ultimately responsible for the regulatory outcome or the volume of regulation.

Surely, then, the combined knowledge of industry associations which develop industry frameworks and guidance (*e.g.* Cobit) should have the answer, right? These associations, however, depend on their members – whether individual professionals or business organisations – who have too limited resources to cover the whole regulatory landscape. Obliged to prioritise their concerns, many of their frameworks are either too generic or too specific to be applicable across multiple regulations and jurisdictions.

There is no simple answer to the question of which are all of the regulations that business organisations must comply with, or how they can most efficiently achieve compliance. And it would seem that most peripheral stakeholders are quite happy with this *status quo*: professionals of every description find full employment – as permanent staff or as contractors – in the regulatory compliance minefield. Professional service firms remain permanently in demand to provide salvation from the never-ending pain. Business associations engage with their members to come up with yet more endorsed and agreed frameworks. Regulators engage in power plays and enjoy endless conferences and ongoing policy-refreshments.

So who are the losers? Do not the industry and consumers have to pay for all this in the end? Certainly, if we deem most regulations "good regulation", then everybody should benefit from a rigorous regulatory framework. If the regulation can reduce bankruptcies and collapses, fraud, waste, abuse and inefficiency, and improve customer satisfaction and boost commerce to boot, then industry benefits as well. The important thing is for the costs not to outweigh the benefits. This is one reason why regulators are obligated to conduct Regulatory Impact Assessments (Reinke, 2012:60-66). There is no guarantee, however, that they will always get it right.

In sum, regulatory compliance can be made simpler, but there are interests that would like to keep things obscure and recondite, as they benefit from this. The present guide was written so as to make a contribution toward easier regulatory compliance.

D. How can the Regulatory Compliance Matrix help?

The Regulatory Compliance Matrix featured in this book is a compendious inventory of regulations currently in force and applicable to the industry. It maps the principal domains of legislation, regulation and legal norms, and their content, together with all ancillary standards, frameworks and guidance. This Matrix is not the sole answer to all compliance issues, but it is the best first step of a successful compliance programme and helps to define priorities and scope.

The Matrix provides international and European as well as UK legal obligations and standards applicable to the financial services (FS) and the information and communication technology (ICTs) industries in particular, as well as generally applicable supplemental norms, at the time of publication. PART I of the Matrix covers laws, regulations and norms specific to the FS industry (applying to banking and insurance). PART II covers laws, regulations and norms specific to the ICT sector (applying not only to the ICT industry as such, but also to IT departments across all industries). PART III covers laws, regulations and norms generally applicable to all industrial sectors, but highly pertinent to FS and ICT in particular. Specific regulations and laws for sub-categories of these major divisions have been identified, and mapped against technical standards, frameworks and guidance. The following diagram illustrates the concept.

Figure 1: Regulatory Compliance Matrix

	LAWS, REGULATIONS and NORMS	STANDARDS, FRAMEWORKS and GUIDANCE
FS SPECIFIC	1. Regulatory Agencies 2. General Regulations 3. Financial Crime and Consumer Protection 4. Retail banking 5. Investment banking 6. Insurance 7. Pensions	- Standards defined and guidance issued by international organisations - Standards defined by standardisation institutes and guidance issued by supervisory authorities at European level - Standards defined by standardisation institutes and guidance issued by regulatory agencies at national level - Technical standards defined by the FS industry and its industry associations - Compliance frameworks developed within industry - Policies, procedures, processes and principles implemented by industry - Other FS-specific guidance
ICT SPECIFIC	1. Market regulation of the Information Society 2. Internet regulation 3. Telecommunications 4. Digital media and content 5. Radio services and equipment 6. Audiovisual services 7. Environmental ("Green IT") 8. Other ICT-specific norms	- Standards defined and guidance issued by international organisations - Standards defined by standardisation institutes and guidance issued by supervisory authorities at European level - Standards defined by standardisation institutes and guidance issued by regulatory agencies at national level - Publicly funded research yield - Technical standards defined by the ICT industry and industry associations - IT Platforms and Protocols - Other ICT-specific guidance

GENERAL	1. Business regulation 2. Consumer protection and employment law 3. Information security 4. Data protection and privacy rights 5. Intellectual property rights 6. Electronic commerce	– Standards defined and guidance issued by international organisations – Standards defined by standardisation institutes and guidance issued by supervisory authorities at European level – Standards defined by standardisation institutes and guidance issued by regulatory agencies at national level – Technical standards defined by industry and industry associations – Compliance frameworks developed within industry – Third-party compliance audits and attestations – Targeted industry self-governance initiatives – Other general guidance

E. How are the most effective regulatory compliance programmes carried out?

The following is an outline of the components of an effective approach to regulatory compliance, starting with the five major goals. A good compliance programme should:

(1) *understand the risk landscape and costs of non-compliance*: Before starting a compliance programme, organisations need to have an overview of the risks of non-compliance in terms of likelihood and impact on their organisation.

(2) *focus on the highest risks*: This requires that regulation is understood in its impact and its risks for the organisation, and prioritised accordingly.

(3) *clearly define the scope*: Although there will be always overlaps between different regulations and laws, at the end of the compliance programme design phase you should have a clear idea of exactly which laws and regulations you need to comply with.

(4) *be structured to leave no room for 'interpretation'*: You should be able to demonstrate to the regulator that you have a robust approach to avoid breaches or non-compliance. This will not only make your programmes more efficient, but should also reduce the risk of regulatory fines if something should go wrong.

(5) *be designed to be repetitive*: If the effort is repeated, it should lead to the same results. You should be able to validate the results, if need be.

The design of an effective compliance programme is most effectively undertaken in the following order:[5]

Phase 1:   Scope and Prioritise

The Matrix is a powerful tool to map out and identify applicable laws, regulations and norms, as well as relevant standards, frameworks and guidance. It kills two birds with one stone by identifying synergies between disparate regulations, thereby saving costs.

Recommended tool: the *Regulatory Compliance Matrix* (RCM)

Phase 2:   Conduct a risk assessment

Risk identification should focus on inherent risk (*i.e.* risk that the organisation will incur losses if it implements no controls) and residual risk (*i.e.* risks that remain after controls have been implemented). Risk is calculated as likelihood of loss multiplied by impact or severity of loss. Senior management should determine the organisation's "risk appetite" and corresponding willingness to spend money to make improvements (assuming they are possible). General and specific regulatory risks are to be identified, and their high/ medium/ low "criticality" (likelihood times impact) estimated and documented.

Recommended tool: *Risks & Controls Matrix* (RCM) (see "risk" and "criticality" fields)

Phase 3:   Define control activities and reporting requirements

To address the risks, specific controls should be defined, for which existing guidance and standards may be consulted. This is when it is important to define reporting requirements, including their format, frequency (*viz.* ongoing/ daily/ weekly/ monthly/ yearly). It should also be specified who is to monitor these controls. All of this forms part of the work programme, and it may include additional guidance for the professional who is conducting the fieldwork. The procedures and evidence required should be specific; for example, obtain a copy of the Information Security policy and check that data protection obligations have been taken into account; request a sample of relevant reports/ alert emails that show

---

5   Further details on this subject can be found in the authors publication "Industry Governance and Regulatory Compliance", Chapter * "Concluding practitioner guidance: A regulatory compliance toolkit." (page 281-295). This Chapter also presents also a number of tools that assist to conduct efficient compliance audits.

that security breaches have been addressed. Controls, reporting, and monitoring should all be documented.

Recommended tool: *Risks & Controls Matrix* (RCM) (see "control specification", "reporting frequency", and "owner" fields)

Phase 4: Undertake an effectiveness review

The effectiveness of the controls, both pre-existing and newly crafted, should be tested for effectiveness, on the basis of which the reviewer or auditor can assess the level of effectiveness.

A control is "designed effective" if a policy and supporting documentation exists and includes the basic elements expected of such a policy; it is "implemented effective" if the policy is not only stored on the Compliance Officer's PC, but has also been communicated, and training and awareness courses have been organised and given. It is also important to test whether staff are adhering to this policy. As with any audit, a random sample must be selected for determination of the extent to which the policy is known and has been followed.

Recommended tool: *Risks & Controls Matrix* (RCM) (see "design/ operational effectiveness" field)

Phase 5: Document findings and make recommendations for improvement

The reviewer should document the findings (*e.g.*, any control weaknesses), then make recommendations for compliance improvement. Such recommendations usually stem from a combination of auditors' experience and judgement; industry best practices; and guides produced by regulators, standards institutes, and industry associations. During this phase, clear recommendations should be made about how to mitigate and manage compliance risks as well.

Recommended tool: *Risks & Controls Matrix* (RCM) (see the "findings" and "recommendations" fields)

Phase 6: Make an assessment of compliance maturity

Professional advisory firms and Governance, Risk and Compliance (GRC) Departments have been using various kinds and uneven qualities of Maturity Model for many years. The typical model distinguishes five levels of compliance:

- *Level 1 Nascent* (*a.k.a.* Naive/ *ad hoc*/ Sub-standard) – compliance is in a reactive state; the organisation is vulnerable.
- *Level 2 Initiative* (*a.k.a.* Basic/ Self-started/ Under construction) – compliance efforts are still lacking in formal documentation and practical consistency.
- *Level 3 Established* (*a.k.a.* Developed/ Formal/ Essential) – compliance policies and procedures are being designed and documented comprehensively.
- *Level 4 Advanced* (*a.k.a.* Competent/ Validated/ Proactive) – compliance policies and procedures are fully implemented.
- *Level 5 Perfected* (*a.k.a.* Excellent/ Monitored/ Transformational) – compliance processes have been optimised and the organisation's employees have adapted to the new order; thenceforward only ongoing monitoring is needed for smooth operation.

The four pillars of compliance control – (1) governance, (2) people, (3) controls, and (4) technology, are covered in the author's Regulatory Compliance Maturity Model, which clearly defines the dimensions of each pillar. This Model was first published in his previous work on the subject of compliance, *Industry Governance and Regulatory Compliance* (Reinke, 2012:531-537). It was elaborated as follows:

- *Governance* (including the dimensions of Senior Management sponsorship; Responsibilities and Accountability; Strategy; Risk Assessment; Monitoring; and Quality Reviews and Audits)
- *People* (including the dimensions of Training and Awareness; Stakeholder Activities; and Ethics and Compliance)
- *Controls* (including the dimensions of Policy; Procedures and Processes; Methodology: Incident-Response Plans; Third-Party Compliance Management; and Systems Support)
- *Technology* (including the dimensions of Automated Tools; Methodological Tools; and Analysis and Business Intelligence)

Recommended tool: *Regulatory Compliance Maturity Model* (see the "maturity level" of each dimension)

Phase 7:   Prioritisation of activities (*via* Heatmaps)

Any effective regulatory compliance strategy must include ways and means for senior management to digest and understand in intuitive form large volumes of information. Heatmaps and roadmaps are such tools: they present data graphically, enabling senior management to take-in at a glance their current compliance status and/or the pathway to higher compliance levels. Both tools facilitate executive actions like prioritisation or decisions on taking the next steps in budget planning, resource allocation and schedule development.

The standard Risk Heatmap is a diagram that plots the likelihood of a risk happening against the severity of its impact, giving a global measure of risk magnitude. Standard Risk Heatmaps are developed at the beginning of a compliance review so as to assess its scope, and are not generally useful after that assessment has been completed.

The more advanced Risk Assessment Heatmap (Reinke, 2012:293) should be used to integrate the results from the Maturity Model. This Heatmap yields a vector for each category of risk by plotting the risk magnitude already given by the standard Heatmap against the maturity of the organisation's effort to contain it. So long as the inputs constituting the Heatmap are accurate, the tool empowers management to decide summarily which steps to take next to achieve the next level of compliance maturity. It is a strategic mainstay useful for clarifying in overview the organisation's current risk and compliance situation.

The Action Quadrant Diagram (Reinke, 2012:294) is the strategic tool next to be deployed. It is compiled to help with the prioritisation of actions, depending on the quadrant in which the risk magnitude values fall. The *Ignore* quadrant contains low-risk, high-maturity issues; the *Monitor* quadrant contains low-risk but low-maturity issues; the *Important* quadrant contains high-risk yet high-maturity issues; the *Urgent* quadrant contains both high-risk and low-maturity issues. Such a Diagram, drawn up by the Chief Compliance Officer, may be presented to upper management, who can then apply their risk appetite to the classed issues to arrive at a plan of action.

Recommended tool: Action Quadrant Diagram (see Risk Assessment Heatmap values indicating risks and maturity levels)

Phase 8: Action Plans (Roadmaps)

Once the strategic decisions have been made, at the end of the compliance audit and risk assessment, the next tool to be applied addresses their tactical execution. This is the Roadmap (Reinke, 2012:294) to higher maturity, to be drafted and executed by the Chief Compliance Officer. It maps in temporal order all specific actions that have been agreed so as to bring the organisation's compliance to (the desired) maturity. Roadmaps plot actions with their "milestones" (or sub-goals, such as reports, check-points/sign-offs and/or completion of specific project "deliverables") against an agreed timeline.

Recommended tool: Roadmap (see actions and milestones *vs.* the agreed timeline).

F. Who should use this *reference guide*?

All who may be concerned with regulatory compliance and related matters should consult this book for advice. Readers who ought to be interested in this book include:

1. Senior Management, or the highest-level executives (*a.k.a.* the "C-suite"), including chief compliance officers (CCOs), chief risk officers (CROs), chief operating officers (COOs), chief information officers (CIOs), chief technology officers (CTOs), chief data officers (CDOs), chief financial officers (CFOs) and chief executive officers (CEOs). It is also of interest to General Counsel and board members. As non-compliance can have big impacts on organisations and cause serious business-disruption, senior management must not turn a blind eye. Many regulators hold Senior Management and Non-Executive Directors now fully accountable for the conduct of the business for which they are responsible.[6] This book will help to: (a) get an overview of regulatory categories, (b) assist with the planning of the regulatory strategy, and (c) prioritise the regulatory focus.

2. Middle Management, including the heads of the departments of risk and compliance, audit, finance, and legal affairs. This book will help to: (a) assess compliance risks, (b) prepare for informed discussions with other stakeholders in the organisation, and (c) identify synergies with other regulatory areas.

3. Subject Matter Experts, including the compliance officers, risk consultants, auditors, and legal advisors who conduct the fieldwork. This book will help to: (a) put their work programmes together based on the legal and regulatory domains in the Regulatory Compliance Matrix and existing guidance, frameworks and standards, and (b) ensure that other regulations in the same domains are identified at an early stage.

---

6   For example, in the UK the Financial Conduct Authority (FCA) and Prudential Regulation Authority (PRA) launched a Senior Management Regime (SMR). Martin Wheatley, Chief Executive of the FCA, said: "Our approach is driven by wanting to ensure firms are managed in a way that reflects good governance and promotes the right culture and behaviours. Having a narrow SMR will also allow the FCA to focus regulatory resources on those responsible for key business areas and board committees. We want those senior individuals to be held accountable for the decisions they make and oversee. This is what people inside and outside the banking sector expect."

4.   Other Stakeholders with an interest in regulatory compliance, including professionals working for outside advisory, audit, tax, or legal services firms; legislators and regulators; as well as scholars interested in this matter. This book will help to: (a) provide them a reference guide, and (b) prepare them for informed discussions with other stakeholders.

G. The main objectives of this guide

This book has three main objectives – to:

(1)   empower professionals to save thousands of euros, man-hours, and consultancy interventions by identifying all the most relevant laws and regulations.

(2)   assist individuals and organisations in categorising [or structuring], scoping, and prioritising the elements of their regulatory compliance programmes, and thereby conduct more efficient compliance programmes.

(3)   reduce the risk of non-compliance and the possible negative consequences thereof.

H. What experience may be required to carry on regulatory compliance?

Those working in regulatory compliance, either for an organisation or independently, should have experience in some of the domains described above. The best work programme or guide will not replace hands-on experience in real life, which alone can avoid mistakes in applying the "tools" and concepts presented in this introduction. Experience is indispensable to *accurately* assessing the likelihood and impact of risks, and how the results of the assessment should be reported. *Guidance is great, but experience is necessary.*

I. How dangerous is this book?

The short answer is, "Not dangerous at all". If this book contributes to saving money, enforcing good conduct and compliance, and educating professionals, regulators and scholars, it is a good book. Nobody needs to worry that it will make employees or professional services redundant, as guidance needs to be tailored to meet a specific purpose and then to be executed by professionals knowledgeable and skilled enough to perform the work.

This book can simplify the conduct of regulatory compliance implementation programmes and reviews. It lays the groundwork for a methodical approach. It can furthermore serve as the basis for more constructive dialogues between regulators and industry, as it helps identify synergies, overlaps and redundant regulations. While the regulator's interest is to enforce "good regulation", organisations are interested in implementing regulatory compliance frameworks that minimise costs.

As a note of caution: This book is dangerous to anyone who would keep business in the dark and benefit from regulatory nebulosity and uncertainty. The new regulatory landscape is complex; however, it can be rendered simpler if organisations can pinpoint what they must comply with and which is the most effective way of complying with it. This book helps organisations in particular with the first task, yet it also gives an overview of the best approaches along with the implications of non-compliance. If certain "professionals" profit from this information's being scattered and inaccessible to persons in need of it, this book just might be their downfall.

ABOUT THE REGULATORY COMPLIANCE MATRIX

The Matrix is divided up in two main columns. On the left hand side are legally binding and compulsory norms (labelled "Laws, Regulations and Norms"), and on the right hand side are voluntary standards and guidelines (labelled "Standards, Frameworks and Guidance").

Each *domain* (or compliance category) consists of at most four dimensions or "levels", as applicable; reflecting the multi-level character of European regulation and governance; to wit:

1. *Global Level* – issued by global organisations like the United Nations and its specialised agencies; international associations; and in certain cases with strong impact on companies in the European Union, the USA.
2. *European Level* – issued by organs of the European Union, pan-European independent regulatory agencies, supervisory bodies or standards organisations with European reach.
3. *National Level* – issued by national parliaments, regulatory agencies or national standards bodies. As it would have been infeasible to compile the national laws and regulations of each country, the United Kingdom was selected as the default example.
4. *Sub-National Level* – issued by regional or local governments or official bodies, or more commonly by influential private organisations.

At the National (*viz.* UK) Level in the binding column of the Matrix, the reader should note the important distinction between Acts of Parliament, or primary legislation, and Statutory Instruments (SIs), or secondary legislation. In the Matrix listings, the secondary legislation has been subordinated to the primary legislation enabling it.

The statutory instrument (SI), taking the form of Regulations, Orders and Rules, is the way delegated legislation is made in the United Kingdom. SIs are governed by the Statutory Instruments Act 1946. Every year, Statutory Instruments may implement the regulatory intent of Acts of Parliament, and in certain conditions specified by the European

Communities Act 1972 may even amend Acts of Parliament in light of EU law. The Regulatory Compliance Matrix mainly lists Statutory Instruments embodying substantive regulation, along with a few key amendments; not every single amendment is covered.

In the other, voluntary column of the ledger are "standards" and "guidelines". In certain contexts the word "standard" is sometimes used rather loosely to mean what is in effect secondary legislation (*e.g.*, the "regulatory technical standards" of the European Banking Authority). In this book, however, the term "standard" is confined to those norms compliance with which, though highly to be recommended and maybe practically indispensable, are not strictly obligatory or enforceable by government sanctions. It might be said that, in this sense, standards are but so many structured guidelines.

PART I

Financial Services Laws and Regulations

It is well enough that people of the nation do not understand our banking and monetary system, for if they did, I believe there would be a revolution before tomorrow morning.
Henry Ford (1863-1947)

Every day is a bank account, and time is our currency. No one is rich, no one is poor, we've got 24 hours each.
Christopher Rice (1978-)

Banking, I would argue, is the most heavily regulated industry in the world. Regulations don't solve things. Supervision solves things.
Wilbur Ross (1937-)

PART 1

FINANCIAL SERVICES LAWS AND REGULATIONS

This Part of the Regulatory Compliance Matrix categorises laws, regulations and norms relevant to the Financial Services Industry, and maps it to the relevant standards, framework and guidance that assist financial institutes to comply with their legal and regulatory requirements. Financial Services covers commercial and investment banking, investment services, insurance, pensions, and other financial services such as electronic payments with credit and debit cards, conglomerates and clearing houses.

Figure 2: Financial Services Regulatory Compliance Matrix

	LAWS, REGULATIONS and NORMS	STANDARDS, FRAMEWORKS and GUIDANCE

· FS SPECIFIC	1. Regulatory Agencies
	  1.1 European Supervisory Authorities
	  1.2 Credit Rating Agencies
	  1.3 Resolution and Recovery
	  1.4 Enforcement procedures
	2. General Regulations
	  2.1 Stability and capital requirements
	  2.2 Capital Markets Union and General banking regulations
	  2.3 Transactions, accounts and payment systems
	  2.4 Corporate conduct, culture and ethics
	  2.5 Markets regulation: record-keeping, transparency and market abuse
		- Standards defined and guidance issued by international organisations
		- Standards defined by standardisation institutes and guidance issued by supervisory authorities at European level
		- Standards defined by standardisation institutes and guidance issued by regulatory agencies at national level
		- Technical standards defined by the FS industry and its industry associations
		- Compliance frameworks developed within industry
		- Policies, procedures, processes and principles implemented by industry
		- Other FS-specific guidance
		-

LAWS, REGULATIONS and NORMS	STANDARDS, FRAMEWORKS and GUIDANCE
2.6 Mergers & Acquisitions (Financial Services specific) 2.7 Insolvency (Financial Services specific) 2.8 Risk Management 3. Financial Crime and consumer protection 2.1 Financial Crime: Anti-Money laundering, sanctions and terrorism 2.2 Consumer protection (Financial Services specific) 4. Retail banking 5.1 Consumer credit, mortgages and lending 5.2 Savings and transactional accounts 5. Investment banking 6.1 Investment products and funds 6.2 Securities and Foreign Exchange 6.3 Derivatives 6. Insurance 7. Pensions	

FINANCIAL SERVICES AUTHORITIES AND KEY INFLUENCERS

(1) Global Level – Authorities (non-US)

International Banking Organisations

- **World Bank Group** is one of the world's largest sources of development assistance, in 2002 it provided $19.5 billion to developing countries and worked in more than 100 developing economies, bringing finance and/or technical expertise (incl. for telecoms). The New York-based bank gives loans and technical assistance to developing countries to reduce poverty and advance sustainable growth. A vital source of these goods to the world's developing countries, it comprises two unique development institutions owned by 185 member countries: the International Bank

for Reconstruction and Development (IBRD) and the International Development Association (IDA).
[Website: http://www.worldbank.org]

- **International Bank for Reconstruction and Development (IBRD)** aims to reduce poverty in middle-income and creditworthy poorer countries by furthering sustainable development through loans, guarantees, risk management products, and analytical and advisory services. Established in 1944 as the original institution of the World Bank Group, IBRD is a cooperative operated for its 185 member countries' benefit.
[Website: http://www.worldbank.org/ibrd]

- **International Development Association (IDA)** is the World Bank unit that lends to the world's poorest countries, it aims to reduce poverty by providing interest-free loans and grants for Programmes; boost economic growth; and reduce inequalities and improve living conditions.
[Website: http://www.worldbank.org/ida]

Global financial supervision authorities

- **Bank for International Settlements (BIS)** promotes international cooperation among monetary authorities and financial supervisory officials through its meetings programmes and through the Basel Process - hosting international committees and standard-setting bodies and facilitating their interaction.
[Website: http://www.bis.org/]

- **International Monetary Fund (IMF)** provides policy advice and financing to members in economic difficulties, and works with developing nations to help them achieve macroeconomic stability and reduce poverty.
[Website: http://www.imf.org/]

Various groupings of central banks and supervisory authorities

- **The Basel Committee on Banking Supervision (BCBS)** provides a forum for regular cooperation on banking supervisory matters. It is the global standard-setter for the prudential regulation of banks, and provides a forum for cooperation on banking supervisory matters. Its mandate is to strengthen the regulation, supervision and practices of banks worldwide with the purpose of enhancing financial stability. The Committee's members come from Argentina, Australia, Belgium, Brazil, Canada, China, France, Germany, Hong Kong SAR, India, Indonesia, Italy, Japan, Korea, Luxembourg, Mexico, the Netherlands, Russia, Saudi Arabia, Singapore, South Africa, Spain, Sweden, Switzerland, Turkey, the United Kingdom and the United States.
[Website: http://www.bis.org/bcbs/]

- **The Committee on the Global Financial System (CGFS)** monitors and analyses the broad issues relating to financial markets and systems.
  [Website: http://www.bis.org/cgfs/]

- **The Committee on Payments and Market Infrastructures (CPMI)** analyses and sets standards for payment, clearing and settlement infrastructures.
  [Website: http://www.bis.org/cpmi/]

- **The Markets Committee** (formerly the Committee on Gold and Foreign Exchange) was established in 1962 following the formation of the so-called Gold Pool. It examines the functioning of financial markets.
  [Website: http://www.bis.org/about/factmktc.htm]

- **The Central Bank Governance Forum (CBGF)** comprises the Central Bank Governance Network, which facilitates the exchange of information on institutional arrangements and the Central Bank Governance Group, which discusses issues related to the design and operation of central banks.
  [Website: http://www.bis.org/cbgov/]

- **The Irving Fisher Committee on Central Bank Statistics (IFC)** addresses statistical issues of concern to central banks, including those relating to economic, monetary and financial stability.
  [Website: http://www.bis.org/ifc/]

The other groups participating in the Basel and other processes each have a separate legal identity and their own governance arrangements:

- **The Financial Stability Board (FSB)** is comprised of senior representatives of national financial authorities (central banks, regulatory and supervisory authorities, and ministries of finance), international financial institutions, standards-setting bodies, and committees of central bank experts. It seeks to enhance global financial stability by developing policies and coordinating the work of national financial authorities and international standards-setting bodies. The FSB develops and promotes effective regulatory supervision and other financial sector policies. It operates under a mandate from the G20 heads of state and government. The Secretariat of the FSB is hosted by the Bank for International Settlements (headquartered in Basel, Switzerland).
  [Website: http://www.financialstabilityboard.org/]

- **The International Association of Insurance Supervisors (IAIS)** is the international standard-setting body for the supervision of the insurance sector. Its membership of insurance supervisors and regulators come from about 140 jurisdictions.
  [Website: http://www.iaisweb.org/]

- **The International Association of Deposit Insurers (IADI)** provides guidance on creating and maintaining effective deposit insurance systems. Its members represent deposit insurance agencies from more than 70 jurisdictions.
  [Website: http://www.iadi.org/]

- **The International Organization of Securities Commissions (IOSCO)** is an international association of securities regulators. IOSCO's membership regulates more than 95% of the world's securities markets.
  [Website: http://www.iosco.org/]

Other general fora are:

- **G-20** consists of the finance ministers and central bank governors of 19 countries: Argentina, Australia, Brazil, Canada, China, France, Germany, India, Indonesia, Italy, Japan, Mexico, Russia, Saudi Arabia, South Africa, South Korea, Turkey, United Kingdom, and the United States of America, as well as representatives from the European Union.
  [Website: https://www.g20.org/]

(2) Global Level – Authorities (US)

Governmental Authorities

- **The Financial Services Committee of the US House of Representatives (HFSC)** oversees all components of the US housing and financial services (banking, insurance, real estate, public and assisted housing, and securities). Various other House committees have concurrent jurisdiction over financial markets (*e.g.* the House Committee on Agriculture).
  [Website: http://financialservices.house.gov/]

- **The Banking Committee of the US Senate (SBC)** oversees the banking, housing and urban affairs sectors.
  [Website: http://www.banking.senate.gov/]

- **US Department of Justice** is the Federal executive department responsible for the enforcement of the law and administration of justice, equivalent to the justice or interior ministries of other countries. [Website: http://www.justice.gov/]

  - **Bureau of Alcohol, Tobacco, Firearms and Explosives (ATF)** is a unique law enforcement agency in the United State Department of Justice that protects our communities from violent criminals, criminal organizations, the illegal use and trafficking of firearms, the illegal use and storage of explosives, acts of arson and bombings, acts of terrorism, and the illegal diversion of alcohol and tobacco products.
    [Website: https://www.atf.gov/]

7

- **US Department of the Treasury** (Foreign Assets and Control Department) is the executive agency responsible for promoting economic prosperity and ensuring the financial security of the United States. The Department is responsible for a wide range of activities such as advising the President on economic and financial issues, encouraging sustainable economic growth, and fostering improved governance in financial institutions. [http://www.treasury.gov/]

  - **Office of the Comptroller of the Currency (OCC)** is an independent agency housed within the Treasury Department. The OCC has primary supervisory responsibility for national banks and federal thrifts.
    [Website: http://www.occ.gov/]

  - **Financial Stability Oversight Council (FSOC)** comprehensively monitors the US financial system to ensure its stability. In addition to identifying threats to financial stability, the Council is charged with promoting market discipline and responding to emerging risks. It is a collaborative body, chaired by the Secretary of the Treasury, which brings together disparate Federal financial regulators and their expertise, along with State regulators and an independent insurance expert appointed by the President.
    [Website: http://www.treasury.gov/initiatives/fsoc]

  - **Office of Financial Research (OFR)** is housed within the Treasury Department and supports the FSOC and its other member agencies by providing better financial data and analysis for a more complete understanding of risk in the financial system.
    [Website: http://www.treasury.gov/initiatives/ofr/about/Pages/default.aspx]

  - **The Office of Foreign Assets Control (OFAC)**, also under the US Department of the Treasury, administers and enforces economic and trade sanctions against targeted foreign countries and regimes, terrorists, international narcotics traffickers, those engaged in activities related to the proliferation of weapons of mass destruction, and other threats to the national security, foreign policy or economy of the United States. OFAC acts under Presidential national emergency powers as well as under authority granted by specific legislation to impose controls on transactions and to freeze assets under US jurisdiction.
    [Website: http://www.treasury.gov/resource-center/sanctions/Pages/default.aspx]

- **US Attorney's Offices** (also known as Federal Prosecutors) represent the United States Federal government in United States District Court and the United States Courts of Appeal. There are 93 U.S. Attorneys stationed throughout the United States [website: http://www.justice.gov/usao/], but by far the most important ones for financial regulatory purposes are the ones located in the following Districts:

- ▪ United States Attorney's Office for the District of Columbia (unique among U.S. Attorney's Offices in the size and scope of its work, it enforces the law and defends the interests of the United States; its location in the seat of the Federal government gives it responsibility for many cases of national importance, including far-reaching challenges to Federal policies.)
  [Website: http://www.justice.gov/usao/dc/]

- ▪ United States Attorney's Office for the Southern District of New York (embracing Manhattan, it is perhaps the most influential and active Federal Districts in the United States, largely because of its jurisdiction over New York's major financial centres, and has distinguished itself as one of the nation's premier legal institutions, successfully prosecuting ground-breaking historic cases.)
  [Website: http://www.justice.gov/usao/nys/]

- ▪ United States Attorney's Office for the Northern District of California (embracing the Bay Area, it is undoubtedly one of the most exceptional districts in the nation, as it hears cases arising in Silicon Valley and in the financial district of San Francisco.).
  [Website: http://www.justice.gov/usao/can/]

- ▪ **Securities and Exchange Commission (SEC)** is an independent agency with a mission to protect investors, maintain fair, orderly, and efficient markets, and facilitate capital formation.
  [Website: http://www.sec.gov/]

- ▪ **Commodity Futures Trading Commission (CFTC)** is an independent agency with a mission to regulate commodity futures and options markets in the US.
  [Website: http://www.cftc.gov/index.htm]

- ▪ **Federal Deposit Insurance Corporation (FDIC)** is an independent agency created by Congress. The FDIC's mission is "to maintain stability and public confidence in the US financial system by insuring deposits, monitoring risks to the insurance deposit funds, and limiting the impact on the economy by a failed bank or thrift."
  [Website: https://www.fdic.gov/]

Non-governmental Authorities

- ▪ **Federal Reserve Board (FRB)** is an independent central bank with a mission to set monetary policy and to supervise financial service holding companies and certain banks.
  [Website: http://www.federalreserve.gov/]

  - ▪ **Consumer Financial Protection Bureau (CFPB)** is a division of the Federal Reserve Board that has jurisdiction over consumer financial products and services in the banking and non-banking sectors. Firms and products regulated

by the SEC and CFTC are exempt from the jurisdiction of the CFPB. The scope and limits of this exemption have not been set or tested.
[Website: http://www.consumerfinance.gov/]

- **Federal Reserve Bank of New York (FRBNY)** is one of the 12 branches of the Federal Reserve Banks. Its mission is "to foster the safety, soundness and vitality of the economic and financial systems."
[Website: http://www.ny.frb.org/]

- **US Financial Accounting Standards Board (FASB)** establishes standards of financial accounting which govern the preparation of financial reports by non-governmental organizations, and which are officially recognised as authoritative by the Securities and Exchange Commission (SEC) and the American Institute of Certified Public Accountants.
[Website: http://www.fasb.org/home]

(3) European Level – Authorities

European Supervisory Authorities (ESAs)

- **European Banking Authority (EBA)** (formerly the Committee of European Banking Supervisors (CEBS)) is an independent EU Authority that contributes to ensuring a high quality, effective, and consistent level of regulation and supervision of banks.
[Website: http://www.eba.europa.eu]

- **European Insurance and Occupational Pensions Authority (EIOPA)** (formerly the Committee of European Insurance and Occupational Pensions Supervisors (EIOPS)) "is an independent advisory body to the European Parliament, the Council of the European Union and the European Commission. EIOPA's core responsibilities are to support the stability of the financial system, transparency of markets and financial products as well as the protection of insurance policyholders, pension scheme members and beneficiaries."
[Website: https://eiopa.europa.eu/]

- **European Securities and Markets Authority (ESMA)** (formerly the Committee of European Securities Regulators (CESR)) is an independent EU Authority that contributes to safeguarding the stability of the European Union's financial system by ensuring the integrity, transparency, efficiency and orderly functioning of securities markets, as well as enhancing investor protection.
[Website: http://www.esma.europa.eu/]

Other European authorities

- **The European Systemic Risk Board (ESRB)** is an independent EU body responsible for macro-prudential oversight of the financial system within the EU. [Website: https://www.esrb.europa.eu/home/html/index.en.html]

European Central Bank and supporting mechanisms for banking supervision

- **European Central Bank (ECB)** is the central bank for the euro and administers monetary policy of the Eurozone, which consists of more than half of EU Member States and is one of the largest currency areas in the world. [Website: https://www.ecb.europa.eu or http://www.ecb.int]

- **Single Supervisory Mechanism (SSM)** is the name of the mechanism that has given the European Central Bank a supervisory role to monitor the financial stability of banks based in participating states, starting from 4 November 2014. [Website: https://www.ecb.europa.eu/ssm/html/index.en.html]

- **Single Resolution Mechanism (SRM)** is one of the main pillars of the European Union's banking union, which centrally implements, in participating Member States, the EU's Bank Recovery and Resolution Directive, the framework for the recovery and resolution of credit institutions and investment firms found to be in danger of failing. [Website: https://www.ecb.europa.eu/ssm]

Specialised European Banks

- **European Investment Bank (EIB)** is the European Union's investment bank. Founded in 1958 under the Treaty of Rome, it contributes to the integration, balanced development, and economic and social cohesion of EU Member States, raising substantial volumes of funds from the markets, which it directs on most favourable terms to capital projects in line with EU objectives. Projects considered for EIB financing must contribute to developing transport, telecommunications, and energy-transmission infrastructure networks with a European Community dimension. In partnership with the European Commission, EIB runs the European Investment Fund (EIF). [Website: http://www.eib.org]

- **European Bank for Reconstruction and Development (EBRD)** was founded in 1991 when communism was crumbling in Central and Eastern Europe. It supports the liberated countries in nurturing a private sector within a democratic environment. [Website: http://www.ebrd.com]

- **European Investment Fund (EIF)** invests equity in venture capital funds and business incubators that support SMEs, particularly early-stage and technology-oriented ones. [Website: http://www.eif.org]

European Institutions

- **European Commission (EC)** is the executive body of the European Union (EU) and consists of 27 Commissioners, one for each Member State of the EU. The EC proposes legislation, administers and implements policy, enforces laws, and negotiates international agreements.
  [Website: http://ec.europa.eu/index_en.htm]

- **European Parliament (EP)** is the directly elected body of the EU and is one part (the other being the Council) of the bicameral legislative branch of the EU institutions.
  [Website: http://www.europarl.europa.eu/]

- **European Council (*a.k.a.* the Council of the European Union)** is made up of relevant ministers from each EU Member State and debates and passes European laws with the Council, scrutinizes other EU institutions (in particular, the Commission), and debates and adopts the EU budget. It consists of the Head of State or Government of the EU Member States together with its President and the President of the Commission and defines general policy directions and priorities.
  [Website: http://www.consilium.europa.eu/en/european-council/]

Other European institutions with influence

- **The Council of Europe** is an organisation of 47 Member States in the European region (also including Russia, Ukraine, Azerbaijan, Armenia, Turkey and Georgia). Its most enduring legacy is the European Convention on Human Rights, adopted in 1950. "The aim of the Council of Europe is to achieve a greater unity between its members for the purpose of safeguarding and realising the ideals and principles which are their common heritage and facilitating their economic and social progress" (Statute of the Council of Europe *a.k.a* Treaty of London (1949), Article 1(a).
  [Website: http://www.coe.int]

(4) National Level (EU Member States) – Authorities

This Matrix focusses on the United Kingdom as the signal example of an advanced financial marketplace in the EU, in lieu of a detailed overview of regulatory authorities in all 28 EU Member States; however, information on financial services regulation by other Member States is available on the following websites.

- **Banking Supervision in the EU** took over supervisory responsibility for banks in the euro area on 4 November 2014. European banking supervision helps to rebuild trust and bolsters the safety and soundness of the banking system.
  [Website: https://www.bankingsupervision.europa.eu/home/html/index.en.html]

- **The European System of Central Banks (ESCB)** is composed of the European Central Bank (ECB) and the national central banks (NCBs) of all 28 European Union (EU) Member States.

  The basic tasks to be carried out by the Euro-system are (Art. 127 TFEU):
  - to define and implement the monetary policy of the Eurozone;
  - to conduct foreign exchange operations;
  - to hold and manage the official foreign reserves of the Member States; and
  - to promote the smooth operation of payment systems.

  In addition, the Euro-system contributes to the smooth conduct of policies pursued by the competent authorities relating to the prudential supervision of credit institutions and the stability of the financial system

The National Banks of the EU Member States are listed below.
[Website: http://www.ecb.europa.eu/home/html/links.en.html]

- **Austria** –
  - Österreichische Nationalbank
    [Website: http://www.oenb.at/]

- **Belgium** –
  - Nationale Bank van België/Banque Nationale de Belgique
    [Website: http://www.bnb.be/]

- **Bulgaria** –
  - Bulgarian National Bank
    [Website: http://www.bnb.bg/]

- **Croatia** –
  - Hrvatska narodna banka
    [Website: http://www.hnb.hr/]

- **Cyprus** –
  - Central Bank of Cyprus
    [Website: http://www.centralbank.gov.cy/]

- **Czech Republic** –
  - Česká národní banka
    [Website: http://www.cnb.cz/]

- **Denmark** –
  - Danmarks Nationalbank
    [Website: http://www.nationalbanken.dk/]

- **Estonia** –
  - Eesti Pank
    [Website: http://www.eestipank.ee/]

- **Finland** –
  - Suomen Pankki – Finland's Bank
    [Website: http://www.suomenpankki.fi/]

- **France** –
  - Banque de France
    [Website: https://www.banque-france.fr/]

- **Germany** –
  - Deutsche Bundesbank
    [Website: http://www.bundesbank.de/]

- **Greece** –
  - Bank of Greece
    [Website: http://www.bankofgreece.gr/]

- **Hungary** –
  - Magyar Nemzeti Bank
    [Website: http://www.mnb.hu/]

- **Ireland** –
  - Central Bank of Ireland/Banc Ceannais na hÉireann
    [Website: http://www.centralbank.ie/]

- **Italy** –
  - Banca d´Italia
    [Website: http://www.bancaditalia.it/]

- **Latvia** –
  - Latvijas Banka
    [Website: http://www.bank.lv/]

- **Lithuania** –
  - Lietuvos bankas
    [Website: http://www.lb.lt/]

- **Luxembourg** –
  - Banque centrale du Luxembourg
    [Website: http://www.bcl.lu/]

- **Malta** –
  - Central Bank of Malta
    [Website: http://www.centralbankmalta.org/]

- **Netherlands** –
  - De Nederlandsche Bank
    [Website: http://www.dnb.nl/]

- **Poland** –
  - Narodowy Bank Polski
    [Website: http://www.nbp.pl/]

- **Portugal** –
  - Banco de Portugal
    [Website: http://www.bportugal.pt/]

- **Romania** –
  - Banca Naţională a României
    [Website: http://www.bnro.ro/]

- **Slovakia** –
  - Národná Banka Slovenska
    [Website: http://www.nbs.sk/]

- **Slovenia** –
  - Banka Slovenije
    [Website: http://www.bsi.si/]

- **Spain** –
  - Banco de España
    [Website: http://www.bde.es/]

- **Sweden** –
  - Sveriges Riksbank
    [Website: http://www.riksbank.se/]

- **United Kingdom** –
  - Bank of England
    [Website: http://www.bankofengland.co.uk/]

European System of Central Banks (ESCB) is composed of the European Central Bank (ECB) and the national central banks (NCBs) of all 28 European Union Member States. The Central Banks play an important role in the supervision of the banking sector.

European Regulatory Authorities regulate financial institutions to certain requirements, restrictions and guidelines, aiming to maintain the integrity of the financial system. The following is a list of financial regulatory authorities by European Member States.

- **Austria –**
  - Austrian National Bank / Österreichische Nationalbank
    [Website: http://www.oenb.at/]

  - FinancialMarketAuthority(FMA)/ÖsterreichischeFinanzmarktaufsichtsbehörde (FMA)
    [Website: http://www.fma.gv.at/]

  - Austrian Takeover Commission / Übernahmekommission
    [Website: http://www.uebkom.at/takeover_new/]

- **Belgium –**
  - National Bank of Belgium (NBB) / Nationale Bank van België / Banque Nationale de Belgique
    [Website: http://www.bnb.be/]

  - Financial Services and Markets Authority (FSMA) / Autorité des services et marchés financiers / Authoriteit voor Financiële Diensten en Markten
    [Website: http://www.fsma.be/]

- **Bulgaria –**
  - Financial Supervision Commission (FSC) / Комисия за финансов надзор
    [Website: http://www.fsc.bg/]

- **Croatia –**
  - Croatian Financial Services Supervisory Agency / Hrvatska Agencija za Nadzor Financijskih Usluga (HANFA)
    [Website: http://www.hanfa.hr/]

- **Cyprus –**
  - Central Bank of Cyprus
    [Website: http://www.centralbank.gov.cy/]

  - Cyprus Securities and Exchange Commission (CYSEC)
    [Website: http://www.cysec.gov.cy/]

  - Cyprus Insurance Companies Control Service
    [Website: http://www.mof.gov.cy/]

- **Czech Republic –**
  - Czech National Bank / Česká Národní Banka (no specific regulator)
    [Website: https://www.cnb.cz/]

- **Denmark** –
  - Financial Supervisory Authority / Finanstilsynet
    [Website: https://www.finanstilsynet.dk/]

- **Estonia** –
  - Financial Supervision Authority / Finantsinspektsioon
    [Website: http://www.fi.ee/]

  - Estonian Bank / Eesti Panga
    [Website: http://www.eestipank.ee/]

- **Finland** –
  - Financial Supervisory Authority (FSA) / Finanssivalvonta (FIN)
    [Website: http://www.finanssivalvonta.fi/]

- **France** –
  - Autorité des marchés financiers (AMF)
    [Website: http://www.amf-france.org/]

  - Registre unique des Intermediaires en Assurance, Banque et Finance (ORIAS)
    [Website: https://www.orias.fr/]

  - Autorité de Contrôle Prudentiel (ACPR)
    [Website: http://acpr.banque-france.fr/]

  - French Takeover Panel / AMF Sociétés cotées et opérations financières – *offres publiques d'acquisition*
    [Website: http://www.amf-france.org/Acteurs-et-produits/Societes-cotees-et-operations-financieres/Offres-publiques-d-acquisition/Presentation.html]

- **Germany** –
  - Federal Financial Supervisory Authority / Bundesanstalt für Finanzdienstleistungsaufsicht (BaFin)
    [Website: http://www.bafin.de/]

- **Greece** –
  - Hellenic Capital Market Commission / Επιτροπή Κεφαλαιαγοράς
    [Website: http://www.hcmc.gr/]

- **Hungary** –
  - The Central Bank of Hungary / Magyar Nemzeti Bank (no specific regulator)
    [Website: http://www.mnb.hu/]

- **Ireland** –
  - Central Bank of Ireland / Banc Ceannais na hÉireann (no specific regulator)
    [Website: http://www.centralbank.ie/]

- Irish Takeover Panel / Painéal Táthcheangail na hÉireann
  [Website: http://irishtakeoverpanel.ie/]

- **Italy** –
  - Commissione Nazionale per le Società e la Borsa (CONSOB)
    [Website: http://www.consob.it/]

  - Institute for the Supervision of Insurance / Istituto per la Vigilanza sulle Assicurazioni Private e di Interesse Collettivo (ISVAP)
    [Website: www.isvap.it]

- **Latvia** –
  - Financial and Capital Market Commission / Finanšu un Kapitāla Tirgus Komisija
    [Website: http://www.fktk.lv/]

- **Lithuania** –
  - Bank of Lithuania / Lietuvos bankas (no specific regulator)
    [Website: http://www.lb.lt/]

- **Luxembourg** –
  - Commission de Surveillance du Secteur Financier (CSSF)
    [Website: http://www.cssf.lu/]

  - Commissariat aux Assurances (CAA)
    [Website: http://www.commassu.lu/]

- **Malta** –
  - Malta Financial Services Authority (MFSA) / Awtorità tas-servizzi finanzjarji f'Malta
    [Website: http://www.mfsa.com.mt/]

- **Netherlands** –
  - Authority for the Financial Markets (AFM) / Autoriteit Financiële Markten
    [Website: http://www.afm.nl/]

- **Poland** –
  - Financial Supervision Authority / Komisja Nadzoru Finansowego (KNF)
    [Website: http://www.knf.gov.pl/]

- **Portugal** –
  - Portuguese Securities Market Commission / Comissão do Mercado de Valores Mobiliários (CMVM)
    [Website: http://www.cmvm.pt/]

- Portuguese Insurance Regulator / Autoridade de Supervisão de Seguros e Fundos de Pensões (ASF)
    [Website: http://www.asf.com.pt/]

- **Romania** –
    - Romanian Financial Supervisory Authority / Autoritatea de Supraveghere Financiară (ASF)
        [Website: http://www.asfromania.ro/]

- **Slovakia** –
    - Slovakian National Bank / Národná Banka Slovenska (no specific regulator)
        [Website: http://www.nbs.sk/en/financial-market-supervision]

- **Slovenia** –
    - Securities Market Agency / Agencija za Trg Vrednostnih Papirjev (ATVP)
        [Website: http://www.a-tvp.si/]

- **Spain** –
    - Spanish Securities Market Commission / Comisión Nacional del Mercado de Valores (CNMV)
        [Website: http://www.cnmv.es/]

    - Insurance sector regulator / Dirección General de Seguros (DGS)
        [Website: http://www.dgsfp.mineco.es/]

    - Banking sector regulator / Banco de España (BdE)
        [Website: http://www.bde.es/]

- **Sweden** –
    - Financial Supervisory Authority / Finansinspektionen (FI)
        [Website: http://www.fi.se/]

- **United Kingdom** –
    - Financial Conduct Authority (FCA)
        [Website: http://www.fca.org.uk/]

    - Prudential Regulation Authority (PRA)
        [Website: http://www.bankofengland.co.uk/pra/]

    - Panel on Takeovers and Mergers (PANEL)
        [Website: http://www.thetakeoverpanel.org.uk/]

(5) National Level (UK) – Authorities

- **The Bank of England (BoE)** is the central bank of the United Kingdom and exists to ensure monetary stability while contributing to and enhancing financial stability.
    [Website: http://www.bankofengland.co.uk/]

- **HM Treasury (HMT** is the UK's economic and finance ministry. It is responsible for formulating and implementing the Government's financial and economic policy. [Website: https://www.gov.uk/government/organisations/hm-treasury]

  - A **Financial Policy Committee (FPC)** has been established in the Bank of England, with responsibility for 'macro-prudential' regulation contributing to the achievement by the BoE of its (revised) financial stability objective.
    [Website: http://www.bankofengland.co.uk/financialstability/Pages/fpc/]

  - The **Prudential Regulation Authority (PRA)** is an operationally independent subsidiary of the Bank of England, which carries out 'micro-prudential' (firm-specific) regulation of financial institutions that manage significant risks on their balance sheets.
    [Website: http://www.bankofengland.co.uk/pra]

- **The Financial Conduct Authority (FCA)** has responsibility for conduct of business and market regulation. The FCA is responsible for conduct issues across the entire spectrum of financial services, the regulation of primary and secondary markets and the prudential regulation of non PRA-regulated firms. The divisions are:
  - Authorisations (assesses and processes applications);
  - Supervision (conduct supervision);
  - Markets (which ensures markets remain stable, efficient and resilient);
  - Policy, Risk and Research (identifies and assesses risks and makes sure that policies protect consumers and eliminate poor practice);
  - Enforcement and Financial Crime (takes action against firms and individuals who are unethical in their practice, investigates misconduct and takes steps to reduce financial crime);
  - Operations (backoffice functions);
  - Communications and International (helps to build confidence); and
  - Corporate Services (supports the FCA Board and its Committees).
  [Website: http://www. fca.org.uk]

- **Jersey Financial Services Commission (the Commission)** is responsible for the regulation, supervision and development of the financial services industry in the Island of Jersey for banking, collective investment funds, fund services business, insurance business, general insurance mediation business, investment business, money service business, and trust and company service providers. Additionally, the Commission is the supervisory body for those sectors that are subject to regulatory oversight of their anti-money laundering and countering the financing of terrorism responsibilities, which includes Accountants, Lawyers, Estate Agents, High Value Goods Dealers, and Non-Profit Organisations.
  [Website: http://www.jerseyfsc.org]

- **Financial Ombudsman (FOS)** was set up by parliament to sort out individual complaints that consumers and financial businesses are not able to resolve themselves. The service is free to consumers and covers banking, insurance, mortgages, credit cards and store cards, loans and credit, payday lending and debt collecting, pensions, savings and investments, hire purchase and pawnbroking, money transfer, financial advice, stocks, shares, unit trusts and bonds.
  [Website: http://www.financial-ombudsman.org.uk]

1.1 REGULATORY AGENCIES

1.1.1 European Supervisory Authorities

GLOBAL LEVEL – Laws, Regulations and Norms

Not applicable: This is an EU regulatory initiative, hence applicable laws, regulations and norms exist only at European Level and below.

GLOBAL LEVEL – Standards, Frameworks and Guidance

General principles set by global financial institutions

- Financial Stability Board (19 December 2014) "Global adherence to regulatory and supervisory standards on international cooperation and information exchange: Status update" (Zurich).
- Financial Stability Board (14 November 2014) "Overview of Progress in the Implementation of the G20 Recommendations for Strengthening Financial Stability: Report of the Financial Stability Board to G20 Leaders"
- Bank for International Settlements, Basel Committee on Banking Supervision (October 2010) "Principles for enhancing corporate governance".

EUROPEAN LEVEL – Laws, Regulations and Norms

This section lists the laws establishing the regulatory authorities in financial services, their responsibilities and enforcement powers. These "constitutional" (or institution-creating) laws do not apply to the subjects of regulation or to the general public, but are laws about who shall make the laws.

European Banking Authority (EBA)

- Regulation (EU) No 1093/2010 "establishing a European Supervisory Authority (European Banking Authority), amending Decision No 716/2009/EC and repealing Commission Decision 2009/78/EC" (*European Supervisory Authority Regulation*) (24 November 2010).

Amendments:
- Regulation (EU) No 1022/2013 "amending Regulation (EU) No 1093/2010 establishing a European Supervisory Authority (European Banking Authority) as regards the conferral of specific tasks on the European Central Bank pursuant to Council Regulation (EU) No 1024/2013" (*EBA (Amendment) Regulation*) (22 October 2013).
- Directive 2010/78/EU "amending Directives 98/26/EC, 2002/87/EC, 2003/6/EC, 2003/41/EC, 2003/71/EC, 2004/39/EC, 2004/109/EC, 2005/60/EC, 2006/48/EC, 2006/49/EC and 2009/65/EC in respect of the powers of the European Supervisory Authority (European Banking Authority), the European Supervisory Authority (European Insurance and Occupational Pensions Authority) and the European Supervisory Authority (European Securities and Markets Authority)" (*European Supervisory Authority Directive (Omnibus 1)*)) (24 November 2010).
  - [UK] SI 2012/916 – Financial Services (Omnibus 1 Directive) Regulations 2012.

European Securities and Markets Authority (ESMA)

- Regulation (EU) No 1095/2010 (24 November 2010) "establishing a European Supervisory Authority (European Securities and Markets Authority), amending Decision No 716/2009/EC and repealing Commission Decision 2009/77/EC" (*ESMA Regulation*) (24 November 2010).

European Insurance and Occupational Pensions Authority (EIOPA)

- Regulation (EU) No 1094/2010 "establishing a European Supervisory Authority (European Insurance and Occupational Pensions Authority), amending Decision No 716/2009/EC and repealing Commission Decision 2009/79/EC" (*EIOPA Regulation*) ((24 November 2010).

The European Systemic Risk Board (ESRB)

- Regulation (EU) No 1092/2010 "on European Union macro-prudential oversight of the financial system and establishing a European Systemic Risk Board" (*ESRB Regulation*) (24 November 2010).

Supervision of institutions for occupational retirement

- Directive 2003/41/EC "on the activities and supervision of institutions for occupational retirement provision" (*IORP Directive*) (3 June 2003).

Single Supervisory Mechanism (SSM)

- Regulation (EU) 2015/534 of the European Central Bank "on reporting of supervisory financial information (ECB/2015/13)" (*SSM and SSMF (Reporting of Supervisory Financial Information) Regulation*) (17 March 2015).
- Regulation (EU) No 806/2014 "establishing uniform rules and a uniform procedure for the resolution of credit institutions and certain investment firms in the framework of a Single Resolution Mechanism and a Single Resolution Fund and amending Regulation" (*Single Resolution Mechanism (SRM) and Single Resolution Fund (SRF) Regulation*) (15 July 2014).
- Regulation (EU) No 468/2014 of the European Central Bank "establishing the framework for cooperation within the Single Supervisory Mechanism between the European Central Bank and national competent authorities and with national designated authorities (*SSM Framework Regulation*)" (*Single Supervisory Mechanism Framework Regulation, SSMF*) (16 April 2014).
- Council Regulation (EU) No 1024/2013 "conferring specific tasks on the European Central Bank concerning policies relating to the prudential supervision of credit institutions" (*Single Supervisory Mechanism Regulation, SSM*) (15 October 2013).

EUROPEAN LEVEL – Standards, Frameworks and Guidance

ESMA Guidance and Technical Advice

- ESMA/2014/298 – "Guidelines on cooperation arrangements and information exchange between competent authorities and between competent authorities and ESMA".
- JC/GL/2014/01 – "Joint Guidelines on the convergence of supervisory practices relating to the consistency of supervisory coordination arrangements for financial conglomerates".

EBA Guidelines

- JC/GL/2014/01 – "Joint Guidelines on the convergence of supervisory practices relating to the consistency of supervisory coordination arrangements for financial conglomerates".
- EBA/GL/2014/13 – "Guidelines on common procedures and methodologies for the supervisory review and evaluation process (SREP)".
- EBA/GL/2013/02 – "Guidelines on capital measures for foreign currency lending to unhedged borrowers under the supervisory review and evaluation process (SREP)".

EIOPA Guidelines and Reports

- EIOPA-BoS-14/146 — "Guidelines on operational functioning of colleges".

- EIOPA-BoS-14/179 — "Guidelines on supervisory review process" (including "SRP Guidelines Diagram").
- EIOPA-BoS-14/262 — "Peer Review on Supervisory Practices in respect of Article 9 of Directive 2003/41/EC ("Conditions of operation") — Final Report".
- EIOPA-BoS-14/262 — "Peer Review on Supervisory Practices in respect of Article 9 of Directive 2003/41/EC ("Conditions of operation") — Final Report".
- JC 2014 004 – "Final Report on mechanistic references to credit ratings in the ESAs' guidelines and recommendations".
- JC/GL/2014/01 — "Joint Guidelines on the convergence of supervisory practices relating to the consistency of supervisory coordination arrangements for financial conglomerates".
- JC/2012/86 – "The Joint Committee Report on the application of AML/CTF obligations to, and the AML/CTF supervision of e-money issuers, agents and distributors in Europe".
- EIOPA (2012) Report on "Comparing Certain Aspects of the Insurance Supervisory and Regulatory Regimes in the European Union and the United States".
- EIOPA-BoS-12092 – "Report on a mapping exercise on Industry Training Standards applied by national competent authorities".
- EIOPA-BoS-12/017 – "Report on the Functioning of Colleges and the Accomplishments of the 2011 Action Plan".
- CEIOPS-OP-68-10 Rev5 – "Report on Reporting Requirements to Supervisory Authorities for IORPs".
- EIOPA-11/026 – "Final Report on the Functioning of Colleges of Supervisors in 2010 & Targets 2011".

ESRB Recommendations and Reports

- ESRB/2014/3 — "ESRB Decision on the extension of the deadline included in Recommendation ESRB/2011/3 on the macro-prudential mandate of national authorities".
- ESRB Recommendation on the macro-prudential mandate of national authorities (ESRB/2011/3) – Follow-up Report — Overall assessment".
- ESRB/2011/3 – "Recommendation on the macro-prudential mandate of national authorities".

1.1.2 Credit Rating Agencies

GLOBAL LEVEL – Laws, Regulations and Norms

Not applicable: Binding laws, regulations and norms exist only at other Levels of governance.

GLOBAL LEVEL – Standards, Frameworks and Guidance

- The International Organization of Securities Commissions, Technical Committee (May 2008) "Code of Conduct Fundamentals for Credit Rating Agencies".
- The International Organization of Securities Commissions, Technical Committee (25 September 2003): "IOSCO Statement of Principles regarding the activities of Credit Rating Agencies".

EUROPEAN LEVEL – Laws, Regulations and Norms

Supervisory regulation in the financial services sector: Financial Conglomerates Directive

- Directive 2002/87/EC "on the supplementary supervision of credit institutions, insurance undertakings and investment firms in a financial conglomerate and amending Council Directives 73/239/EEC, 79/267/EEC, 92/49/EEC, 92/96/EEC, 93/6/EEC and 93/22/EEC, and Directives 98/78/EC and 2000/12/EC of the European Parliament and of the Council" (*Financial Conglomerates Directive (FICOD)*) (16 December 2002).
  Amendment:
  - Directive 2011/89/EU "amending Directives 98/78/EC, 2002/87/EC, 2006/48/EC and 2009/138/EC as regards the supplementary supervision of financial entities in a financial conglomerate" (*Financial Conglomerates (Amendment) Directive*) (16 November 2011).
  - [UK] SI 2013/1162 — Financial Conglomerates and Other Financial Groups (Amendment) Regulations 2013.
  - Directive 2008/25/EC "amending Directive 2002/87/EC on the supplementary supervision of credit institutions, insurance undertakings and investment firms in a financial conglomerate, as regards the implementing powers conferred on the Commission" (*Financial Conglomerates (Amendment) Directive*) (11 March 2008).

Regulation of Credit Rating Agencies (CRAs)

- Regulation (EC) No 1060/2009 "on credit rating agencies" (*Credit Rating Agencies (CRA)*) (16 September 2009).
  Amendments and Supplements:
  - Regulation (EU) No 462/2013 "amending Regulation (EC) No 1060/2009 on credit rating agencies" (*Credit Rating Agencies (Amendment) Regulation*) (21 May 2013).
  - Commission Delegated Regulation (EU) No 946/2012 "supplementing Regulation (EC) No 1060/2009 of the European Parliament and of the Council with regard to rules of procedure on fines imposed to credit rating

agencies by the European Securities and Markets Authority, including rules on the right of defence and temporal provisions" (*Credit Rating Agencies (Rules of Procedure on Fines) Regulation*) (12 July 2012).

- Commission Delegated Regulation (EU) No 449/2012 "supplementing Regulation (EC) No 1060/2009 of the European Parliament and of the Council with regard to regulatory technical standards on information for registration and certification of credit rating agencies Text with EEA relevance" (*Credit Rating Agencies (Registration and Certification) Regulation*) (21 March 2012).
- Delegated Regulation (EU) No 448/2012 "supplementing Regulation (EC) No 1060/2009 of the European Parliament and of the Council with regard to regulatory technical standards for the presentation of the information that credit rating agencies shall make available in a central repository established by the European Securities and Markets Authority Text with EEA relevance" (*Credit Rating Agencies (Central Repository Information) Regulation*) (21 March 2012).
- Commission Delegated Regulation (EU) No 447/2012 "supplementing Regulation (EC) No 1060/2009 of the European Parliament and of the Council on credit rating agencies by laying down regulatory technical standards for the assessment of compliance of credit rating methodologies" (*Credit Rating Agencies (Methodologies) Regulation*) (21 March 2012).
- Commission Delegated Regulation (EU) No 446/2012 "supplementing Regulation (EC) No 1060/2009 of the European Parliament and of the Council with regard to regulatory technical standards on the content and format of ratings data periodic reporting to be submitted to the European Securities and Markets Authority by credit rating agencies" (*Credit Rating Agencies (Content and Format of Ratings) Regulation*) (21 March 2012).
- Commission Delegated Regulation (EU) No 272/2012 "supplementing Regulation (EC) No 1060/2009 of the European Parliament and of the Council with regard to fees charged by the European Securities and Markets Authority to credit rating agencies" (*Credit Rating Agencies (Fees) Regulation*) (7 February 2012).
- Regulation (EU) No 513/2011 "amending Regulation (EC) No 1060/2009 on credit rating agencies" (*Credit Rating Agencies (Amendment) Regulation*) (11 May 2011).
- [UK] SI 2013/1637 – Credit Rating Agencies (Civil Liability) Regulations 2013.
- [UK] SI 2010/906 – Credit Rating Agencies Regulations 2010.

EUROPEAN LEVEL – Standards, Frameworks and Guidance

Technical Standards for Credit Rating Agencies (Regulation (EC) No 1060/2009)

- Commission Delegated Regulation (EU) 2015/3 "supplementing Regulation (EC) No 1060/2009 of the European Parliament and of the Council with regard to regulatory technical standards on disclosure requirements for structured finance instruments" (*CRA (Disclosure Requirements for Structured Finance Instruments — Regulatory Technical Standards) Regulation*) (30 September 2014).

- Commission Delegated Regulation (EU) 2015/2 "supplementing Regulation (EC) No 1060/2009 of the European Parliament and of the Council with regard to regulatory technical standards for the presentation of the information that credit rating agencies make available to the European Securities and Markets Authority" (*CRA (Presentation of Information made available to ESMA — Regulatory Technical Standards) Regulation*) (30 September 2014).

- Commission Delegated Regulation (EU) 2015/1 "supplementing Regulation (EC) No 1060/2009 of the European Parliament and of the Council with regard to regulatory technical standards for the periodic reporting on fees charged by credit rating agencies for the purpose of ongoing supervision by the European Securities and Markets Authority" (*CRA (Periodic Reporting on Fees — Regulatory Technical Standards) Regulation*) (30 September 2014).

ESMA Guidance and Technical Advice

- ESMA/2015/609 – Final Report – "Guidelines on periodic information to be submitted to ESMA by Credit Rating Agencies".
- ESMA/2015/280 – "ESMA supervision of Credit Rating Agencies and Trade Repositories – Annual report 2014 and work plan".
- ESMA/2014/1524 — "Credit Rating Agencies – ESMA's investigation into structured finance ratings".
- ESMA/2014/850rev – "Technical Advice in accordance with Article 39(b) 2 of the CRA Regulation regarding the appropriateness of the development of a European creditworthiness assessment for sovereign debt [Revised Version]".
- ESMA/2014/850 – "Technical Advice in accordance with Article 39(b) 2 of the CRA Regulation regarding the appropriateness of the development of a European creditworthiness assessment for sovereign debt".
- ESMA/2014/685 – "Final Report on Draft Regulatory Technical Standards under the CRA3 Regulation".
- ESMA/2014/151 – "Credit Rating Agencies Annual Report 2013".
- JC 2014 004 "Final Report on mechanistic references to credit ratings in the ESAs' guidelines and recommendations".
- ESMA/2013/1775 – "Credit Rating Agencies — Sovereign ratings investigation – ESMA's assessment of governance, conflicts of interest, resourcing adequacy and confidentiality controls".
- ESMA/2013/720 – "Guidelines and Recommendations on the Scope of the CRA Regulation".
- ESMA/2013/308 – "Annual report on the application of the Regulation on credit rating agencies – 2012".

- ESMA/2011/188 – "Cooperation including delegation between ESMA, the competent authorities and the sectoral-competent authorities under Regulation (EU) No 513/2011 on credit rating agencies".
- ESMA/2011/139 – "Final Report: Guidelines on the application of the endorsement regime under Article 4 (3) of the Credit Rating Agencies Regulation No 1060/2009".

NATIONAL LEVEL (UK) – Laws, Regulations and Norms

Cross-reference: No Act of Parliament is directly applicable. See applicable UK Statutory Instruments ("[UK] SI") implementing EU law in the corresponding European Level sub-section.

1.1.3. Resolution and Recovery

GLOBAL LEVEL – Laws, Regulations and Norms

Not applicable: Binding laws, regulations and norms exist only at other Levels of governance.

GLOBAL LEVEL – Standards, Frameworks and Guidance

- Financial Stability Board (15 October 2014) "Key Attributes of Effective Resolution Regimes for Financial Institutions".
- European Central Bank (6 August 2014) "Opinion on resolution of credit institutions and investment firms (CON/2014/62)".
- International Monetary Fund (27 August 2012) "The Key Attributes of Effective Resolution Regimes for Financial Institutions— Progress to Date and Next Steps", Prepared by the Legal Department and the Monetary and Capital Markets Department.
- Committee on Payment and Settlement Systems, Board of the International Organization of Securities Commissions (July 2012) "Recovery and resolution of financial market infrastructures", Consultative Report.

EUROPEAN LEVEL – Laws, Regulations and Norms

Resolution and Recovery

- Directive 2014/59/EU "establishing a framework for the recovery and resolution of credit institutions and investment firms and amending Council Directive 82/891/EEC, and Directives 2001/24/EC, 2002/47/EC, 2004/25/EC, 2005/56/EC, 2007/36/EC, 2011/35/EU, 2012/30/EU and 2013/36/EU, and Regulations (EU) No 1093/2010 and (EU) No 648/2012, of the European Parliament and of the Council" (*Bank Recovery and Resolution Directive (BRRD)*) (15 May 2014).

- Regulation (EU) No 806/2014 "establishing uniform rules and a uniform procedure for the resolution of credit institutions and certain investment firms in the framework of a Single Resolution Mechanism and a Single Resolution Fund and amending Regulation (EU) No 1093/2010" (*Single Resolution Mechanism (SRM) and Single Resolution Fund (SRF)*) (15 July 2014).
- Council Directive 2001/24/EC on "the reorganisation and winding up of credit institutions" (4 April 2001).
  Supplementing legislation:
  - Commission Delegated Regulation (EU) 2015/63 "supplementing Directive 2014/59/EU of the European Parliament and of the Council with regard to ex ante contributions to resolution financing arrangements" (*BRRD (Ex Ante Contributions to Resolution Financing Arrangements) Regulation*) (21 October 2014).
  - [UK] SI 2014/3329 — Bank Recovery and Resolution Order 2014 [*amending* the UK Banking Act 2009 c. 1].
  - [UK] SI 2014/3348 — Bank Recovery and Resolution (No 2) Order 2014 [*amending* the UK Banking Act 2009 c. 1].
  - [UK] SI 2007/830 – Credit Institutions (Reorganisation and Winding Up) (Amendment) Regulations 2007.
  - [UK] SI 2004/1045 – Credit Institutions (Reorganisation and Winding Up) Regulations 2004.

EUROPEAN LEVEL – Standards, Frameworks and Guidance

Recovery and Resolution

- Financial Stability Board (16 July 2013) "Recovery and Resolution Planning for Systemically Important Financial Institutions: Guidance on Identification of Critical Functions and Critical Shared Services".

EBA Guidelines

- EBA/GL/2014/11 – "Guidelines on the specification of measures to reduce or remove impediments to resolvability and the circumstances in which each measure may be applied under Directive 2014/59/EU" (Bank Recovery and Resolution Directive).
- EBA/GL/2014/09 – "Guidelines on the types of tests, reviews or exercises that may lead to support measures under Article 32(4)(d)(iii) of the Bank Recovery and Resolution Directive".
- EBA/GL/2014/06 – "Guidelines on the range of scenarios to be used in recovery plans".

ESRB Recommendations and Reports related to Resilience

- ESRB (2013) – "Occasional Paper No. 3 – The Structure and Resilience of the European Interbank Market".
- ESRB (2013) – "Report of the Advisory Scientific Committee on Forbearance, Resolution and Deposit Insurance".

NATIONAL LEVEL (UK) – Laws, Regulations and Norms

Resolution and Recovery

Cross-reference: No Act of Parliament is directly applicable. See applicable UK Statutory Instruments ("[UK] SI") implementing EU law in the corresponding European Level sub-section.

- The Banking Act 2009 c.1.

1.1.4 Enforcement procedures

GLOBALE LEVEL – Laws, Regulations and Norms

Not applicable: Binding laws, regulations and norms exist only at other Levels of governance.

EUROPEAN LEVEL – Laws, Regulations and Norms

Not applicable: Binding laws, regulations and norms exist only at other Levels of governance.

- Council Regulation (EC) No 44/2001 "on jurisdiction and the recognition and enforcement of judgments in civil and commercial matters" (22 December 2000).

EUROPEAN LEVEL – Standards, Frameworks and Guidance

- Communication COM(2009) 175 "Green Paper on the review of Council Regulation (EC) No 44/2001 on jurisdiction and the recognition and enforcement of judgments in civil and commercial matters" (21 April 2009).

NATIONAL LEVEL (UK) – Laws, Regulations and Norms

Enforcement

- Criminal Justice Act 1993 c. 36.
  Secondary legislation:
  - SI 1994/187 – Insider Dealing (Securities and Regulated Markets) Order 1994.
- FCA: Decision Procedure and Penalties Manual (DEPP), release 146, February 2014.

- Financial Services and Markets Act 2000
  - Section 169(7): Investigations etc. in support of overseas regulator.

Penalties (examples)

Penalties are usually defined in the Acts of Parliament and implemented by statutory instruments. The list below provides a few examples.

- Financial Services Act 2012 c. 21.
  Secondary legislation implementing penalties:
  - SI 2013/429 – Payment to Treasury of Penalties Regulations 2013.
- Data Protection Act 1998 c. 29.
  Secondary legislation implementing penalties:
  - SI 2010/31 – Data Protection (Monetary Penalties) (Maximum Penalty and Notices) Regulations 2010.
  - SI 2010/910 – Data Protection (Monetary Penalties) Order 2010.
- Companies Act 2006 c. 46.
  Secondary legislation implementing penalties:
  - SI 2008/497 – Companies (Late Filing Penalties) and Limited Liability Partnerships (Filing Periods and Late Filing Penalties) Regulations 2008.
- European Commission Regulation
  - Commission Delegated Regulation (EU) No 667/2014 European Market Infrastructure Regulation (EMIR) (Penalties Imposed on Trade Repositories by ESMA) Regulation.
- Financial Services Act 2012 c. 21.
  Secondary legislation implementing penalties:
  - SI 2013/487 – Payment to Treasury of Penalties (Enforcement Costs of the Payment Systems Regulator) Order 2015.

NATIONAL LEVEL (UK) – Standards, Frameworks and Guidance

- Combined View: Decision Procedure and Penalties Manual (DEPP)
  A description of the FCA's procedures for taking statutory notice decisions, the FCA's policy on the imposition and amount of penalties and the conduct of interviews to which a direction under section 169(7) of the Act has been given or the FSA is considering giving with effect from 28 August 2007.
  - DEPP 1 – Application and Purpose
  - DEPP 2 – Statutory notices and the allocation of decision making
  - DEPP 3 – The nature and procedure of the Regulatory Decisions Committee (RDC)
  - DEPP 4 – Decisions by FCA staff under executive procedures1
  - DEPP 5 – Settlement decision procedure

- DEPP 6 – Penalties
- DEPP 6A – The power to impose a suspension or restriction
- DEPP 7 – Statement of policy on interviews conducted on behalf of overseas and EEA regulators
- Combined View: The Enforcement Guide (EG) (1 April 2014)
  This guide describes the FCA's approach to exercising the main enforcement powers given to it by the Financial Services and Markets Act 2000 (the Act) and by regulation 12 of the Unfair Terms Regulations.

1.2   GENERAL REGULATIONS

1.2.1 Stability and capital requirements

GLOBAL LEVEL – Laws, Regulations and Norms

Note: The Basel Accords were approved and in that sense "ratified" at the (Annual) General Meetings of the Bank for International Settlements (BIS), and thereby became international law. These agreements between the central banks members of the BIS and the commercial banks regulated by them (all of which are private corporations) constitute *private* not public international law.

Until 2009 the Basel Committee consisted of representatives from central banks and regulatory authorities from the Group of Ten countries (Belgium, Canada, France, Italy, Japan, the Netherlands, the UK, US, Germany and Sweden) plus Luxembourg and Spain. Since 2009 all of the other G-20 countries have also been represented as well as certain other major banking centres such as Hong Kong and Singapore.

Cross-reference: For further information, see 1.7 "Insurance": the Insurance and Reinsurance Directive (Solvency II) (2009/138/EC).

Capital Requirements Regulation (CRR)

- Regulation (EU) No 575/2013 on "prudential requirements for credit institutions and investment firms and amending Regulation (EU) No 648/2012" (*Capital Requirements Regulation (CRR)*) (26 June 2013).
  Amendments:
  - Commission Implementing Regulation (EU) 2015/880 "on the extension of the transitional periods related to own funds requirements for exposures to central counterparties set out in Regulations (EU) No 575/2013 and (EU) No 648/2012 of the European Parliament and of the Council" (*CRR (Own Funds Requirements for Exposures to Central Counterparties — Extension of Transitional Periods) Regulation)* (4 June 2015).

- Commission Delegated Regulation (EU) 2015/850 "amending Delegated Regulation (EU) No 241/2014 supplementing Regulation (EU) No 575/2013 of the European Parliament and of the Council with regard to regulatory technical standards for Own Funds requirements for institutions" (*CRR (Own Funds Requirements for Institutions) (Amendment) Regulation*) (30 January 2015).
- Commission Delegated Regulation (EU) 2015/62 "amending Regulation (EU) No 575/2013 of the European Parliament and of the Council with regard to the leverage ratio" (*CRR (Leverage Ratio) Regulation*) (10 October 2014).
- Commission Delegated Regulation (EU) 2015/61 "to supplement Regulation (EU) No 575/2013 of the European Parliament and the Council with regard to liquidity coverage requirement for Credit Institutions" (*CRR (Liquidity Coverage Requirement for Credit Institutions) Regulation*) (10 October 2014).
- Commission Implementing Regulation (EU) No 1317/2014 "on the extension of the transitional periods related to own funds requirements for exposures to central counterparties in Regulations (EU) No 575/2013 and (EU) No 648/2012" (*CRR (Own Funds Requirements for Exposures to Central Counterparties — Extension of Transitional Periods) Regulation*) (11 December 2014).
- Commission Implementing Regulation (EU) No 591/2014 "on the extension of the transitional periods related to own funds requirements for exposures to central counterparties in Regulation (EU) No 575/2013 and Regulation (EU) No 648/2012 of the European Parliament and of the Council" (*CRR and EMIR (Extension of Transitional Periods) Regulation*) (3 June 2014).

Capital Requirements Directive (CRD IV)

- Directive 2013/36/EU "on access to the activity of credit institutions and the prudential supervision of credit institutions and investment firms, amending Directive 2002/87/EC and repealing Directives 2006/48/EC and 2006/49/EC" (*Capital Requirements Directive (CRD IV)*) (26 June 2013).
  - [UK] SI 2015/19 — Capital Requirements (Capital Buffers and Macroprudential Measures) (Amendment) Regulations 2015.
  - [UK] SI 2014/894 – Capital Requirements (Capital Buffers and Macroprudential Measures) Regulations.
  - [UK] SI 2013/3118 – Capital Requirements (Country-by-Country Reporting) Regulations 2013.
  - [UK] SI 2013/3115 – Capital Requirements Regulations 2013.

Capital adequacy of investment firms and credit institutions (Directive 2006/49/EC), Basel II Accord

- Directive 2006/49/EC "on the capital adequacy of investment firms and credit institutions (recast)" (*recast as part of Capital Requirements Directive (CRD)*) (14 June 2006). [Repealed]

The taking-up and pursuit of the business of credit institutions (Directive 2006/48/EC), Basel II Accord

- Directive 2006/48/EC "relating to the taking up and pursuit of the business of credit institutions" (*recast as part of Capital Requirements Directive (CRD)*) (14 June 2006). [Repealed]
  Amendments:
  - Directive 2010/76/EU "amending Directives 2006/48/EC and 2006/49/EC as regards capital requirements for the trading book and for re-securitisations, and the supervisory review of remuneration policies" (*Capital Requirements Directive IV (CRD IV) with its Corrigendum 1*) (24 November 2010).
  - Directive 2009/111/EC "amending Directives 2006/48/EC, 2006/49/EC and 2007/64/EC as regards banks affiliated to central institutions, certain own funds items, large exposures, supervisory arrangements, and crisis management" (*Capital Requirements and Payment Services (Amendment) Directive (CRD II)*) (16 September 2009).
  - Directive 2007/18/EC "amending Directive 2006/48/EC of the European Parliament and of the Council as regards the exclusion or inclusion of certain institutions from its scope of application and the treatment of exposures to multilateral development banks" (*CRD) Institutions Revision Directive*) (27 March 2007).

Further regulation related to Financial Stability

- Council Directive 89/646/EEC "on the coordination of laws, regulations and administrative provisions relating to the taking up and pursuit of the business of credit institutions and amending Directive 77/780/EEC" (Second Banking Directive) (15 December 1989).

GLOBAL LEVEL – Standards, Frameworks and Guidance

Basel Committee on Banking Supervision Guidance

- Basel Committee on Banking Supervision "Annex 1: Summary description of the LCR" (January 2013).

- Basel Committee on Banking Supervision "Annex 2: Complete set of agreed changes to the Liquidity Coverage Ratio (LCR)" (January 2013).
- Committee on Banking Supervision "Operational Risk – Supervisory Guidelines for the Advanced Measurement Approaches, Consultative Document" (25 February 2011).
- Basel Committee on Banking Supervision/ Bank for International Settlement "Operational Risk – Supervisory Guidelines for the Advanced Measurement Approaches, Consultative Document" (25 February 2011).
- Basel Committee on Banking Supervision/ Bank for International Settlement "Operational Risk – Sound Practices for the Management and Supervision of Operational Risk, Consultative Document" (25 February 2011).
- New Basel Capital Accord (Basel II)/ Capital Requirements Directive (CRD; "International Convergence of Capital Measurement and Capital Standards - A Revised Framework Comprehensive Version" (June 2006).

EUROPEAN LEVEL – Laws, Regulations and Norms

Cross-reference: For further information, see Global Level.

EUROPEAN LEVEL – Standards, Frameworks and Guidance

Implementing Technical Standards with regard to supervisory reporting of institutions: The European Commission has adopted (16/04) an implementing technical standard (ITS) which harmonises the content and format of data to be reported by 8000 European banks to their supervisors in order to comply with the Capital Requirements Regulation (575/2013) and Capital Requirements Directive (2013/36).

The European Banking Authority (EBA) is responsible for developing a Single Rulebook. The Single Rulebook aims to provide a single set of harmonised prudential rules which institutions throughout the EU must respect. The European Council coined the term Single Rulebook in 2009 in order to refer to the goal of a unified regulatory framework for the EU financial sector that would complete the Single Market in financial services. This will ensure uniform application of Basel III in all Member States. It will close regulatory loopholes, and will thus contribute to a more effective functioning of the Single Market. This is primarily achieved through the use of implementing technical standards (ITS).

Technical Standards for CRR (Regulation (EU) 575/2013)

- Commission Delegated Regulation (EU) 2015/585 "supplementing Regulation (EU) No 575/2013 of the European Parliament and of the Council with regard to regulatory technical standards for the specification of margin periods of risk" (*CRR (Specification of Margin Periods of Risk — Regulatory Technical Standards) Regulation*) (18 December 2014).
- Commission Implementing Regulation (EU) 2015/233 "laying down implementing technical standards with regard to currencies in which there is an extremely narrow

definition of central bank eligibility pursuant to Regulation (EU) No 575/2013" (*CRR (Implementing Technical Standards) Regulation*) (13 February 2015).

- Commission Implementing Regulation (EU) 2015/227 "amending Implementing Regulation (EU) No 680/2014 laying down implementing technical standards with regard to supervisory reporting of institutions according to Regulation (EU) No 575/2013" (*CRR (Supervisory Reporting of Institutions) (Amendment) Regulation*) (9 January 2015).

- Commission Delegated Regulation (EU) No 183/2014 "supplementing Regulation (EU) No 575/2013 of the European Parliament and of the Council on prudential requirements for credit institutions and investment firms, with regard to regulatory technical standards for specifying the calculation of specific and general credit risk adjustments" (*CRR (Specific and General Credit Risk Adjustments — Regulatory Technical Standards) Regulation*) (20 December 2013).

- Commission Delegated Regulation (EU) No 1187/2014 "supplementing Regulation (EU) No 575/2013 of the European Parliament and of the Council as regards regulatory technical standards for determining the overall exposure to a client or a group of connected clients in respect of transactions with underlying assets" (*CRR (Overall Exposure to a Client or Connected Clients in respect of Transactions with Underlying Assets — Regulatory Technical Standards) Regulation*) (2 October 2014).

- Commission Implementing Regulation (EU) 2015/79 amending Implementing Regulation (EU) No 680/2014 laying down implementing technical standards with regard to supervisory reporting of institutions according to Regulation (EU) No 575/2013 of the European Parliament and of the Council as regards asset encumbrance, single data point model and validation rules" (*CRR (Supervisory Reporting – Implementing Technical Standards) Regulation*) (18 December 2014).

- Commission Implementing Regulation (EU) No 1030/2014 "laying down implementing technical standards with regard to the uniform formats and date for the disclosure of the values used to identify global systemically important institutions according to Regulation (EU) No 575/2013 of the European Parliament and of the Council" (*CRR (Identification of Global Systemically Important Institutions (G-SIIs) — Implementing Technical Standards) Regulation*) (29 September 2014).

- Commission Implementing Regulation (EU) No 945/2014 "laying down implementing technical standards with regard to relevant appropriately diversified indices according to Regulation (EU) No 575/2013 of the European Parliament and of the Council" (*CRR (Relevant Indices — Implementing Technical Standards) Regulation*) (4 September 2014).

- Commission Implementing Regulation (EU) No 680/2014 "laying down implementing technical standards with regard to supervisory reporting of institutions according to Regulation (EU) No 575/2013 of the European Parliament and of the Council" (*CRR (Supervisory Reporting of Institutions — Implementing Technical Standards) Regulation*) (16 April 2014).

- Commission Delegated Regulation (EU) No 625/2014 "supplementing Regulation (EU) No 575/2013 of the European Parliament and of the Council by way of regulatory technical standards specifying the requirements for investor, sponsor, original lenders and originator institutions relating to exposures to transferred credit risk" (*CRR (Requirements relating to Exposures to Transferred Credit Risk — Regulatory Technical Standards) Regulation*) (13 March 2014).

- Commission Delegated Regulation (EU) No 529/2014 "supplementing Regulation (EU) No 575/2013 of the European Parliament and of the Council with regard to regulatory technical standards for assessing the materiality of extensions and changes of the Internal Ratings Based Approach and the Advanced Measurement Approach" (*CRR (Extensions and Changes of Internal Ratings Based Approach and Advanced Measurement Approach — Regulatory Technical Standards) Regulation*) (12 March 2014).

- Commission Delegated Regulation (EU) No 528/2014 "supplementing Regulation (EU) No 575/2013 of the European Parliament and of the Council with regard to regulatory technical standards for non-delta risk of options in the standardised market risk approach" (*CRR (Non-Delta Risk of Options in the Standardised Market Risk Approach — Regulatory Technical Standards) Regulation*) (12 March 2014).

- Commission Delegated Regulation (EU) No 526/2014 "supplementing Regulation (EU) No 575/2013 of the European Parliament and of the Council with regard to regulatory technical standards for determining proxy spread and limited smaller portfolios for credit valuation adjustment risk" (*CRR (Proxy Spread and Limited Smaller Portfolios for Credit Valuation Adjustment Risk — Regulatory Technical Standards) Regulation*) (12 March 2014).

- Commission Delegated Regulation (EU) No 525/2014 "supplementing Regulation (EU) No 575/2013 of the European Parliament and of the Council with regard to regulatory technical standards for the definition of market" (*CRR (Definition of Market — Regulatory Technical Standards) Regulation*) (12 March 2014).

- Commission Delegated Regulation (EU) No 523/2014 "supplementing Regulation (EU) No 575/2013 of the European Parliament and of the Council with regard to regulatory technical standards for determining what constitutes the close correspondence between the value of an institution's covered bonds and the value of the institution's assets" (*CRR (Close Correspondence between the Value of an Institution's Covered Bonds and the Value of the Institution's Assets — Regulatory Technical Standards) Regulation*) (12 March 2014).

- Commission Delegated Regulation (EU) No 342/2014"supplementing Directive 2002/87/EC of the European Parliament and of the Council and Regulation (EU) No 575/2013 of the European Parliament and of the Council with regard to regulatory technical standards for the application of the calculation methods of capital adequacy requirements for financial conglomerates" (FCD and CRR (*Calculation Methods of Capital Adequacy Requirements for Financial Conglomerates — Regulatory Technical Standards) Regulation*) (21 January 2014).
- Commission Delegated Regulation (EU) No 241/2014 "supplementing Regulation (EU) No 575/2013 of the European Parliament and of the Council with regard to regulatory technical standards for Own Funds requirements for institutions" (*CRR (Own Funds Requirements for Institutions — Regulatory Technical Standards) Regulation*) (7 January 2014).
  Amendments:
    - Commission Delegated Regulation (EU) 2015/488 "amending Delegated Regulation (EU) No 241/2014 as regards own funds requirements for firms based on fixed overheads" (*CRR (Own Funds Requirements for Firms based on Fixed Overheads) (Amendment) Regulation*) (4 September 2014).

Technical Standards for CRD (Directive 2013/36/EU)

- Commission Delegated Regulation (EU) No 1222/2014 "supplementing Directive 2013/36/EU of the European Parliament and of the Council with regard to regulatory technical standards for the specification of the methodology for the identification of global systemically important institutions and for the definition of subcategories of global systemically important institutions" (*CRD (Identification and Definition of Subcategories of Global Systemically Important Institutions - Regulatory Technical Standards) Regulation*) (8 October 2014).
- Commission Delegated Regulation (EU) No 1152/2014 "supplementing Directive 2013/36/EU of the European Parliament and of the Council with regard to regulatory technical standards on the identification of the geographical location of the relevant credit exposures for calculating institution-specific countercyclical capital buffer rates" (*CRD (Identification of Location of Credit Exposures — Regulatory Technical Standards) Regulation*) (4 June 2014).
- Commission Delegated Regulation (EU) No 1151/2014 "supplementing Directive 2013/36/EU of the European Parliament and of the Council with regard to regulatory technical standards on the information to be notified when exercising the right of establishment and the freedom to provide services" (*CRD (Information when Exercising the Right of Establishment and Freedom to Provide Services — Regulatory Technical Standards) Regulation*) (4 June 2014).
- Commission Implementing Regulation (EU) No 710/2014 "laying down implementing technical standards with regard to conditions of application of the joint decision process for institution-specific prudential requirements according to

Directive 2013/36/EU of the European Parliament and of the Council" (*CRD (Joint Decision Process for Institution-Specific Prudential Requirements — Implementing Technical Standards) Regulation*) (23 June 2014).

- Commission Implementing Regulation (EU) No 650/2014 "laying down implementing technical standards with regard to the format, structure, contents list and annual publication date of the information to be disclosed by competent authorities in accordance with Directive 2013/36/EU of the European Parliament and of the Council" (*CRD (Information to be Disclosed by Competent Authorities — Implementing Technical Standards) Regulation*) (4 June 2014).

- Commission Implementing Regulation (EU) No 620/2014 "laying down implementing technical standards with regard to information exchange between competent authorities of home and host Member States, according to Directive 2013/36/EU of the European Parliament and of the Council" (*CRD (Information Exchange — Implementing Technical Standards) Regulation*) (4 June 2014).

- Commission Implementing Regulation (EU) No 926/2014 "laying down implementing technical standards with regard to standard forms, templates and procedures for notifications relating to the exercise of the right of establishment and the freedom to provide services according to Directive 2013/36/EU of the European Parliament and of the Council" (*CRD (Right of Establishment and Freedom to Provide Services — Forms, Templates and Procedures for Notifications — Implementing Technical Standards) Regulation*) (27 August 2014).

- Commission Delegated Regulation (EU) No 604/2014 "supplementing Directive 2013/36/EU of the European Parliament and of the Council with regard to regulatory technical standards with respect to qualitative and appropriate quantitative criteria to identify categories of staff whose professional activities have a material impact on an institution's risk profile" (*CRD (Qualitative and Quantitative Criteria to Identify Staff that Impact on An Institution's Risk Profile — Regulatory Technical Standards) Regulation*) (4 March 2014).

- Commission Delegated Regulation (EU) No 530/2014 "supplementing Directive 2013/36/EU of the European Parliament and of the Council with regard to regulatory technical standards further defining material exposures and thresholds for internal approaches to specific risk in the trading book" (*CRD (Material Exposures and Thresholds to Specific Risk in the Trading Book — Regulatory Technical Standards) Regulation*) (12 March 2014).

- Commission Delegated Regulation (EU) No 527/2014 "supplementing Directive (EU) No 2013/36/EU of the European Parliament and of the Council with regard to regulatory technical standards specifying the classes of instruments that adequately reflect the credit quality of an institution as a going concern and are appropriate to be used for the purposes of variable remuneration" (*CRD (Classes of Instruments — Regulatory Technical Standards) Regulation*) (12 March 2014).

- Commission Delegated Regulation (EU) No 524/2014 "supplementing Directive 2013/36/EU of the European Parliament and of the Council with regard to regulatory technical standards specifying the information that competent authorities of home and host Member States supply to one another" (*CRD (Supply of Information by and to Competent Authorities of Home and Host Member States — Regulatory Technical Standards) Regulation*) (12 March 2014).

ESMA Guidance related to Capital Requirements

- ESMA/2014/1293 — "ESMA Guidelines on enforcement of financial information".
- ESMA/2014/1571 — "Final Report on draft Implementing Technical Standards on main indices and recognised exchanges under the Capital Requirements Regulation".
- ESMA/2014/807 — "Final Report on ESMA Guidelines on enforcement of financial information".
- ESMA/2013/1965 — "ESMA's Technical Advice to the Commission on procedural rules to impose fines and periodic penalty payments to Trade Repositories".
- ESMA/2013/1545 — "14th Extract from the EECS' Database of Enforcement".

EBA Guidelines and Options related to Capital Requirements

- EBA/GL/2014/14 — "Guidelines on materiality, proprietary and confidentiality and on disclosure frequency under Articles 432(1), 432(2) and 433 of Regulation (EU) No 575/2013" (*Capital Requirements Regulation (CRR) Guidelines*).
- EBA/GL/2014/10 – "Guidelines On the criteria to determine the conditions of application of Article 131(3) of Directive 2013/36/EU (CRD) in relation to the assessment of other systemically important institutions (O-SIIs)" (*Capital Requirements Directive (CRD IV) Guidelines*).
- EBA/Op/2014/10 (15 October 2014) "Opinion of the European Banking Authority on the application of Directive 2013/36/EU (Capital Requirements Directive) regarding the principles on remuneration policies of credit institutions and investment firms and the use of allowances." (European Banking Authority, London).
- EBA/GL/2014/05 — "Guidelines on Significant Credit Risk Transfer relating to Articles 243 and Article 244 of Regulation 575/2013" (*Capital Requirements Regulation (CRR) Guidelines*).
- EBA/GL/2013/01 — "Guidelines on retail deposits subject to different outflows for purposes of liquidity reporting under Regulation (EU) No 575/2013, on prudential requirements for credit institutions and investment firms and amending Regulation (EU) No 648/2012" (*Capital Requirements Regulation (CRR) Guidelines*).

EBA Guidelines related to Financial Stability

- EBA/GL/2014/02 — "Guidelines on disclosure of indicators of global systemic importance".

- EBA/GL/2012/3 – "Guidelines on Incremental Default and Migration Risk Charge (IRC)"
- EBA/GL/2012/2 – "Guidelines on Stressed Value-At-Risk (Stressed VaR)".
- EBA (2013) – "Guidelines on Advanced Measurement Approach (AMA) – Extensions and Changes (GL45)".

EIOPA Guidelines and Reports related to Financial Stability

- EIOPA-FS-12-097 – "Financial Stability Report 2012: Second half-year report".
- EIOPA-FS-12-042) – "Financial Stability Report 2012: First half-year report EIOPA".
- EIOPA-FSC-11/057 – "Financial Stability Report 2011: Second half-year report (EIOPA-FSC-11/057)".
- EIOPA-FSC-11-026 – "Financial Stability Report 2011: First half-year report".

ESRB Recommendations and Reports related to Financial Stability

- ESRB/2014/4 — "Decision on the extension of certain deadlines set by Recommendation ESRB/2012/2 on funding of credit institutions".
- ESRB/2014/1 — "ESRB Recommendation on guidance for setting countercyclical buffer rates".
- ESRB (2014) – "Extension of reporting deadlines for ESRB Recommendation 2012/2 on bank funding".
- ESRB (2014) – "Reports of the Advisory Scientific Committee, No.5: Allocating macro-prudential powers".
- ESRB (2014) – "Occasional Paper No. 5 — Operationalising the countercyclical capital buffer: indicator selection, threshold identification and calibration options".
- ESRB/2013/1 – "Recommendation of the ESRB of 4 April 2013 on intermediate objectives and instruments of macro-prudential policy".
- ESRB/2012/2 – "Recommendation of the ESRB of 20 December 2012 on funding of credit institutions".
- ESRB (2014) – "ESRB's reply to the European Commission's Green Paper on Shadow Banking".

EIOPA Guidelines and Reports related to Stability

- EIOPA-FS-14/105 — "Financial Stability Report — December 2014".
- EIOPA-FS-14-044 — "Financial Stability Report — May 2014".
- EIOPA-FS-13/075 – "Financial Stability Report — Second Half-Year Report — Autumn 2013".
- JC-2013-77 – "Joint Position of the European Supervisory Authorities on Manufacturers' Product Oversight & Governance Processes".

- EIOPA-FS-13/041 – "Financial Stability Report 2013 — First Half Year Report".

NATIONAL LEVEL (UK) – Laws, Regulations and Norms

Cross-reference: For further information, see Global and European Level.

NATIONAL LEVEL (UK) – Standards, Frameworks and Guidance

FCA Handbook/ PRD Handbook:
- BIPRU 12.2 – Adequacy of liquidity resources
- BIPRU 12.2.1R – The overall liquidity adequacy rule
- BIPRU 12.2.2R – Branch liquidity resources
- BIPRU 12.2.3R and BIPRU 12.2.4G – Branch liquidity resources
- BIPRU 12.2.5G – BIPRU 12.2.7G – Liquidity resources: general
- BIPRU 12.2.8R - BIPRU 12.2.13G – Liquid assets buffer and funding profile
- BIPRU 12.2.14G - BIPRU 12.2.18G – Individual assessments of liquidity adequacy
- FCA Handbook: GENPRU 2.1 – Calculation of capital resources requirements

SUB-NATIONAL LEVEL – Laws, Regulations and Norms

Capital risk is defined as the risk that the Group has a sub-optimal amount or quality of capital or that capital is inefficiently deployed across the Financial Institute.

- Group Capital Policy
- Regulatory Capital Requirements Policy
- Model Governance Policy
- Business Planning & Stress Testing Policy
- Capital Transfer Pricing Policy

SUB-NATIONAL LEVEL – Standards, Frameworks and Guidance

- The financial institution will maintain a Board-approved capital-risk appetite by setting target levels of capital with reference to key regulatory capital ratios and taking account of:
  - Company Strategy – including targets for the amount and distribution of Risk Weighted Averages (RWAs) across business units.
  - Regulatory expectations – including meeting current and expected future regulatory capital requirements.
  - Market expectations of investors and rating agencies.
  - Stressed forecasts – prescribing minimum acceptable capital levels required in Board approved stress scenarios.

- The company will ensure the business operates within its stated capital risk appetite – this will include the monitoring of actuals, forecasting of future positions and using comprehensive stress testing to understand potential threats to the company's capital adequacy and to develop appropriate mitigating actions.
- The company operates a centralised capital management model – subsidiaries must hold sufficient but not excessive capital buffers that will ensure that minimum regulatory expectations are met or, if the entity is not regulated, will ensure that the entity remains solvent. Surplus capital above the buffers must be held centrally.
- The company will ensure that capital usage is efficient – The company, divisions and business units must consider the costs and availability of capital when forming business plans and strategies, ensuring the optimisation of returns. This will include a Capital Transfer Pricing mechanism and consideration of risk/ return measures.

1.2.2 Capital Markets Union and General banking regulation

EUROPEAN LEVEL – Laws, Regulations and Norms

Not applicable: Binding laws, regulations and norms exist only at other Levels of governance.

EUROPEAN LEVEL – Standards, Frameworks and Guidance

Capital Markets Union

- Commission COM/2015/063 final "Green Paper Building a Capital Markets Union" (18 February 2015).
- Commission Staff Working Document SWD(2015) 13 final "Initial reflections on the obstacles to the development of deep and integrated EU capital markets – Accompanying the document Green Paper Building a Capital Markets Union; COM(2015) 63 final" (18 February 2015)
- Communication COM(2012) 510 final "A Roadmap towards a Banking Union" (12 September 2012).
- Communication COM(2012) 102 final "Green Paper: Shadow Banking" (19 March 2012).
- Commission, European Parliament, the Council the European Economic and Social Committee and the European Central Bank COM(2010) 301 final "Regulating Financial Services for sustainable Growth" (2 June 2010).
- Communication COM(2005) 177 "Green Paper on Financial Services Policy (2005 - 2010)" (May 2005).
- Communication COM(96) 209 "Green Paper on Financial Services: Meeting Consumer's Expectations" (22 May 1996)

<u>NATIONAL LEVEL (UK) – Laws, Regulations and Norms</u>

Applicable to the whole sector

For further information, see 1.1.1 "European Supervisory Authorities", and sub-section Financial Conglomerates.

Credit Institutions

- Directive 2000/28/EC on "amending Directive 2000/12/EC relating to the taking up and pursuit of the business of credit institutions" (18 September 2000).
  - [UK] SI 2002/765 – Electronic Money (Miscellaneous Amendments) Regulations 2002.

General Banking Regulation

- Financial Services (Banking Reform) Act 2013 c. 33.
  Secondary legislation:
  - SI 2015/492 — Financial Services (Banking Reform) Act 2013 (Transitional and Savings Provisions) Order 2015.
  - SI 2015/487 — Payment to Treasury of Penalties (Enforcement Costs of the Payment Systems Regulator) Order 2015.
  - SI 2014/3344 — Building Societies (Bail-in) Order 2014.
  - SI 2014/882 — Financial Services (Banking Reform) Act 2013 (Disclosure of Confidential Information) Regulations 2014.
  - SI 2014/378 — Financial Services (Banking Reform) Act 2013 (Transitional Provision) Order 2014.
- Financial Services Act 2012 c. 21.
  Secondary legislation:
  - SI 2013/2984 — Financial Services Act 2012 (Consequential Amendments and Transitional Provisions) (No 4) Order 2013.
  - SI 2013/1765 — Financial Services Act 2012 (Consequential Amendments and Transitional Provisions) (No 3) Order 2013.
  - SI 2013/642 — Financial Services Act 2012 (Consequential Amendments and Transitional Provisions) (No 2) Order 2013.
  - SI 2013/637 — Financial Services Act 2012 (Misleading Statements and Impressions) Order 2013.
  - SI 2013/636 — Financial Services Act 2012 (Consequential Amendments) Order 2013.
  - SI 2013/496 — Financial Services Act 2012 (Mutual Societies) Order 2013.
  - SI 2013/472 — Financial Services Act 2012 (Consequential Amendments and Transitional Provisions) Order 2013.

- SI 2013/442 — Financial Services Act 2012 (Transitional Provisions) (Miscellaneous Provisions) Order 2013.
- SI 2013/441 — Financial Services Act 2012 (Transitional Provisions) (Enforcement) Order 2013.
- SI 2013/440 — Financial Services Act 2012 (Transitional Provisions) (Permission and Approval) Order 2013.
- SI 2013/423 — Financial Services Act 2012 (Commencement No 2) Order 2013.
- SI 2013/161 — Financial Services Act 2012 (Transitional Provisions) (Rules and Miscellaneous Provisions) Order 2013.
- SI 2013/113 — Financial Services Act 2012 (Commencement No 1) Order 2013.

- Banking Act 2009 c. 1.
  Secondary legislation:
  - SI 2014/3350 — Banking Act 2009 (Restriction of Special Bail-in Provision, etc.) Order 2014.
  - SI 2014/3330 — Banking Act 2009 (Mandatory Compensation Arrangements Following Bail-in) Regulations 2014.
  - SI 2014/1832 — Banking Act 2009 (Exclusion of Investment Firms of a Specified Description) Order 2014.
  - SI 2014/1831 — Banking Act 2009 (Banking Group Companies) Order 2014.
  - SI 2014/1830 — Banking Act 2009 (Third Party Compensation Arrangements for Partial Property Transfers) (Amendment) Regulations 2014.
  - SI 2014/1828 — Banking Act 2009 (Restriction of Partial Property Transfers) (Recognised Central Counterparties) Order 2014.
  - SI 2010/828 – Banking Act 2009 (Inter-Bank Payment Systems) (Disclosure and Publication of Specified Information) Regulations 2010.
  - SI 2010/35 – Banking Act 2009 (Exclusion of Insurers) Order 2010.
  - SI 2009/312 – Banking Act 2009 (Bank Administration) (Modification for Application to Banks in Temporary Public Ownership) Regulations 2009.

- Banking (Special Provisions) Act 2008 c. 2.
- Financial Services and Markets Act 2000 (FSMA) c. 8 and Companies Act 1989 c. 40.
  Secondary legislation:
  - SI 2015/547 – Financial Services and Markets Act 2000 (Banking Reform) (Pensions) Regulations 2015.
  - SI 2015/369 — Financial Services and Markets Act 2000 (Regulated Activities) (Amendment) Order 2015.
  - SI 2015/61 — Financial Services and Markets Act 2000 (Regulation of Auditors and Actuaries) (PRA Specified Powers) Order 2015.
  - SI 2014/3340 — Financial Services and Markets Act 2000 (Carrying on Regulated Activities by Way of Business) (Amendment) Order 2014.
  - SI 2014/3081 — Financial Services and Markets Act 2000 (Market Abuse) Regulations 2014.

- 2014/2632 — Financial Services and Markets Act 2000 (Consumer Credit) (Transitional Provisions) (No 4) Order 2014.
- SI 2014/2080 — Financial Services and Markets Act 2000 (Excluded Activities and Prohibitions) Order 2014.
- SI 2014/1960 — Financial Services and Markets Act 2000 (Ring-fenced Bodies and Core Activities) Order 2014.
- SI 2014/1850 — Financial Services and Markets Act 2000 (Regulated Activities) (Green Deal) (Amendment) Order 2014.
- SI 2014/1740 — Financial Services and Markets Act 2000 (Regulated Activities) (Amendment) (No 3) Order 2014.
- SI 2014/1448 — Financial Services and Markets Act 2000 (Regulated Activities) (Amendment) (No 2) Order 2014.
- SI 2014/1446 — Financial Services and Markets Act 2000 (Consumer Credit) (Transitional Provisions) (No 3) Order 2014.
- SI 2014/905 — Financial Services and Markets Act 2000 (Over the Counter Derivatives, Central Counterparties and Trade Repositories) (Amendment) Regulations 2014.
- SI 2014/883 — Financial Services and Markets Act 2000 (Disclosure of Confidential Information) (Amendment) Regulations 2014.
- SI 2014/506 — Financial Services and Markets Act 2000 (Consumer Credit) (Miscellaneous Provisions) (No 2) Order 2014.
- SI 2014/376 – Financial Services and Markets Act 2000 (Consumer Credit) (Transitional Provisions) Order.
- SI 2014/366 — Financial Services and Markets Act 2000 (Regulated Activities) (Amendment) Order 2014.
- SI 2014/334 — Financial Services and Markets Act 2000 (Consumer Credit) (Designated Activities) Order 2014.
- SI 2014/208 — Financial Services and Markets Act 2000 (Consumer Credit) (Miscellaneous Provisions) Order 2014.
- SI 2014/206 — Financial Services and Markets Act 2000 (Appointed Representatives) (Amendment) Regulations 2014.
- SI 2013/3191 — Financial Services and Markets Act 2000 (Designated Consumer Bodies) Order 2013.
- SI 2013/3128 — Financial Services and Markets Act 2000 (Consumer Credit) (Transitional Provisions) Order 2013.
- SI 2013/3116 — Financial Services and Markets Act 2000 (Qualifying EU Provisions) (No 2) Order 2013.
- SI 2013/1908 — Financial Services and Markets Act 2000 (Over the Counter Derivatives, Central Counterparties and Trade Repositories) (No 2) Regulations 2013.

Amendment:

- SI 2015/348 — Financial Services and Markets Act 2000 (Over the Counter Derivatives, Central Counterparties and Trade Repositories) (Amendment) Regulations 2015.
- SI 2013/1882 — Financial Services Act 2012 (Consumer Credit) Order 2013.
- SI 2013/1881 — Financial Services and Markets Act 2000 (Regulated Activities) (Amendment) (No 2) Order 2013 (*the RAO Amendment No. 2 Order*).
- SI 2013/655 — Financial Services and Markets Act 2000 (Regulated Activities) (Amendment) Order 2013.
- SI 2013/598 — Financial Services and Markets Act 2000 (Financial Services Compensation Scheme) Order 2013.
- SI 2013/556 — Financial Services and Markets Act 2000 (PRA-regulated Activities) Order 2013.
- SI 2013/555 — Financial Services and Markets Act 2000 (Threshold Conditions) Order 2013.
- SI 2013/504 — Financial Services and Markets Act 2000 (Over the Counter Derivatives, Central Counterparties and Trade Repositories) Regulations 2013.
- SI 2013/439 — Financial Services and Markets Act 2000 (EEA Passport Rights) (Amendment) Regulations 2013.
- SI 2013/431 — Financial Services and Markets Act 2000 (Exercise of Powers under Part 4A) (Consultation with Home State Regulators) Regulations 2013.
- SI 2013/165 — Financial Services and Markets Act 2000 (Prescribed Financial Institutions) Order 2013.
- SI 2012/2554 – Financial Services and Markets Act 2000 (Short Selling) Regulations 2012.
- SI 2012/916 – Financial Services (Omnibus 1 Directive) Regulations 2012.
- SI 2007/108 – Financial Services (EEA State) Regulations 2007.
- SI 2005/1529 – Financial Services and Markets Act 2000 (Financial Promotion) Order 2005.
- SI 2001/3632 – Financial Services and Markets Tribunal (Legal Assistance) Regulations 2001.
- SI 2001/3084 – Financial Services and Markets Act 2000 (Gibraltar) Order 2001.
- SI 2001/2511 – Financial Services and Markets Act 2000 (EEA Passport Rights) Regulations 2001.
- SI 2001/995 – Financial Services and Markets Act 2000 (Recognition Requirements for Investment Exchanges and Clearing Houses) Regulations 2001.
- SI 2001/544 – The Financial Services and Markets Act 2000 (Regulated Activities) Order.

- Bank of England Act 1998 c. 11.
  Secondary legislation:
  - SI 2013/1189 – Cash Ratio Deposits (Value Bands and Ratios) Order 2013.
  - SI 2013/721 – Bank of England (Call Notice) (Benchmark Rate of Interest) Order.
  - SI 2013/644 – Bank of England Act 1998 (Macro-prudential Measures) Order.
  - SI 1998/1130 – Cash Ratio Deposits (Eligible Liabilities) Order 1998.

NATIONAL LEVEL (UK) – Standards, Frameworks and Guidance

The Handbook Online contains provisions made by the Financial Conduct Authority (FCA) and the Prudential Regulation Authority (PRA). [Website: http://fshandbook.info/FS/index.jsp]

The FCA (Financial Conduct Authority) Handbook provides access to FCAs provisions, legal rules and guidance which apply to FCA-regulated firms:

(1) High Level Standards (the standards applying to all firms and approved persons)
   - Principles for Businesses: the fundamental obligations of all firms under the regulatory system
   - Senior Management Arrangements, Systems and Controls: the responsibilities of directors and senior management
   - Threshold Conditions: the minimum standards for becoming and remaining authorised
   - Statements of Principle and Code of Practice for Approved Persons: the fundamental obligations of approved persons
   - The Fit and Proper test for Approved Persons: the minimum standards for becoming and remaining an approved person
   - Financial Stability and Market Confidence Sourcebook: Provisions relating to financial stability, market confidence and short selling
   - Training and Competence: the commitments and requirements concerning staff competence
   - General Provisions: interpreting the Handbook, fees, approval by the FCA and PRA, emergencies, status disclosure, the FSA logo and insurance against fines
   - Fees Manual: the fees provisions for funding the FCA and PRA, FOS and FSCS

(2) Prudential Standards (sets out the prudential requirements for firms)
   - General Prudential sourcebook: Sourcebook for Banks, Building Societies, Insurers and Investment Firms
   - Prudential sourcebook for Banks, Building Societies and Investment Firms
   - Prudential sourcebook for Investment Firms

- Prudential sourcebook for Insurers
- Prudential sourcebook for Mortgage and Home Finance Firms, and Insurance Intermediaries
- Prudential sourcebook for UCITS Firms (21/07/2014 is the last day this material was in force)
- Interim Prudential sourcebook for Friendly Societies
- Interim Prudential sourcebook for Insurers
- Interim Prudential sourcebook for Investment Businesses

(3) Business Standards (the detailed requirements relating to firms' day-to-day business)
- Conduct of Business Sourcebook: the conduct of business requirements applying to firms with effect from 1 November 2007
- Insurance: Conduct of Business sourcebook: (the non-investment insurance conduct of business requirements)
- Mortgages and Home Finance: Conduct of Business sourcebook (the requirements applying to firms with mortgage business customers)
- Banking: Conduct of Business sourcebook
- Client Assets: the requirements relating to holding client assets and client money
- Market Conduct: Code of Market Conduct, Price stabilising rules, Inter-professional conduct, Support of the Takeover Panel's Functions, Alternative Trading Systems, what is acceptable market conduct and what is market abuse

(4) Regulatory Processes (the manuals describing the operation of the FCA's and PRA's authorisation, supervisory and disciplinary functions)
- Supervision: supervisory provisions including those relating to auditors, waivers, individual guidance, notifications and reporting
- Decision Procedure and Penalties Manual: a description of the FCA's procedures for taking statutory notice decisions, the FCA's policy on the imposition and amount of penalties and the conduct of interviews to which a direction under section 169(7) of the Act has been given or the FSA is considering giving with effect from 28 August 2007

(5) Redress (the processes for handling complaints and compensation)
- Dispute Resolution: Complaints: the detailed requirements for handling complaints and the Financial Ombudsman Service arrangements
- Consumer Redress Schemes sourcebook: the requirements for all firms that advised, arranged or managed investments in an Arch cru fund
- Compensation: the rules governing eligibility under, and levies for, the Financial Services Compensation Scheme

(6) Specialist sourcebooks (requirements applying to individual business sectors)
- Collective Investment Schemes: requirements for collective investment schemes (replaced CIS)
- Credit Unions sourcebook: requirements applying to credit unions
- Consumer Credit sourcebook: The specialist sourcebook for credit-related regulated activities
- Investment Funds sourcebook: Requirements for firms covered by AIFMD
- Professional Firms: requirements applying to professional firms (whether exempt or authorised)
- Regulated Covered Bonds: requirements relating to regulated covered bonds
- Recognised Investment Exchanges: requirements applying to recognised bodies

(7) Listing, Prospectus and Disclosure (United Kingdom Listing Authority rules)
- Listing Rules: United Kingdom Listing Authority listing rules
- Prospectus Rules: United Kingdom Listing Authority prospectus rules
- Disclosure Rules and Transparency Rules: United Kingdom Listing Authority disclosure rules

(8) Handbook Guides (guides to the Handbook that aims to give a basic overview of certain topics and points firms in the direction of material in the Handbook applicable to them)
- Energy Market Participants
- Oil Market Participants
- Service companies
- General guidance on Benchmark Submission and Administration

(9) Regulatory Guides (These are guides to regulatory topics)
- The Building Societies Regulatory Guide
- The Collective Investment Scheme Information Guide
- The Enforcement Guide
- Financial Crime: a guide for firms
- The Perimeter Guidance Manual
- The Responsibilities of Providers and Distributors for the Fair Treatment of Customers
- The Unfair Contract Terms Regulatory Guide

[Website: http://fshandbook.info/FS/html/FCA]

The PRA (Prudential Regulation Authority) Handbook contains rules and directions made by the PRA that apply to PRA-authorised firms:

Cross-reference: For further information, see also Financial Conduct Authority Handbook above.

(1)   High Level Standards (the standards applying to all firms and approved persons)
-    Senior Management Arrangements, Systems and Controls
-    Statements of Principle and Code of Practice for Approved Persons
-    The Fit and Proper test for Approved Persons
-    General Provisions
-    Fees Manual

(2)   Prudential Standards (sets out the prudential requirements for firms)
-    General Prudential sourcebook
-    Prudential sourcebook for Banks, Building Societies and Investment Firms
-    Prudential sourcebook for Insurers
-    Prudential sourcebook for Mortgage and Home Finance Firms, and Insurance Intermediaries
-    Interim Prudential sourcebook for Friendly Societies
-    Interim Prudential sourcebook for Insurers
-    Interim Prudential sourcebook for Investment Businesses

(3)   Business Standards (the detailed requirements relating to firms' day-to-day business)
-    Conduct of Business Sourcebook

(4)   Regulatory Processes (the manuals describing the operation of the FCA's and PRA's authorisation, supervisory and disciplinary functions)
-    Supervision

(5)   Redress (the processes for handling complaints and compensation)
-    Compensation

(6)   Specialist sourcebooks (requirements applying to individual business sectors)
-    Building Societies sourcebook
-    Credit Unions sourcebook

(7)   Regulatory Guides (These are guides to regulatory topics)
-    The Building Societies Regulatory Guide

(8)   Rulebook Glossary
-    Glossary

(9)   Rulebook Interpretation
-      Interpretation

(10)   Rulebook CRR Firms [CRR = Capital Requirements Regulation]
-      Fundamental Rules
-      Remuneration Reporting Requirements
-      Housing
-      Internal Capital Adequacy Assessment
-      Definition of Capital
-      Benchmarking of Internal Approaches
-      Credit Risk
-      Counterparty Credit Risk
-      Market Risk
-      Groups
-      Large Exposures
-      Public Disclosure
-      Waivers Transitional Provisions
-      Permissions
-      Recovery and Resolution
-      Related Party Transaction Risk
-      Capital Buffers
-      Information Gathering
-      Permissions and Waivers
-      Auditors
-      Lloyd's: Actuaries and Auditors
-      Skilled Persons
-      Notifications

(11)   Rulebook Non-CRR Firms
-      Fundamental Rules
-      Remuneration Reporting Requirements
-      Housing
-      Recovery and Resolution
-      Information Gathering
-      Permissions and Waivers
-      Auditors
-      Lloyd's: Actuaries and Auditors
-      Skilled Persons
-      Incoming Firms and Third Country Firms
-      Notifications

(12)   Rulebook SII Firms [SII = Solvency II]]
- Fundamental Rules
- Information Gathering
- Permissions and Waivers
- Auditors
- Lloyd's: Actuaries and Auditors
- Skilled Persons
- Notifications

(13)   Rulebook Non-SII Firms
- Fundamental Rules
- Information Gathering
- Permissions and Waivers
- Auditors
- Lloyd's: Actuaries and Auditors
- Skilled Persons
- Notifications

(14)   Non-authorised persons
- Auditors
- Lloyd's: Actuaries and Auditors

[Website: http://fshandbook.info/FS/html/PRA]

The PRA Rulebook contains rules and directions made by the PRA which apply only to PRA-authorised firms:

(1)   CRR Firms
- Fundamental Rules
- Housing
- Internal Capital Adequacy Assessment
- Definition of capital
- Benchmarking of internal approaches
- Credit risk
- Counterparty credit risk
- Market risk
- Groups
- Large exposures
- Public disclosure
- Waivers Transitional Provisions
- Permissions
- Recovery and Resolution

- Related Party Transaction Risk
- Capital buffers
- Information Gathering
- Permissions and Waivers
- Auditors
- Lloyd's Actuaries and Auditors
- Skilled Persons
- Notifications

(2) SII Firms
- Fundamental Rules
- Information Gathering
- Permissions and Waivers
- Auditors
- Lloyd's Actuaries and Auditors
- Skilled Persons
- Notifications

(3) Non-CRR Firms
- Fundamental Rules
- Housing
- Recovery and Resolution
- Information Gathering
- Permissions and Waivers
- Auditors
- Lloyd's Actuaries and Auditors
- Skilled Persons
- Incoming Firms and Third Country Firms
- Notifications

(4) Non-SII Firms
- Fundamental Rules
- Information Gathering
- Permissions and Waivers
- Auditors
- Lloyd's Actuaries and Auditors
- Skilled Persons
- Notifications

(5) Non-authorised Persons
- Auditors
- Lloyd's Actuaries and Auditors

[Website: http://fshandbook.info/FS/prarulebook.jsp]

The Combined View provides an overview of the FCA Handbook and the PRA Handbook in a single view:

Cross-reference: For further information, see also Financial Conduct Authority Handbook above.

(1)   High Level Standards (the standards applying to all firms and approved persons)
- Principles for Businesses
- Senior Management Arrangements, Systems and Controls
- Threshold Conditions
- Statements of Principle and Code of Practice for Approved Persons
- The Fit and Proper test for Approved Persons
- Financial Stability and Market Confidence Sourcebook
- Training and Competence
- General Provisions
- Fees Manual

(2)   Prudential Standards (sets out the prudential requirements for firms)
- Integrated Prudential sourcebook (31/12/2006 is the last day this material was in force): prudential requirements for insurers, groups, mortgage firms and insurance intermediaries and, in relation to liquidity risk, for banks, building societies and own account dealers
- General Prudential sourcebook
- Prudential sourcebook for Banks, Building Societies and Investment Firms
- Prudential sourcebook for Investment Firms
- Prudential sourcebook for Insurers
- Prudential sourcebook for Mortgage and Home Finance Firms, and Insurance Intermediaries
- Prudential sourcebook for UCITS Firms (21/07/2014 is the last day this material was in force)
- Interim Prudential sourcebook for Banks (31/10/2010 is the last day this material was in force)
- Interim Prudential sourcebook for Building Societies (30/09/2010 is the last day this material was in force)
- Interim Prudential sourcebook for Friendly Societies
- Interim Prudential sourcebook for Insurers
- Interim Prudential sourcebook for Investment Businesses

(3)   Business Standards (the detailed requirements relating to firms' day-to-day business)
- Conduct of Business (31/10/2007 is the last day this material was in force): the requirements applying to firms with investment business customers

- Conduct of Business Sourcebook: the conduct of business requirements applying to firms with effect from 1 November 2007
- Insurance: Conduct of Business (05/01/2008 is the last day this material was in force): the requirements applying to firms with insurance business customers
- Insurance: Conduct of Business sourcebook
- Mortgages and Home Finance: Conduct of Business sourcebook
- Banking: Conduct of Business sourcebook
- Client Assets
- Market Conduct
- Money Laundering (30/08/2006 is the last day this material was in force): the requirements for anti-money laundering systems and controls

(4) Regulatory Processes (the manuals describing the operation of the FCA's and PRA's authorisation, supervisory and disciplinary functions)
- Authorisation (to see AUTH derivations and destinations tables, go to Useful links) (30/12/2006 is the last day this material was in force): guidance on whether authorisation is needed, how to apply for it and related issues
- Supervision
- Enforcement (27/08/2007 is the last day this material was in force): details of the FSA's disciplinary and enforcement arrangements
- Decision Procedure and Penalties Manual
- Decision Making (27/08/2007 is the last day this material was in force): the FSA's decision-making processes

(5) Redress (the processes for handling complaints and compensation)
- Dispute Resolution: Complaints
- Consumer Redress Schemes sourcebook
- Compensation
- Complaints against the FSA (31/03/2013 is the last day this material was in force): details of the scheme for handling complaints against the FSA

(6) Specialist sourcebooks (requirements applying to individual business sectors)
- Building Societies sourcebook: guidance for building societies
- Collective Investment Schemes (11/02/2007 is the last day this material was in force): requirements for collective investment schemes
- Collective Investment Schemes
- Credit Unions (07/01/2012 is the last day this material was in force): requirements applying to credit unions
- Credit Unions sourcebook
- Consumer Credit sourcebook

- Investment Funds sourcebook
- Electronic Commerce Directive (31/10/2007 is the last day this material was in force): requirements for firms providing financial services by electronic means
- Electronic Money (29/04/2012 is the last day this material was in force): requirements for firms issuing electronic money
- Lloyd's (30/12/2006 is the last day this material was in force): requirements applying to Lloyd's and members of Lloyd's
- Professional Firms
- Regulated Covered Bonds
- Recognised Investment Exchanges

(7) Listing, Prospectus and Disclosure (United Kingdom Listing Authority rules)
  - Listing Rules
  - Prospectus Rules
  - Disclosure Rules and Transparency Rules

(8) Handbook Guides (guides to the Handbook that aims to give a basic overview of certain topics and points firms in the direction of material in the Handbook applicable to them)
  - Energy Market Participants
  - Small Friendly Societies (12/06/2005 is the last day this material was in force): (See FREN instruments for various in force dates). Prudential requirements for insurers, groups, mortgage firms and insurance intermediaries
  - Oil Market Participants
  - Service companies
  - General guidance on Benchmark Submission and Administration
  - Using the FSA Handbook: an Overview for small IFA firms (30/08/2006 is the last day this material was in force)
  - Small Mortgage and Insurance Intermediaries: Part I - General Rules (30/08/2006 is the last day this material was in force)
  - Small Mortgage and Insurance Intermediaries: Part II - Mortgage Intermediaries (additional rules) (30/08/2006 is the last day this material was in force)
  - Small Mortgage and Insurance Intermediaries: Part III - Insurance Intermediaries (additional rules) (30/08/2006 is the last day this material was in force)

(9) Regulatory Guides (These are guides to regulatory topics)
  - The Building Societies Regulatory Guide
  - The Collective Investment Scheme Information Guide

- The Credit Rating Agencies Guide (08/12/2011 is the last day this material was in force)
- The Enforcement Guide
- Financial Crime: a guide for firms
- The Perimeter Guidance Manual
- The Responsibilities of Providers and Distributors for the Fair Treatment of Customers
- The Unfair Contract Terms Regulatory Guide

(10) Rulebook Glossary
- Glossary

(11) Rulebook Interpretation
- Interpretation

(12) Rulebook CRR Firms
- Fundamental Rules
- Remuneration Reporting Requirements
- Housing
- Internal Capital Adequacy Assessment
- Definition of Capital
- Benchmarking of Internal Approaches
- Credit Risk
- Counterparty Credit Risk
- Market Risk
- Groups
- Large Exposures
- Public Disclosure
- Waivers Transitional Provisions
- Permissions
- Recovery and Resolution
- Related Party Transaction Risk
- Capital Buffers
- Information Gathering
- Permissions and Waivers
- Auditors
- Lloyd's: Actuaries and Auditors
- Skilled Persons
- Notifications

(13)   Rulebook Non-CRR Firms
- Fundamental Rules
- Remuneration Reporting Requirements
- Housing
- Recovery and Resolution
- Information Gathering
- Permissions and Waivers
- Auditors
- Lloyd's: Actuaries and Auditors
- Skilled Persons
- Incoming Firms and Third Country Firms
- Notifications

(14)   Rulebook SII Firms
- Fundamental Rules
- Information Gathering
- Permissions and Waivers
- Auditors
- Lloyd's: Actuaries and Auditors
- Skilled Persons
- Notifications

(15)   Rulebook Non-SII Firms
- Fundamental Rules
- Information Gathering
- Permissions and Waivers
- Auditors
- Lloyd's: Actuaries and Auditors
- Skilled Persons
- Notifications

(16)   Non-authorised persons
- Auditors
- Lloyd's: Actuaries and Auditors

[Website: http://fshandbook.info/FS/html/handbook]

Financial Conduct Authority Handbook – The Principles [for business] (PRIN 2.1)

- Principle 1: Integrity
  A firm must conduct its business with integrity.

- Principle 2: Skill, care and diligence
  A firm must conduct its business with due skill, care and diligence.
- Principle 3: Management and control
  A firm must take reasonable care to organise and control its affairs responsibly and effectively, with adequate risk management systems.
- Principle 4: Financial prudence
  A firm must maintain adequate financial resources.
- Principle 5: Market conduct
  A firm must observe proper standards of market conduct.
- Principle 6: Customers' interests
  A firm must pay due regard to the interests of its customers and treat them fairly.
- Principle 7: Communications with clients
  A firm must pay due regard to the information needs of its clients, and communicate information to them in a way which is clear, fair and not misleading.
- Principle 8: Conflicts of interest
  A firm must manage conflicts of interest fairly, both between itself and its customers and between a customer and another client.
- Principle 9: Customers: relationships of trust
  A firm must take reasonable care to ensure the suitability of its advice and discretionary decisions for any customer who is entitled to rely upon its judgment.
- Principle 10 Clients' assets
  A firm must arrange adequate protection for clients' assets when it is responsible for them.
- Principle 11: Relations with regulators
  A firm must deal with its regulators in an open and cooperative way, and must disclose to the appropriate regulator appropriately anything relating to the firm of which that regulator would reasonably expect notice.

1.2.3 Transactions, accounts and payment systems

GLOBAL LEVEL – Laws, Regulations and Norms

Not applicable: Binding laws, regulations and norms exist only at other Levels of governance.

GLOBAL LEVEL – Standards, Frameworks and Guidance

Corporate Governance, Audit and Compliance for Financial Services

- Basel Committee on Banking Supervision (April 2005) "Compliance and the compliance function in banks" (Bank for International Settlements).

- Basel Committee on Banking Supervision (June 2012) "The internal audit function in banks" (Bank for International Settlements).
- Basel Committee on Banking Supervision (March 2014) "External audits of banks" (Bank for International Settlements).
- Basel Committee on Banking Supervision (October 2014) "Guidelines – Corporate governance principles for banks", Issued for comments by 9 January 2015 (Bank for International Settlements).
- EBA (2013) Report on "Benchmarking Practices at Union Level" (EBA, London).
- EBA/Op/2014/10 (15 October 2014) "Opinion of the European Banking Authority on the application of Directive 2013/36/EU (Capital Requirements Directive) regarding the principles on remuneration policies of credit institutions and investment firms and the use of allowances." (European Banking Authority, London).

Standards

- NACHA – The electronic Payments Association (December 2014) "Payments Innovation Alliance White Paper: The Future of Corporate Payments" (NACHA).
- International Payments Framework Association (IPFA) guidance.
- United Nations Commission on International Trade Law (UNCITRAL) "Model Law on Electronic Commerce with Guide to Enactment" (1996).
- PCI Data Security Standard (PCI DSS):
  - Validated Point-to-Point Encryption (P2PE) standards and procedures: P2PE Hardware/Hardware Solution Requirements and Testing Procedures, P2PE Vendor Release Agreement, P2PE HW-HW Solution P-ROV Reporting Instructions
  - Approved PIN Transaction Security (PTS) standards: PIN Security Requirements and Test procedures, Point of Interaction (POI) Modular Security Requirements, Unattended Payment Terminal (UPT) Security Requirements, Device Testing and Approval Program Guide
  - Card production standards: Card Production Logical Security Requirements, Card Production Summary of Changes
  - Further documents: Self Assessment Questionnaires, Lifecycle for Changes to the PCI DSS and PA-DSS, Overview of the PCI DSS Wireless Guideline, Penetration Testing Guidance, Mobile Payment Acceptance Security Guidelines for Merchants as End-Users, PCI DSS V3.0 Best Practices for Maintaining PCI DSS Compliance, Third-Party Security Assurance, PCI DSS 2.0 eCommerce Guidelines, PCI DSS 2.0 Cloud Computing Guidelines, PCI DSS 2.0 Risk Assessment Guidelines, PCI DSS 2.0 Wireless Guidelines, PCI DSS Tokenization Guidelines, Protecting Telephone-based Payment Card Data, PCI DSS Applicability in an EMV Environment and PCI DSS Virtualization Guidelines

EUROPEAN LEVEL– Laws, Regulations and Norms

For further information, see 1.1.1 "European Supervisory Authorities" and 1.2.1 "Stability and Capital Requirements".

Single Euro Payments Area (SEPA)

- Regulation (EU) No 260/2012 "establishing technical and business requirements for credit transfers and direct debits in euro and amending Regulation (EC) No 924/2009" (*the SEPA Regulation*) (14 March 2012).
  Secondary legislation:
  - [UK] SI 2012/3122 – The Payments in Euro (Credit Transfers and Direct Debits) Regulations 2012.
  - [UK] SI 2012/1791 – Payment Services Regulations 2012.
  - [UK] SI 2009/209 – Payment Services Regulations 2009.
  Amendments:
  - Regulation (EU) No 248/2014 "amending Regulation (EU) No 260/2012 as regards the migration to Union-wide credit transfers and direct debits" (*SEPA Credit Transfers (SCT) and SEPA Direct Debits (SDD) in Euro (Amendment) Regulation*) (26 February 2014).
- Council Regulation (EC) No 924/2009 on "cross-border payments in the Community and repealing Regulation (EC) No 2560/2001" (*Single Euro Payments Area (SEPA)*)) (16 September 2009).

Payment and Settlement

- Regulation (EU) 2015/751 "on interchange fees for card-based payment transactions" (*Card-Based Payment Transactions (Interchange Fees) Regulation*) (29 April 2015).
- Regulation (EU) 2015/847 "on information accompanying transfers of funds and repealing Regulation (EC) No 1781/2006" (*Wire Transfer Regulation*) (20 May 2015).
- Directive 2002/47/EC on "financial collateral arrangements" (*Collateral Arrangements Directive (FCD)*)) (6 June 2002).
  Amendments:
  - Directive 2009/44/EC "amending Directive 98/26/EC on settlement finality in payment and securities settlement systems and Directive 2002/47/EC on financial collateral arrangements as regards linked systems and credit claims" (*Settlement Finality and Financial Collateral Arrangements (Amendment) Directive*) (6 May 2009).
- Council Directive 89/117/EEC "on the obligations of branches established in a Member State of credit institutions and financial institutions having their head

PART 1 FINANCIAL SERVICES LAWS AND REGULATIONS

offices outside that Member State regarding the publication of annual accounting documents" (*Branch Accounts Directive*) (13 February 1989).

- Directive 98/26/EC on "settlement finality in payment and securities settlement systems" (*Settlement Finality Directive (SFD)*) (19 May 1998). [Repealed with effect from 1 January 2016]
  Secondary legislation:
  - [UK] SI 2009/1972 – The Financial Markets and Insolvency (Settlement Finality) (Amendment) Regulations 2009.
  - [UK] SI 1999/2979 – The Financial Markets and Insolvency (Settlement Finality) Regulations 1999.
  Amendment:
  - [UK] SI 2015/347 — Financial Markets and Insolvency (Settlement Finality) (Amendment) Regulations 2015.

Organisation: Committees

- Directive 2005/1/EC "amending Council Directives 73/239/EEC, 85/611/EEC, 91/675/EEC, 92/49/EEC and 93/6/EEC and Directives 94/19/EC, 98/78/EC, 2000/12/EC, 2001/34/EC, 2002/83/EC and 2002/87/EC in order to establish a new organisational structure for financial services committees" (*Financial Services Committees Directive*) (9 March 2005).

Payment Service Directive

- Directive 2007/64/EC on "payment services in the internal market amending Directives 97/7/EC, 2002/65/EC, 2005/60/EC and 2006/48/EC and repealing Directive 97/5/EC" (*Payment Services Directive (PSD)*) (13 November 2007).
  - [UK] SI 2012/1791 – Payment Services Regulations 2012.
  - [UK] SI 2009/209 – Payment Services Regulations 2009.

Electronic Money Directive

- Directive 2009/110/EC "on the taking up, pursuit and prudential supervision of the business of electronic money institutions amending Directives 2005/60/EC and 2006/48/EC and repealing Directive 2000/46/EC" (*Second Electronic Money Directive (2EMD)*) (16 September 2009).
  - [UK] SI 2011/99 – Electronic Money Regulations 2011.

Accounts Directive

- Directive 2014/92/EU "on the comparability of fees related to payment accounts, payment account switching and access to payment accounts with basic features" (*Payment Accounts Directive*) (23 July 2014).

- Council Directive 86/635/EEC "on the annual accounts and consolidated accounts of banks and other financial institutions" (*Bank Accounts Directive*) (8 December 1986).
  - [UK] SI 2008/567 – Bank Accounts Directive (Miscellaneous Banks) Regulations 2008.

Encryption/conditional access

- Directive 98/84/EC on "the legal protection of services based on, or consisting of, conditional access" (20 November 1998).

EUROPEAN LEVEL – Standards, Frameworks and Guidance

- Communication COM(2011) 941 "Green Paper: Towards an integrated European market for card, internet and mobile payments" (11 January 2012).

EBA Guidelines and Governance

- EBA/GL/2015/01 — "Final report — Guidelines on national provisional lists of the most representative services linked to a payment account and subject to a fee under the Payment Accounts Directive (2014/92/EU)".
- EBA/GL/2014/12 — "Final guidelines on the security of internet payments".
- GL44 — EBA Guidelines on Internal Governance
- EBA(2012) – Revision of the Common Reporting Framework

EIOPA Guidelines and Reports related to Governance and Undertakings

- EIOPA-BoS-14/180 — "Guidelines on the use of internal models".
- EIOPA-BoS-14-248 — "Progress Report on the Follow-up to the Peer Reviews on Pre-application of Internal Models".
- EIOPA-BoS-14/178 — "Guidelines on undertaking-specific parameters".
- EIOPA-BoS-14/170 — "Guidelines on treatment of related undertakings, including participations".
- EIOPA-CCPFI-13/100 — "Report on Good Practices on Comparison Website"
- EIOPAOPC12/046 – "2012 Report on Market Developments".

ESMA Guidance

- ESMA/2013/322 — "Guidelines and Recommendations for establishing consistent, efficient and effective assessments of interoperability arrangements".
- ESMA/2013/323 — "Guidelines and Recommendations for establishing consistent, efficient and effective assessments of interoperability arrangements".

Various Guidance

- European Commission "The Payment Services Directive: What it means for consumers".
- Payment Card Industry Data Security Standards (PCI DSS, Dec 2004) "Data Security Standards".

NATIONAL LEVEL (UK) – Laws, Regulations and Norms

Single Euro Payments Area (SEPA)

Cross-reference: No Act of Parliament is directly applicable. See applicable UK Statutory Instruments ("[UK] SI") implementing EU law in the corresponding European Level sub-section.

Electronic Money

- Electronic Money Directive and the Electronic Money Regulations 2011 (EMRs).
  Secondary legislation:
  - SI 2011/99 – Electronic Money Regulations 2011.

Accounts

- Companies (Audit, Investigations and Community Enterprise) Act 2004 and Companies Act 2006.
  Secondary legislation:
  - SI 2012/1439 – Supervision of Accounts and Reports (Prescribed Body) and Companies (Defective Accounts and Directors' Reports) (Authorised Person) Order 2012.

Other Payments Regulation

- SI 2014/3293 — Payments to Governments and Miscellaneous Provisions Regulations 2014.
- SI 2014/3209 — Reports on Payments to Governments Regulations 2014.

NATIONAL LEVEL (UK) – Standards, Frameworks and Guidance

Financial Services Authority

- FSA (2012) "Bank accounts: Know your rights – What to know where you stand with your bank or building society? We explain your rights and how to use them?"
- FSA (March 2011) "The FSA's role under the Electronic Money Regulations 2011: Our approach".
- FSA Handbook – Chapter 3A (February 3013) "Guidance on the scope of the Electronic Money Regulations 2011".

Banking industry standards

- British Bankers' Association, The Building Societies Association and APACS (March 2008) "The Banking Code: Setting standards for banks, building societies and other banking service providers".
- British Bankers' Association and APACS (2008) "The Business Banking Code: Setting the standards of banking practice - Guidance for subscribers".

1.2.4 Corporate conduct, culture and ethics

This covers conduct, Treating Customers Fairly and other matters relating to corporate culture.

Cross-reference: For further information, see 3.1.3. "Corporate governance, accounting, audit and risk management".

GLOBAL LEVEL – Laws, Regulations and Norms

Not applicable: Binding laws, regulations and norms exist only at other Levels of governance.

GLOBAL LEVEL – Standards, Frameworks and Guidance

- United Nations "UN Global Compact" for Human Rights, Labour, Environment and Anti-corruption. [Website at https://www.unglobalcompact.org/].
- ISO 26000: ISO 26000:2010 – Guidance on social responsibility.
- OECD "Guidelines for Multinational Enterprises (MNEs)" [Website at http://www.oecd.org/daf/inv/mne/].

EUROPEAN LEVEL – Laws, Regulations and Norms

Not applicable: Binding laws, regulations and norms exist only at other Levels of governance.

EUROPEAN LEVEL– Standards, Frameworks and Guidance

- Communication COM(2010) 284 "Green Paper: Corporate governance in financial institutions and remuneration policies" (2 June 2010).
- Commission Recommendation C(2001) 477on "pre-contractual information to be given to consumers by lenders offering home loans" (1 March 2001).
- European Business Ethics Forum (EBEF) (2013) "The Evolving Responsibilities &Liabilities of Ethics Representatives: A practical guide".

ESMA Guidance related to Euribor

- JC/2014/62 — "The Joint Committee of the ESAs reminds financial institutions of their responsibilities when placing their own financial products with consumers".

- ESMA/2014/207 — "Review of the Implementation of EBA-ESMA Recommendations to Euribor-EBF".

EBA Guidance

- EBA/BS/2013/002 — "Report on the administration and management of Euribor".
- EBA/GL/2012/06 – "Guidelines on the assessment of the suitability of members of the management body and key function holders".

NATIONAL LEVEL – Laws, Regulations and Norms

Skilled Persons Reviews (s166 and s166A)

- Financial Services & Markets Act 2001, Section 166.
- Two types:
  - s166 Reports by Skilled Persons; and/or
  - s166A Appointment of Skilled Person to collect and update information.

NATIONAL LEVEL (UK) – Standards, Frameworks and Guidance

Senior Management Regime (SMR)

- FCA (23 February 2015) "Approach to Non-Executive Directors and the Senior Managers Regime".

Skilled Persons Reviews (s166 and s166A)

- FCA Handbook/ PRD Handbook: SUP 5 – Reports by skilled persons
  Reports by skilled persons (SUP 5):
  - SUP 5.1 – Application and purpose
  - SUP 5.2 – The appropriate regulator's power
  - SUP 5.3 – Policy on the use of skilled persons
  - SUP 5.4 – Appointment and reporting process
  - SUP 5.5 – Duties of firms
  - SUP 5.6 – Confidential information and privilege
  - SUP 5 Annex 1 – Non-exhaustive list of examples of when the FCA may use the skilled person tool (This Annex belongs to SUP 5.3.1AG)

Code of Business Sourcebook (COBS)

- Financial Conduct Authority Handbook "Conduct of Business Sourcebook (COBS)"

Treating Customers Fairly (TCF)

- FSA (July 2007) "Treating customers fairly (TCF), the FSA's principles-based approach to regulation".
- FSA (July 2007) "Treating customers fairly – guide to management information".
- FSA (2002) "FSA Ethical Framework for Financial Services".

Various Guidance

- British Banking Association (September 2013) Industry Guidance for FCA Banking Conduct of Business Sourcebook.

FCA Handbook

- FCA Handbook: Market Conduct (MAR)
  - MAR 1 – The Code of Market Conduct (including market abuse such as insider dealing, improper disclosure, manipulating transactions, misleading behaviours)
  - MAR 7 – Disclosure of information on certain trades undertaken outside a regulated market or MTF
  - MAR 8 – Benchmarks

SUB-NATIONAL LEVEL (UK) – Laws, Regulations and Norms

Conduct

Conduct Risk is defined as the risk of customer detriment or censure and/or a reduction in earnings/value, through financial or reputational loss, from inappropriate or poor customer treatment or business conduct.

Corporate Conduct Policies

- Customer Treatment Policy
- Complaint Handling Policy
- Product Governance Policy

SUB-NATIONAL LEVEL (UK) – Standards, Frameworks and Guidance

Corporate Conduct Procedures and Processes:

List of operational principles:

- Conduct
- Regulatory
- People

- Operational (Process & Security)
- Governance

1.2.5 Markets regulation: records-keeping, transparency and market abuse

<u>EUROPEAN LEVEL – Laws, Regulations and Norms</u>

Markets in Financial Instrument Directives (MiFiD) II

- Directive 2014/65/EU on "markets in financial instruments and amending Directive 2002/92/EC and Directive 2011/61/EU" (*Markets in Financial Instruments Directive – MiFID II*) (15 May 2014).
  Implementation:
  - Regulation (EU) No 600/2014 "on markets in financial instruments and amending Regulation (EU) No 648/2012" (*Markets in Financial Instruments Regulation (MiFIR)*) (15 May 2014).
- Proposal for a Directive on "markets in financial instruments repealing Directive 2004/39/EC, and for a Regulation on markets in financial instruments and amending Regulation [EMIR] on OTC derivatives, central counterparties and trade repositories" (*MiFID II Proposal Directive*) (20 October 2011).

Markets in Financial Instrument Directives (MiFID)

- Directive 2004/39/EC on "markets in financial instruments amending Council Directives 85/611/EEC and 93/6/EEC and Directive 2000/12/EC of the European Parliament and of the Council and repealing Council Directive 93/22/EEC" (*MiFID I*) (21 April 2004). [Repealed with effect from 3 January 2017]
  Implementation and Amendments:
  - Directive 2008/10/EC "amending Directive 2004/39/EC on markets in financial instruments, as regards the implementing powers conferred on the Commission" (*MiFID (Amendment) Directive*) (11 March 2008). [Repealed with effect from 3 January 2017]
  - [UK] SI 2007/126 – The Financial Services and Markets Act 2000 (Markets in Financial Instruments) Regulations 2007.
  - Commission Regulation (EC) No 1287/2006 "implementing Directive 2004/39/EC as regards record-keeping obligations for investment firms, transaction reporting, market transparency, admission of financial instruments to trading, and defined terms for the purposes of that Directive" (*MiFID (Implementing) Regulation*) (10 August 2006).
  - Commission Directive 2006/73/EC "implementing Directive 2004/39/EC as regards organisational requirements and operating conditions for investment

firms and defined terms for the purposes of that Directive" (*MiFID Implementing Directive*) (10 August 2006).

- Council Directive 2006/31/EC "amending Directive 2004/39/EC on markets in financial instruments, as regards certain deadlines" (*MiFID Deadline Extension Directive*) (5 April 2006). [Repealed with effect from 3 January 2017]
- [UK] SI 2008/3053 – Definition of Financial Instrument Order 2008.

Market Transparency and Prospectus Directives

- Commission Regulation (EC) No 1569/2007 "establishing a mechanism for the determination of equivalence of accounting standards applied by third country issuers of securities pursuant to Directives 2003/71/EC and 2004/109/EC of the European Parliament and of the Council" (*Prospectus and Transparency (Third Country Accounting Standards Equivalence) Regulation*) (21 December 2007).
  Amendments:
  - Commission Delegated Regulation (EU) No 310/2012 "amending Regulation (EC) No 1569/2007 establishing a mechanism for the determination of equivalence of accounting standards applied by third country issuers of securities pursuant to Directives 2003/71/EC and 2004/109/EC" (*Prospectus and Transparency (Third Country Accounting Standards Equivalence) (Amendment) Regulation*) (21 December 2011).
- Commission Regulation (EC) No 809/2004 "implementing Directive 2003/71/EC of the European Parliament and of the Council as regards information contained in prospectuses as well as the format, incorporation by reference and publication of such prospectuses and dissemination of advertisements" (*Prospectus (Implementation) Regulation*) (29 April 2004).
  Amendments:
  - Commission Delegated Regulation (EU) No 759/2013 "amending Regulation (EC) No 809/2004 as regards the disclosure requirements for convertible and exchangeable debt securities" (*Prospectus (Amendment) Regulation*) (30 April 2013).
  - Commission Delegated Regulation (EU) No 862/2012 " amending Regulation (EC) No 809/2004 as regards information on the consent to use of the prospectus, information on underlying indexes and the requirement for a report prepared by independent accountants or auditors" (*Prospectus (Amendment) Regulation*) (4 June 2012).
  - Commission Delegated Regulation (EU) No 486/2012 "amending Regulation (EC) No 809/2004 as regards the format and the content of the prospectus, the base prospectus, the summary and the final terms and as regards the disclosure requirements" (*Prospectus (Amendment) Regulation*) (30 March 2012).
  - Commission Delegated Regulation (EU) No 311/2012 "amending Regulation (EC) No 809/2004 implementing Directive 2003/71/EC of the European

Parliament and of the Council as regards elements related to prospectuses and advertisements" (Prospectus (Amendment) Regulation) (21 December 2011).

- Commission Regulation (EC) No 1289/2008 "amending Commission Regulation (EC) No 809/2004 implementing Directive 2003/71/EC of the European Parliament and of the Council as regards elements related to prospectuses and advertisements" (*Prospectus (Amendment) Regulation*) (12 December 2008).
- Commission Regulation (EC) No 211/2007 "amending Regulation (EC) No 809/2004 implementing Directive 2003/71/EC of the European Parliament and of the Council as regards financial information in prospectuses where the issuer has a complex financial history or has made a significant financial commitment (Text with EEA relevance)" (*Prospectus (Financial Information) Regulation*) (27 February 2007).
- Commission Regulation (EC) No 1787/2006 "amending Commission Regulation (EC) No. 809/2004 implementing Directive 2003/71/EC of the European Parliament and of the Council as regards information contained in prospectuses as well as the format, incorporation by reference and publication of such prospectuses and dissemination of advertisements" (Prospectus (*Third-Country GAAP) Regulation*) (4 December 2006).

- Directive 2001/34/EC "on the admission of securities to official stock exchange listing and on information to be published on those securities" (*Consolidated Admissions and Reporting Directive (CARD)*) (28 May 2001).
Amendments:
  - Directive 2004/109/EC "on the harmonisation of transparency requirements in relation to information about issuers whose securities are admitted to trading on a regulated market and amending Directive 2001/34/EC" (*Transparency Directive*) (15 December 2004).
  Amendments and supplements:
    - Directive 2013/50/EU "amending Directive 2004/109/EC of the European Parliament and of the Council on the harmonisation of transparency requirements in relation to information about issuers whose securities are admitted to trading on a regulated market, Directive 2003/71/EC of the European Parliament and of the Council on the prospectus to be published when securities are offered to the public or admitted to trading, and Commission Directive 2007/14/EC laying down detailed rules for the implementation of certain provisions of Directive 2004/109/EC" (*Transparency (Amendment) Directive*) (22 October 2013).
    - [UK] SI 2014/1261 – Financial Services and Markets Act 2000 (Transparency) Regulations 2014.

- Directive 2008/22/EC "amending Directive 2004/109/EC on the harmonisation of transparency requirements in relation to information about issuers whose securities are admitted to trading on a regulated market, as regards the implementing powers conferred on the Commission" (*Transparency Implementing (Amendment) Directive*) (11 March 2008).
- Directive 2007/14/EC "laying down detailed rules for the implementation of certain provisions of Directive 2004/109/EC on the harmonisation of transparency requirements in relation to information about issuers whose securities are admitted to trading on a regulated market" (*Transparency Implementing Directive*) (8 March 2007).

- Directive 2003/71/EC "on the prospectus to be published when securities are offered to the public or admitted to trading and amending Directive 2001/34/EC" (*Prospectus Directive*) (4 November 2003).
  Amendments:
  - Directive 2010/73/EU "amending Directives 2003/71/EC on the prospectus to be published when securities are offered to the public or admitted to trading and 2004/109/EC on the harmonisation of transparency requirements in relation to information about issuers whose securities are admitted to trading on a regulated market" (*Prospectus (Amendment) Directive*) (24 November 2010).
  - Directive 2008/11/EC "amending Directive 2003/71/EC on the prospectus to be published when securities are offered to the public or admitted to trading, as regards the implementing powers conferred on the Commission" (*Prospectus (Amendment) Directive*) (11 March 2008).

Market Abuse Directive II (MAD II)

- Directive 2014/57/EU on "criminal sanctions for market abuse (market abuse directive)" (*Market Abuse Directive II (MAD II)*) (16 April 2014).
  Implementing:
  - Council Regulation (EU) No 596/2014 "on market abuse (market abuse regulation) and repealing Directive 2003/6/EC of the European Parliament and of the Council and Commission Directives 2003/124/EC, 2003/125/EC and 2004/72/EC" (*Market Abuse Regulation (MAR)*) (16 April 2014).

Market Abuse Directive I (MAD I)

- Directive 2003/6/EC "on insider dealing and market manipulation (market abuse)" (*Market Abuse Directive I (MAD I)*) (28 January 2003). [Repealed with effect from 3 July 2016]

Implementation and Amendments:

- [UK] SI 2009/3128 – Financial Services and Markets Act 2000 (Market Abuse) Regulations 2009.
- [UK] SI 2005/381 – Financial Services and Markets Act 2000 (Market Abuse) Regulations 2005.
- Directive 2008/26/EC "amending Directive 2003/6/EC on insider dealing and market manipulation (market abuse), as regards the implementing powers conferred on the Commission" (*Market Abuse (Amendment) Directive*) (11 March 2008).
- Directive 2004/72/EC "implementing Directive 2003/6/EC of the European Parliament and of the Council as regards accepted market practices, the definition of inside information in relation to derivatives on commodities, the drawing up of lists of insiders, the notification of managers' transactions and the notification of suspicious transactions" (*Market Abuse Implementation Directive*) (29 April 2004). [Repealed with effect from 3 July 2016]
- Directive 2003/125/EC "implementing Directive 2003/6/EC of the European Parliament and of the Council as regards the fair presentation of investment recommendations and the disclosure of conflicts of interest" (*Market Abuse (Investment Recommendations) Directive*) (22 December 2003). [Repealed with effect from 3 July 2016]
- Directive 2003/124/EC "implementing Directive 2003/6/EC of the European Parliament and of the Council as regards the definition and public disclosure of inside information and the definition of market manipulation" (*Market Abuse (Inside Information) Directive*) (22 December 2003). [Repealed with effect from 3 July 2016]
- Commission Regulation (EC) No 2273/2003 "implementing Directive 2003/6/EC of the European Parliament and of the Council as regards exemptions for buy-back programmes and stabilisation of financial instruments" (*Market Abuse (Implementing) Regulation (MAR)*)) (22 December 2003).

EUROPEAN LEVEL – Standards, Frameworks and Guidance

Transparency initiative

- Communication COM(2006) 194 "Green Paper: European Transparency Initiative" (3 May 2006).

Technical Standards for Transparency Directive (Directive 2004/109/EC)

- Commission Delegated Regulation (EU) 2015/761 "supplementing Directive 2004/109/EC of the European Parliament and of the Council with regard to certain regulatory technical standards on major holdings" (*Transparency (Major Holdings — Regulatory Technical Standards) Regulation*) (17 December 2014).

Technical Standards for Prospectus Directive (Directive 2003/71/EC)

- Commission Delegated Regulation (EU) No 382/2014 "supplementing Directive 2003/71/EC of the European Parliament and of the Council with regard to regulatory technical standards for publication of supplements to the prospectus" (*Prospectus (Publication of Supplements to the Prospectus — Regulatory Technical Standards) Regulation*) (7 March 2014).

ESMA Technical Advice

- ESMA/2015/224 — "Final Report on ESMA's technical advice on possible delegated acts concerning the Market Abuse Regulation".
- ESMA/2015/592 — "Automated Trading Guidelines: ESMA peer review among National Competent Authorities".
- ESMA/2014/1569 — "Final Report on ESMA's Technical Advice to the Commission on MiFID II and MiFIR".
- ESMA/2014/1485 — "Peer Review Report — MiFID — Conduct of Business, fair, clear and not misleading information".
- ESMA/2014/1187 — "Final Report on draft Regulatory Technical Standards on major shareholdings and an indicative list of financial instruments subject to notification requirements under the revised Transparency Directive".
- ESMA/2013/606 — "Guidelines on remuneration policies and practices (MiFID)".
- ESMA/2013/319 — "The consistent implementation of Commission Regulation (EC) No 809/2004 implementing the Prospectus Directive".
- ESMA/2013/1940 — "Final report — Draft technical standards under Article 10a(8) of MiFID on the assessment of acquisitions and increases in qualifying holdings in investment firms".
- ESMA/2013/619 — "Report: Comparison of liability regimes in Member States in relation to the Prospectus Directive".
- ESMA/2012/388 — "Guidelines on certain aspects of the MiFID compliance function requirements".
- ESMA/2012/387 — "Guidelines on certain aspects of the MiFID suitability requirements".
- ESMA/2011/456 — "Final Report: Guidelines on systems and controls in an automated trading environment for trading platforms, investment firms and competent authorities".

<u>NATIONAL LEVEL (UK) – Laws, Regulations and Norms</u>

Market Abuse

Cross-reference: No Act of Parliament is directly applicable. See applicable UK Statutory Instruments ("[UK] SI") implementing EU law in the corresponding European Level sub-section.

MiFID

Cross-reference: No Act of Parliament is directly applicable. See applicable UK Statutory Instruments ("[UK] SI") implementing EU law in the corresponding European Level sub-section.

Market Transparency and Prospectus

- Financial Services and Markets Act 2000 c. 8.
  Secondary legislation:
  - SI 2013/1125 — Prospectus Regulations 2013.
  - SI 2012/1538 – Prospectus Regulations 2012.
  - SI 2011/1668 – Prospectus Regulations 2011.

<u>NATIONAL LEVEL (UK) – Standards, Frameworks and Guidance</u>

- London Stock Exchange (LSE) "Introduction to the Rulebook and the Markets in Financial Instruments Directive (MiFID or "the Directive")".
- FCA Handbook: Prospectus Rules (PR)
  - PR1 [Preliminary] – PR5 [Other provisions]
- FCA Handbook: Disclosure Rules and Transparency Rules (DRT)
  - DTR1 [Introduction] – TRT8 [Primary Information Providers]

<u>SUB-NATIONAL – Laws, Regulations and Norms</u>

Group Market Risk Principles: Market risk is defined as the risk that unfavourable market moves (including changes in and increased volatility of interest rates, market-implied inflation rates, credit spreads and prices for bonds, foreign exchange rates, equity, property and commodity prices and other instruments) lead to reductions in earnings and/or value.

- Market Risk Policy
- Trading Book Policy
- Foreign Exchange Policy
- Interest Rate Risk [in the market]
- Banking Book Policy
- Policy for Management [of market risk]

- Risks in the Defined Benefit Pension Schemes
- Banking Volatility Policy

1.2.6 Mergers & Acquisitions (Financial Services specific)

EUROPEAN LEVEL – Laws, Regulations and Norms

- Council Regulation (EC) No 139/2004 "on the control of concentrations between undertakings (*the EC Merger Regulation*)" (20 January 2004).
- Directive 2007/44/EC "amending Council Directive 92/49/EEC and Directives 2002/83/EC, 2004/39/EC, 2005/68/EC and 2006/48/EC as regards procedural rules and evaluation criteria for the prudential assessment of acquisitions and increase of holdings in the financial sector" (5 September 2007).

NATIONAL LEVEL (UK) – Laws, Regulations and Norms

- Banking Act 2009 c. 1.
  Secondary legislation:
  - SI 2011/245 – Investment Bank Special Administration Regulations 2011.
  - SI 2009/314 – Bank Administration (Sharing Information) Regulations 2009.

1.2.7 Insolvency (Financial Services specific)

EUROPEAN LEVEL – Laws, Regulations and Norms

- Directive 2008/94/EC "on the protection of employees in the event of the insolvency of their employer (Codified version)" (22 October 2008).
  - Council regulation (EC) No 1346/2000 "on insolvency proceedings" (*EU Insolvency Regulation*) (29 May 2000).

NATIONAL LEVEL (UK) – Laws, Regulations and Norms

- Insolvency Act 1986 c. 45.
  Secondary legislation:
  - SI 2011/1301 – Investment Bank Special Administration (England and Wales) Rules 2011.
  - SI 2009/357 – Bank Administration (England and Wales) Rules 2009.
- Company Directors Disqualification Act 1986 c. 46.
- Insolvency Act 1986 c. 45.
  Secondary legislation:
  - SI 1996/1909 – Insolvent Companies (Reports on Conduct of Directors) Rules 1996.
- Council Directive 2001/24/EC on "the reorganisation and winding up of credit institutions" (4 April 2001).

Secondary legislation:
- SI 2004/1045 – Credit Institutions (Reorganisation and Winding up) Regulations 2004.

1.2.8 Risk Management

EUROPEAN LEVEL – Laws, Regulations and Norms

The regulations establishing the European Supervisory Authorities (ESAs) and the European Systemic Risk Board (ESRB) include provisions for the Commission to publish a general report on the experience acquired as a result of the operation of the Authorities within the ESFS and the ESFS as a whole.
Cross-reference: For further information, see 1.1.1 "European Supervisory Authorities".

EUROPEAN LEVEL – Standards, Frameworks and Guidance

ESMA Technical Advice related to Risk

- ESMA/2015/527 – "ESMA Risk Dashboard No. 1, 2015".
- ESMA/2015/526 – "Trends Risks Vulnerabilities".
- JC/2014/63 – " Joint Committee Report on Risk and Vulnerabilities in the EU Financial System".
- ESMA/2014/884 – "Trends Risks Vulnerabilities No. 2, 2014".
- ESMA/2014/883 – "ESMA Risk Dashboard No. 3, 2014".
- ESMA/2014/536 – "ESMA Risk Dashboard No. 2, 2014".
- JC/2014/18 – "Report on risks and vulnerabilities in the EU financial system March 2014".
- ESMA/2014/188 – "Trends Risks Vulnerabilities No.1, 2014".
- ESMA/2014/0197 – "ESMA Risk Dashboard No. 1, 2014".
- ESMA/2013/1454 – "ESMA Risk Dashboard No. 4".
- ESMA (August 2013) "Joint Committee Report On Risks And Vulnerabilities In The EU Financial System".
- ESMA/2013/1138 – "Trends, Risks, Vulnerabilities No. 2, 2013".
- ESMA/2013/712 – "ESMA Risk Dashboard No. 2, 2013".
- JC 2013-010 – "Joint Committee Report on Risks and Vulnerabilities in the European Union's (EU) Financial System".
- ESMA/2013/213 – "ESMA Risk Dashboard".
- ESMA/2013/212 – "Trends, Risks, Vulnerabilities".

EIOPA Guidelines and Reports related to Risk

- EIOPA-BoS-14/172 – "Guidelines on basis risk".
- EIOPA-BoS-14/176 – "Guidelines on health catastrophe risk sub-module".

- EIOPA-BoS-14/174 – "Guidelines on the treatment of market and counterparty risk exposures in the standard formula".
- EIOPA-BoS-14/166 – "Guidelines on valuation of technical provisions" (various Annexes).
- EIOPA-FS-15/209 (March 2015) – "EIOPA Risk Dashboard – Q4 2014 data PUBLIC".
- EIOPA-FS-15/209 – "EIOPA Risk Dashboard – March 2015 – Q4 2014 data PUBLIC".
- EIOPA-FS-14/108 – "EIOPA Risk Dashboard – December 2014 – Q3 2014 data"
- EIOPA-FS-14/109 – "EIOPA Risk Dashboard – December 2014 – Q3 2014 data – Background note".
- EIOPA-FS-14/083 – "EIOPA Risk Dashboard – September 2014 – Q2 2014 data".
- EIOPA-FS-14/057 – "EIOPA Risk Dashboard – June 2014 – Q1 2014 data".
- EIOPA-FS-14/028 – "EIOPA Risk Dashboard – March 2014".
- EIOPA-FS-14/034 – "EIOPA Risk Dashboard – March 2014 – Background Note".
- EIOPA-FS-13-081 – "EIOPA Risk Dashboard – December 2013".
- EIOPA (August 2013) "Joint Committee Report On Risks And Vulnerabilities In The EU Financial System".
- EIOPA-FS-13-022 – "EIOPA Risk Dashboard March 2013".
- EIOPA-FS-13-029 – "EIOPA Risk Dashboard March 2013 – Background Note".
- EIOPA-BoS-13/011 – "Report on the Functioning of Colleges and the Accomplishments of the 2012 Action Plan".
- EIOPA-BoS-13/012 – "EIOPA's Action Plan 2013 for Colleges".
- EIOPA-FS-12-110 – "EIOPA Risk Dashboard – December 2012".
- EIOPA-FS-12-076 – "EIOPA Risk Dashboard – September 2012".
- EIOPA-BoS/025 – "Report on Risk Mitigation Mechanisms for Defined Contribution Related Risks".
- CEIOPS-BOS-11/024 – "Report on Risks Related to Defined Contribution Pension Plan Members".

Joint Committee of the European Supervisory Authorities (ESMA/ EBA/ EIOPA)

- JC/2014/63 – "Joint Committee Report on Risk and Vulnerabilities in the EU Financial System".
- JC 2013-010 – "Joint Committee Report on Risks and Vulnerabilities in the European Union's (EU) Financial System".

ESRB Recommendations and Reports related to Risk

- ESRB (2014) – "ESRB Risk Dashboard – Issue 10 (December 2014)".
- ESRB (2014) – "ESRB Risk Dashboard – Issue 9 (25 September 2014)".
- ESRB (2014) – "ESRB Risk Dashboard – Issue 8 (18 June 2014)".
- ESRB (2014) – "ESRB Risk Dashboard – Issue 7 (31 March 2014)".

- ESRB (2014) – "ESRB Risk Dashboard – Issue 6 (28 January 2014)".
- ESRB (2013) – "ESRB Risk Dashboard – Issue 5 (2 September 2013)".
- ESRB (2013) – "Occasional Paper No. 4 – Assessing contagion risks from the CDS market".
- ESRB (2013) – "ESRB Risk Dashboard – Issue 4 (3 June 2013)".
- ESRB (2013) – "ESRB Risk Dashboard – Issue 3 (1 March 2013)".
- ESRB (2014) – "ESRB Risk Dashboard – Issue 2 (30 November 2012)".
- ESRB (2014) – "ESRB Risk Dashboard (20 September 2012)".

NATIONAL LEVEL – Standards, Frameworks and Guidance

System and Controls

- FCA Handbook: Principles for Businesses (PRIN 2.1.1R [The Principles], Principle 3 [Rules about application]).
- FCA Handbook: Senior Management Arrangements, Systems and Controls (SYSC 4.1.1R [General requirements; SYSC 4.1.4R [Mechanisms and procedures for a firm] and SYSC 9.1.1R [Record-keeping]).
- FCA Handbook: SYSC Senior Management Arrangements, Systems and Controls (SYSC 7.1 [Risk control]).

SUB-NATIONAL – Laws, Regulations and Norms

Organisations implement a wide range of policies and procedures regarding reporting, transparency, reducing fraud and improving business operations. Examples include.

Credit Risk Principles

Credit risk is defined as the risk that parties with whom the Group has contracted fail to meet their obligations (both on or off balance sheet).

- Commercial Credit Risk Policy
- Retail & Wealth Credit Risk Policy
- Country Risk & Sovereign Risk Policy
- Large Exposures and Connected Counterparty (Inter-Group) Lending Policy

Funding and Liquidity Risk Principles

Funding risk is defined as the risk that the company does not have sufficiently stable and diverse sources of funding or the funding structure is inefficient.
Liquidity risk is defined as the risk that the company has insufficient financial resources to meet its commitments as they fall due, or can only secure them at excessive cost.

- Funding & Liquidity Policy.
- UK Defined Liquidity Group Funding & Liquidity Policy.
- Liquidity Transfer Pricing Policy.
- Securitisation Policy.

Financial Reporting Risk Principles

Financial Reporting risk is defined as the risk that the company suffers reputational damage, loss of investor confidence and/or financial loss arising from the adoption of inappropriate accounting policies, ineffective controls over financial reporting, failure to manage the associated risks of changes in taxation rates, law, ownership or corporate structure and the failure to disclose accurate and timely information.

- Financial & Prudential Regulatory Reporting Policy.
- Delegated Authorities Policy.
- Pillar 3 Disclosure Policy.
- Internal Rate Of Return (IRR) Policy.
- Disclosure Policy.
- Accounting Policy.
- Tax Policy.

Operational Risk Principle

Operational risk is defined as the risk of loss resulting from inadequate or failed internal processes, people and systems or from external events.

- Security Policies
  - Information Security Policy.
  - Internet Usage Policy.
  - Business Continuity Policy.
  - IT Disaster Recovery Policy.
  - Physical and People Security Policy.
- Anti-Fraud Policies
  - Fraud Policy.
  - Investigations Policy.
  - Whistle blowing Policy.
- Process Policies
  - Records Management Policy.
  - Data Privacy Policy.
  - Insurable Risk Policy.
  - Sourcing Policy.
  - Operational Risk Policy.

- Health and Safety Policy.
- Business Operations Policies
  - Business Continuity Management (BCM) Policy.
  - IT Disaster Recovery Policy.
- HR Policies
  - Employment Manual.
  - Expense Policy.

SUB-NATIONAL LEVEL – Standards, Frameworks and Guidance

Processes and Key Performance Indicators (KPIs)

- Governance Process, including accountability; assurance monitoring, identification, documentation and maintenance and inventories; risk assessments/ Business Impact Assessments (BIAs).
- Compliance matrices, including Critical Information Security Assets Register; 3rd Party Supplier Management.
- Management and resolution of issues
- Incident and reporting of policy breaches
- Risk Management
- Change Management
- Education and Awareness

1.3   FINANCIAL CRIME AND CONSUMER PROTECTION

1.3.1   FINANCIAL CRIME: ANTI-MONEY LAUNDERING, SANCTIONS AND TERRORISM

Cross-reference: For further information, see 3.1.5 "Anti-bribery and corruption ("ABC")".

GLOBAL LEVEL – Laws, Regulations and Norms

Not applicable: Binding laws, regulations and norms exist only at other Levels of governance.

GLOBAL LEVEL – Standards, Frameworks and Guidance

Fighting Terrorism Guidance

- Organisation for Security and Co-operation in Europe (OSCE) "Overview of OSCE Counter-Terrorism Related Commitments" (2 February 2015).

- Organisation for Security and Co-operation in Europe (OSCE) "Preventing Terrorism and Countering Violent Extremism and Radicalization that Lead to Terrorism: A Community-Policing Approach" (17 March 2014).
- Organisation for Security and Co-operation in Europe (OSCE) "OSCE Consolidated Framework for the Fight against Terrorism", Permanent Council Decision No. 1063 (7 December 2012).
- Organisation for Security and Co-operation in Europe (OSCE) "OSCE Handbook on Data Collection in Support of Money Laundering and Terrorism Financing, National Risk Assessments" (16 October 2012).

International Sanction Lists (incl. United States)

Major worldwide sanction lists which are regularly updates include:
International Organisations

- United Nations, UN Office for Disarmament Affairs (UNODA): "UN Register of Conventional Arms"
  [Website: http://www.un.org/disarmament/convarms/Register/].

- United Nations "Consolidated United Nations Security Council Sanctions List: Individuals, entities and other groups"
  [Website: http://www.un.org/spanish/sc/committees/consolidated.htm].

- The World Bank, International Development Association (IDA): "IDA Borrowing Countries"
  [Website: http://www.worldbank.org/ida/borrowing-countries.html].

- World Bank "World Bank Listing of Ineligible Firms & Individuals"
  [Website: http://web.worldbank.org/].

- Interpol "Most Wanted Persons"
  [Website: http://www.interpol.int/notice/search/wanted]

United States Sanctions Lists

- Office of Foreign Assets Control (OFAC), part of the US Department of the Treasury, administers and enforces economic and trade sanctions
  [Website: http://www.treas.gov/ofac]:

  - Specially Designated Nationals (SDN) and Blocked Persons List
  - Foreign Sanctions Evaders List
  - Sectoral Sanctions Identifications (SSI) List
  - Palestinian Legislative Council (PLC) List
- Office of the Comptroller of the Currency (OCC), US Department of Treasury "Rescinded Banking Circulars".
  [Website: http://www.occ.gov/]

- Bureau of Industry and Security, US Department of Commerce "Consolidated Screening List" [Website: http://www.bis.doc.gov/].
    - Department of Commerce, Bureau of Industry and Security:
        - Denied Persons List – Individuals and entities that have been denied export privileges.
        - Unverified List – End-users who BIS (Bureau of Industry and Security) has been unable to verify in prior transactions.
        - Entity List – Parties whose presence in a transaction can trigger a license requirement supplemental to those elsewhere in the Export Administration Regulations (EAR).
    - Department of State, Bureau of International Security and Non-proliferation: Nonproliferation Sanctions – Parties that have been sanctioned under various statutes.
    - Department of State, Directorate of Defense Trade Controls: Arms Export Control Act (AECA) Debarred List – Entities and individuals prohibited from participating directly or indirectly in the export of defense articles, including technical data and defense services.
- Federal Bureau of Investigations (FBI) "FBI Top Ten Most Wanted" [Website: http://www.fbi.gov/wanted].

- U.S. Immigrations and Customs Enforcement "ICE Most Wanted List" – Homeland security Investigations, Enforcement and Removal, and Human Trafficking [Website: https://www.ice.gov/most-wanted].

Sanctions Lists from other countries

- State Secretariat for Economic Affairs SECO, Schweizer Eidgenossenschaft "Sanctions / Embargos List" [Website: http://www.seco.admin.ch/themen/00513/00620/].

- Central Bureau of Investigations (CBI) "CBI List", India [Website: http://cbi.nic.in/wantedbycbi.php].

EURPEAN LEVEL – Laws, Regulations and Norms

Anti-Money Laundering Directive

- Directive (EU) 2015/849 "on the prevention of the use of the financial system for the purposes of money laundering or terrorist financing, amending Regulation (EU) No 648/2012 of the European Parliament and of the Council, and repealing Directive 2005/60/EC of the European Parliament and of the Council and Commission Directive 2006/70/EC" (*Fourth Anti-Money Laundering Directive (AMLD4)*) (20 May 2015).

- Directive 2005/60/EC on "the prevention of the use of the financial system for the purpose of money laundering and terrorist financing" (*Third Anti-Money Laundering Directive (AMLD3)*) (26 October 2005).
  Implementing measures and Amendments:
  - Directive 2008/20/EC "amending Directive 2005/60/EC on the prevention of the use of the financial system for the purpose of money laundering and terrorist financing, as regards the implementing powers conferred on the Commission" (*Third Anti-Money Laundering (Amendment) Directive*) (11 March 2008).
  - [UK] SI 2007/2157 – Monday Laundering Regulations 2007.
  - Directive 2006/70/EC "laying down implementing measures for Directive 2005/60/EC of the European Parliament and of the Council as regards the definition of 'politically exposed person' and the technical criteria for simplified customer due diligence procedures and for exemption on grounds of a financial activity conducted on an occasional or very limited basis" (*Third Anti-Money Laundering Implementing Directive*) (1 August 2006).
- Directive 91/308/EEC on "prevention of the use of the financial system for the purpose of money laundering" (*First Anti-Money Laundering Implementing Directive*) (10 June 1991).
  - Directive 2001/97/EC "amending Council Directive 91/308/EEC on prevention of the use of the financial system for the purpose of money laundering" (*Second Anti-Money Laundering Implementing Directive*) (4 December 2001).

Anti-Terrorism Regulation

- Council Regulation (EC) No 881/2002 "imposing certain specific restrictive measures directed against certain persons and entities associated with Usama bin Laden, the Al-Qaida network and the Taliban, and repealing Council Regulation (EC) No 467/2001 prohibiting the export of certain goods and services to Afghanistan, strengthening the flight ban and extending the freeze of funds and other financial resources in respect of the Taliban of Afghanistan" (*Taliban and Al-Qaida Regulation*)(27 May 2002).
  Amendments:
  - Council Regulation (EU) No 754/2011 "amending Regulation (EC) No 881/2002 imposing certain specific restrictive measures directed against certain persons and entities associated with Usama bin Laden, the Al-Qaida network and the Taliban" (*the Al-Qaida Regulation*) (1 August 2011).
  - Council Regulation (EU) No 753/2011 "concerning restrictive measures directed against certain individuals, groups, undertakings and entities in view of the situation in Afghanistan" (*the Taliban Regulation*) (1 August 2011).
  - [UK] SI 2011/2649 – The Export Control (Al-Qaida and Taliban Sanctions) Regulations 2011.

- Council Regulation (EC) No 2580/2001 "on specific restrictive measures directed against certain persons and entities with a view to combating terrorism" (*Anti-Terrorism Regulation*) (27 December 2001).
  - Commission Implementing Regulation (EU) No 1250/2012 "amending Council Regulation (EC) No 2580/2001 on specific restrictive measures directed against certain persons and entities with a view to combating terrorism" (20 December 2012).

Sanctions related regulations

- Council Regulation (EU) No 833/2014 "concerning restrictive measures in view of Russia's actions destabilising the situation in Ukraine" (31 July 2014).

EJROPEAN LEVEL – Standards, Frameworks and Guidance

- Communication COM(2010)386 final "The EU Counter-Terrorism Policy: main achievements and future challenges (SEC(2010)911)" (20 July 2010).

EIOPA Guidelines and Reports related to AML

- JC/2011/096 AMLTF/2011/05 – "Report on the legal, regulatory and supervisory implementation across EU Member States in relation to the Beneficial Owners Customer Due Diligence requirements under the Third Money Laundering Directive [2005/60/EC]".
- EIOPA (2012) "Report on the legal and regulatory provisions and supervisory expectations across EU Member States of Simplified Due Diligence requirements where the customers are credit and financial institutions under the Third Money Laundering Directive [2005/60/EC]".

European Sanction Lists

- European Union "Consolidated list of persons, groups and entities subject to EU financial sanctions" [Website: http://eeas.europa.eu/cfsp/sanctions/consol-list/index_en.htm].
- Common Foreign and Security Policy (CFSP) of the European Union [Regular updates on website: http://eeas.europa.eu/cfsp/index_en.htm].

NATIONAL LEVEL (UK) – Laws, Regulations and Norms

Anti-Terrorism

- Terrorist Asset-Freezing etc. Act 2010 c. 38.

- Council Regulation (EC) No 881/2002 *Taliban and Al-Qaida Regulation* (27 May 2002).

  Secondary legislation:
  - SI 2010/1197 – Al-Qaida and Taliban (Asset-Freezing) Regulations 2010.
- Counter-Terrorism Act 2008 c.28, Schedule 7 [Terrorist financing and money laundering].
- Council Directive 2005/60/EC on "the prevention of the use of the financial system for the purpose of money laundering and terrorist financing" *Third Anti-Money Laundering Directive (AMLD3)* (26 October 2005).

  Secondary legislation:
  - SI 2015/11 — Money Laundering (Amendment) Regulations 2015.
  - SI 2012/2298 – Money Laundering (Amendment) Regulations 2012.
  - SI 2015/11 — Money Laundering (Amendment) Regulations 2015.
  - SI 2007/2157 – Money Laundering Regulations 2007.
- Terrorism Act 2006 c. 11.
- Serious Organised Crime and Police Act 2005 c. 15.
- Anti-terrorism, Crime and Security Act 2001 c. 24.
- Terrorism Act 2000 c. 11.

  Secondary legislation:
  - SI 2011/2701 – Terrorism Act 2000 and Proceeds of Crime Act 2002 (Business in the Regulated Sector) Order 2011.
  - SI 2007/3288 – Terrorism Act 2000 (Business in the Regulated Sector and Supervisory Authorities) Order 2007.

NATIONAL LEVEL (UK) – Standards, Frameworks and Guidance

FCA/ FSA Handbook

- Financial Conduct Authority Handbook: PRIN 2.1 – The Principles [for Businesses]
  - Principle 1. Integrity A firm must conduct its business with integrity.
  - Principle 2. Skill, care and diligence A firm must conduct its business with due skill, care and diligence.
  - Principle 3. Management and control A firm must take reasonable care to organise and control its affairs responsibly and effectively, with adequate risk management systems.
- The FSA's financial crime and AML rules and guidance are set out
  - SYSC 3.2.6 R [Systems and controls in relation to compliance, financial crime and money laundering] – SYSC 3.2.6J G [The money laundering reporting officer] (for insurers and managing agents)

- SYSC 6.1.1R [Compliance, internal audit and financial crime, compliance] and SYSC 6.3 1R [Compliance, internal audit and financial crime, financial crime] (for other firms)
- SYSC 6.3.9 R [The money laundering reporting officer]
- SUP 10A.7.10 and SUP 10A.7.11 [Money laundering reporting function]

FCA Guidance

- FCA "FCA's Financial Crime: a guide for firms - Part 1 : A firm's guide to preventing financial crime (Chapter 6 Bribery and Corruption)" (2015).
- FCA "Thematic Review TR13/9 Anti-Money Laundering and Anti-Bribery and Corruption Systems and Controls: Asset Management and Platform Firms" (January 2014).
- FCA "Thematic Review TR13/9 Anti-Money Laundering and Anti-Bribery and Corruption Systems and Controls: Asset Management and Platform Firms" (2013).
- FCA "Financial Crime: a guide for firms - Part 2: Financial crime thematic reviews" (2013).
- FSA "Anti-bribery and corruption systems and controls in investment banks" (2012).
- FSA "Anti-bribery and corruption in commercial insurance broking - Reducing the risk of illicit payments or inducements to third parties" (2010).
- FCA "Anti-bribery and corruption in commercial insurance broking: Reducing the risk of illicit payments or inducements to third parties" (May 2010).

Anti-money laundering Guidance

- HM Revenue and Customs (July 2010) "Anti-money laundering guidance for trust or company service providers".
- Consultative Committee of Accountancy Bodies (August 2008) "Anti-money Laundering guidance for the accountancy sector".
- Prevention of money laundering / combating terrorist financing – guidance for the UK financial sector Parts I & II, Joint Money Laundering Steering Group (JMLST) Guidance (December 2007).

United Kingdom Sanction Lists

- Her Majesty Treasury (HM) List "Financial sanctions: consolidated list of targets" – consolidated list of asset freeze targets and a list of persons subject to restrictive measures.
  [Website: https://www.gov.uk/government/publications/financial-sanctions-consolidated-list-of-targets/consolidated-list-of-targets].

ESMA Report

- JC-2013-72 — Joint Committee Report — Preliminary report on anti-money laundering and counter financing of terrorism Risk Based Supervision

<u>SUB-NATIONAL LEVEL – Laws, Regulations and Norms</u>

Group Regulatory Risk Principle

- Anti-Money Laundering (AML) Policy
- Insurance/ on boarding Anti-Money Laundering Policy

1.3.2 Consumer protection (Financial Services specific)

<u>EUROPEAN LEVEL – Laws, Regulations and Norms</u>

See also Markets in Financial Instrument Directives (MiFiD) regulation (1.2.5 Markets regulation: records-keeping, transparency and market abuse).

- Council Directive 93/13/EEC on "unfair terms in consumer contracts" (Unfair Terms Directive) (5 April 1993).
  Secondary legislation:
  - [UK] SI 1999/2083 – Unfair Terms in Consumer Contracts Regulations 1999.
- Directive 2002/65/EC "concerning the distance marketing of consumer financial services and amending Council Directive 90/619/EEC and Directives 97/7/EC and 98/27/EC" (*Distance Marketing Directive (DMD)*) (23 September 2002).
  - [UK] SI 2004/2095 – Financial Services (Distance Marketing) Regulations 2004.

<u>EUROPEAN LEVEL – Standards, Frameworks and Guidance</u>

Joint Committee of the European Supervisory Authorities (ESMA/ EBA/ EIOPA)

- JC/2014/43 — Joint Committee Final Report on guidelines for complaints-handling for the securities (ESMA) and banking (EBA) sectors

EIOPA Guidelines and Reports on consumer protection

- JC/2014/62 — "The Joint Committee of the ESAs reminds financial institutions of their responsibilities when placing their own financial products with consumers".
- JC/2014/43 — "Joint Committee Final Report on guidelines for complaints-handling for the securities (ESMA) and banking (EBA) sectors".

- EIOPA-BoS-13/164 – "Guidelines on complaints-handling by insurance intermediaries".
- EIOPA-CCPFI-12-037 – "Methodology Report for Collecting, Analysing and Reporting on Consumer Trends".
- EIOPA-BoS-12/074 – "Updated Survey of the Competences of National Competent Authorities in the field of Consumer Protection".
- EIOPA-Bos-12/069 – "Guidelines on Complaints-Handling by Insurance Undertakings".
- EIOPA-BoS-12/070 – "Report on Best Practices by Insurance Undertakings in Handling Complaints".
- EIOPA-CP-11/007 – "Report on Good Practices for Disclosure and Selling of Variable Annuities".
- EIOPA-CCPFI-11/029 – "Initial Overview of Key Consumer Trends in the EU".

NATAIONAL LEVEL (UK) – Laws, Regulations and Norms

Cross-reference: No Act of Parliament is directly applicable. See applicable UK Statutory Instruments ("[UK] SI") implementing EU law in the corresponding European Level sub-section.

- Consumer Protection Act 1987 c. 43.
- Supply of Goods and Services Act 1982 c. 29.
- Sale of Goods Act 1979 c. 54
- Unfair Contract Terms Act 1977 c. 50.
  Secondary legislation:
  - SI 1999/2083 – Unfair Terms in Consumer Contracts Regulations 1999.

NATIONAL LEVEL (UK) – Standards, Frameworks and Guidance

London Stock Exchange Guidance

- London Stock Exchange (LSE) "Rules of the London Stock Exchange – Rule Book" (January 2015)
- London Stock Exchange (LSE) "Rules of the London Stock Exchange – Derivatives Market" Attachment 1 to Market Notice 09/13 (September 2013).
- London Stock Exchange (LSE) "A Guide to Capital Markets – Your Route to the heart of global finance" (August 2007).

SUB-NATIONAL LEVEL – Laws, Regulations and Norms

- Customer Complaint Policy
- Customer Compensation Policy
- General Terms and Conditions
- Service Agreement

Employment contract: Many employees have contracts with their employers, setting out the employment conditions and the rights, responsibilities and duties of the parties. This may include details of matters like pay, holidays and working hours.

1.4   RETAIL BANKING

Includes savings and transactional accounts, mortgages, personal loans, debit cards and credit cards.

1.4.1   Consumer credit, mortgages and lending

Cross-reference: For further information, see 1.1.2 "Credit Rating Agencies".

EUROPEAN LEVEL– Laws, Regulations and Norms

- Directive 2014/17/EU on "credit agreements for consumers relating to residential immovable property and amending Directives 2008/48/EC and 2013/36/EU and Regulation (EU) No 1093/2010" (*Consumer Credit Directive – CCD (Residential Immovable Property Agreements)/ Mortgage Credit Directive*) (4 February 2014).
  - 2015/910 — Mortgage Credit Directive Order 2015.
- Directive 2011/90/EU "amending Part II of Annex I to Directive 2008/48/EC of the European Parliament and of the Council providing additional assumptions for the calculation of the annual percentage rate of charge" (*Consumer Credit (Amendment) Directive*) (14 November 2011).
- Directive 2008/48/EC "on credit agreements for consumers and repealing Council Directive 87/102/EEC" (*Consumer Credit Directive*) (23 April 2008).
  - [UK] SI 2010/1013 – Consumer Credit (Disclosure of Information) Regulations 2010. (and [the pre-contractual information requirements in] Directive 2002/65/EC "concerning the distance marketing of consumer financial services and amending Council Directive 90/619/EEC and Directives 97/7/EC and 98/27/EC" (*Distance Marketing Directive (DMD)*)) (23 September 2002).
  - [UK] SI 2010/1010 – The Consumer Credit (EU Directive) Regulations 2010.
  - [UK] SI 2004/506 – Financial Services and Markets Act 2000 (Consumer Credit) (Miscellaneous Provisions) (No 2) Order.

Building Societies

- Directive 2014/59/EU *Bank Recovery and Resolution Directive (BRRD* (15 May 2014).
  - [UK] SI 2014/3486 — Banks and Building Societies (Depositor Preference and Priorities) Order 2014.

Cooperative Society

- Council Regulation (EC) No. 1435/2003 on "the Statute for a European Cooperative Society (SCE)" (22 July 2003).
  Secondary legislation:
  - [UK] SI 2006/2078 – European Cooperative Society Regulations 2006.

EUROPEAN LEVEL – Standards, Frameworks and Guidance

- Communication COM(2007) 226 "Green Paper on Retail Financial Services in the Single Market" (30 April 2007).
- Communication COM(2005) 327 "Mortgage Credit in the EU" (19 July 2005).

Technical Standards for Consumer Credit Directive (2014/17/EU)

- Commission Delegated Regulation (EU) No 1125/2014 "supplementing Directive 2014/17/EU of the European Parliament and of the Council with regard to regulatory technical standards on the minimum monetary amount of the professional indemnity insurance or comparable guarantee to be held by credit intermediaries" (*Consumer Credit (Residential Immovable Property Agreements — Minimum Monetary Amount — Regulatory Technical Standards) Regulation*) (19 September 2014).

NATIONAL LEVEL (UK) – Laws, Regulations and Norms

- Financial Services Act 2012 c. 21.
  Secondary legislation:
  - SI 2013/1882 – Financial Services Act 2012 (Consumer Credit) Order 2013.
- Consumer Credit Act 1974 c. 39 and The Consumer Credit Act 2006 c. 14.
  Secondary legislation:
  - SI 2014/2369 – Consumer Credit (Information Requirements and Duration of Licences and Charges) (Amendment) Regulations 2014.
  - SI 2012/2798 – Consumer Credit (Green Deal) Regulations 2012.
  - SI 2010/1014 – Consumer Credit (Agreements) Regulations 2010.
  - SI 2004/3236 – Consumer Credit Act 1974 (Electronic Communications) Order 2004 (and Electronic Communications Act 2000).
  - SI 2004/1481 – Consumer Credit (Disclosure of Information) Regulations 2004.
  - SI 2000/290 – Consumer Credit (Credit Reference Agency) Regulations 2000 (and Data Protection Act 1998).
  - SI 1983/1553 – Consumer Credit (Agreements) Regulations 1983.
  - SI 1983/1561 – Consumer Credit (Enforcement, Default and Termination Notices) Regulations 1983.
  - SI 1983/1553 – The Consumer Credit (Agreements) Regulations 1983.
  - SI 1974/139 – The Consumer Credit Act 1974 (Fees) Order 2010.

Credit Unions

- Credit Unions Act 1979 c. 34.
  Secondary legislation:
  - SI 2013/2589 — Credit Unions (Maximum Interest Rate on Loans) Order 2013.

1.4.2 Savings and transactional accounts

EUROPEAN LEVEL – Laws, Regulations and Norms

- Council Directive 2003/48/EC on "taxation of savings income in the form of interest payments" (*Savings Taxation Directive*) (3 June 2003).
  Amendments:
  - Directive 2014/48/EU "amending Directive 2003/48/EC on taxation of savings income in the form of interest payments" (*Savings Taxation (Amendment) Directive*) (24 March 2014).
- Council Directive 86/635/EEC "on the annual accounts and consolidated accounts of banks and other financial institutions" (*Bank Accounts Directive*) (8 December 1986).
  - [UK] SI 2008/567 – Bank Accounts Directive (Miscellaneous Banks) Regulations 2008 (Directive 2006/43/EC on "statutory audits of annual accounts and consolidated accounts, amending Council Directives 78/660/EEC and 83/349/EEC and repealing Council Directive 84/253/EEC" (17 May 2006).

Deposits

- Directive 2014/49/EU on "deposit guarantee schemes (recast)" (*Deposit Guarantee Scheme Directive, DGS*) (16 April 2014).
- Directive 94/19/EC on "deposit-guarantee schemes" (*Deposit Guarantee Schemes Directive (DGS)*) (30 May 1994). [Repealed with effect from 4 July 2016]
  - [UK] SI 1995/1442 – Credit Institutions (Protection of Depositors) Regulations 1995.

NATIONAL LEVEL (UK) – Laws, Regulations and Norms

Cross-reference: No Act of Parliament is directly applicable. See applicable UK Statutory Instruments ("[UK] SI") implementing EU law in the corresponding European Level subsection.

- Saving Gateway Accounts Act 2009 c. 8.

Taxation on income

- Income Tax (Trading and other Income) Act 2005 ("ITTOIA 2005") c.5.
  Secondary legislation:
  - SI 2015/608 — Individual Savings Account (Amendment) Regulations 2015.
  - SI 2014/1450 — Individual Savings Account (Amendment No 2) Regulations 2014.
- Income Tax (Trading and Other Income) Act 2005 and Taxation of Chargeable Gains Act 1992.
  Secondary legislation:
  - SI 2014/654 — Individual Savings Account (Amendment) Regulations 2014.
  - SI 2013/1743 — Individual Savings Account (Amendment No 3) Regulations 2013.
  - SI 2013/267 — Individual Savings Account (Amendment) Regulations 2013.
- Income and Corporation Taxes Act 1988, Taxation of Chargeable Gains Act 1992, and Finance Act 1998.
  Secondary legislation:
  - SI 1998/1870 – Individual Savings Account Regulations 1998.

Transfer of Funds

- Financial Services and Markets Act 2000 c.8.
  Secondary legislation:
  - SI 2007/3298 – Transfer of Funds (Information on the Payer) Regulations 2007.
- Dormant Bank and Building Society Accounts Act 2008 Act (the "2008 Act") c.31.
  Secondary legislation:
  - SI 2011/1799 – Distribution of Dormant Account Money (Apportionment) Order 2011.

1.5 INVESTMENT BANKING

1.5.1 Investment products and funds

GLOBAL LEVEL – Laws, Regulations and Norms

Not applicable: Essentially all regulation of investment banking, especially Alternative Investment Funds which is an EU regulatory initiative, takes place (hence applicable laws, regulations and norms exist) only at European Level and below.

EUROPEAN LEVEL – Laws, Regulations and Norms

- Regulation (EU) 2015/760 "on European long-term investment funds" (*European Long-Term Investment Funds Regulation*) (29 April 2015).
- Regulation (EU) No 1286/2014 "on key information documents for packaged retail and insurance-based investment products (PRIIPs)" (*Packaged Retail and Insurance-Based Investment Products Regulation (PRIIPs)*) ((26 November 2014).
- Directive 2013/14/EU "amending Directive 2003/41/EC on the activities and supervision of institutions for occupational retirement provision, Directive 2009/65/EC on the coordination of laws, regulations and administrative provisions relating to undertakings for collective investment in transferable securities (UCITS) and Directive 2011/61/EU on Alternative Investment Funds Managers in respect of over-reliance on credit ratings" (*IORP, UCITS & AIFM (Amendment) Directive*) (21 May 2013).
- Regulation (EU) No 346/2013 "on European social entrepreneurship funds" (*European Social Entrepreneurship Funds Regulation (EuSEF)*) (17 April 2013).
- Regulation (EU) No 345/2013 "on European venture capital funds" (*European Venture Capital Funds Regulation (EuVECA)*) (17 April 2013).
- Directive 2003/87/EC "establishing a scheme for greenhouse gas emission allowance trading within the Community and amending Council Directive 96/61/EC" (*Greenhouse Gas Emission Allowance Trading Directive*) (13 October 2003).
- Directive 97/9/EC "on investor-compensation schemes" (*Investor Compensation Schemes Directive (ICS)*) (3 March 1997).

Money Market Funds

- Proposal for a Regulation COM/2013/0615 final on "Money Market Funds" (4 September 2013).
  Note: This is currently the only regulatory initiative at European Level.

Alternative Investment Funds (AIF)

- Directive 2011/61/EU "on Alternative Investment Fund Managers and amending Directives 2003/41/EC and 2009/65/EC and Regulations (EC) No 1060/2009 and (EU) No 1095/2010" (*Alternative Investment Fund Managers Directive (AIFMD)*) (8 June 2011).
  Secondary legislation:
  - Commission Delegated Regulation (EU) 2015/514 "on the information to be provided by competent authorities to the European Securities and Markets Authority pursuant to Article 67(3) of Directive 2011/61/EU of the European Parliament and of the Council" (*AIFM (Information to be Provided by Competent Authorities to ESMA) Regulation*) (18 December 2014).

- Commission Implementing Regulation (EU) No 448/2013 "establishing a procedure for determining the Member State of reference of a non-EU AIFM pursuant to Directive 2011/61/EU of the European Parliament and of the Council" (*AIFM (Non-EU Member State Procedure) Regulation*) (15 May 2013).
- Commission Implementing Regulation (EU) No 447/2013 "establishing the procedure for AIFMs which choose to opt in under Directive 2011/61/EU of the European Parliament and of the Council" (*AIFM (Opt In Procedure) Regulation*) (15 May 2013).
- [UK] SI 2014/1313 — Alternative Investment Fund Managers (Amendment) Order 2014.
- [UK] SI 2014/1292 — Alternative Investment Fund Managers Order 2014.
- [UK] SI 2013/1797 — Alternative Investment Fund Managers (Amendment) Regulations 2013.
- [UK] SI 2013/1773 – Alternative Investment Fund Managers Regulations 2013.
- FCA 2013/54 - Alternative Investment Fund Managers Directive (No 2) Instrument 2013.
- Commission Delegated Regulation (EU) No 231/2013 "supplementing Directive 2011/61/EU of the European Parliament and of the Council with regard to exemptions, general operating conditions, depositaries, leverage, transparency and supervision" (*AIFM (Exemptions, General Operating Conditions, Depositaries, Leverage, Transparency and Supervision) Regulation*) (19 December 2012).

EUROPEAN LEVEL – Standards, Frameworks and Guidance

European Commission

- Communication COM(2011) 818 "Green Paper on the feasibility of introducing Stability Bonds" (23 November 2011).
- Communication COM(2005) 314 "Green Paper on the enhancement of the EU framework for investment funds" (12 July 2005).

Technical Standards for alternative investment fund managers (Directive 2011/61/EU)

- Commission Delegated Regulation (EU) No 694/2014 "supplementing Directive 2011/61/EU of the European Parliament and of the Council with regard to regulatory technical standards determining types of alternative investment fund managers" (*AIFM (Types of AIFM — Regulatory Technical Standards) Regulation*) (17 December 2013).

Technical Standards for European social entrepreneurship funds (Regulation (EU) No 346/2013)

▪ Commission Implementing Regulation (EU) No 594/2014 "laying down implementing technical standards with regard to the format of the notification according to Article 17(1) of Regulation (EU) No 346/2013 of the European Parliament and of the Council on European social entrepreneurship funds" (*EuSEF (Notification Format — Implementing Technical Standards) Regulation*) (3 June 2014).

Technical Standards for European venture capital funds (Regulation (EU) No 345/2013)

▪ Commission Implementing Regulation (EU) No 593/2014 "laying down implementing technical standards with regard to the format of the notification according to Article 16(1) of Regulation (EU) No 345/2013 of the European Parliament and of the Council on European venture capital funds" (*EuVECA (Notification Format — Implementing Technical Standards) Regulation*) (3 June 2014).

ESMA Guidelines

▪ ESMA/2015/227 — "Final report on ESMA's technical advice to the European Commission on the delegated acts of the Regulations on European Social Entrepreneurship Funds and European Venture Capital Funds".
▪ ESMA/2014/869 — "Guidelines on reporting obligations under Articles 3(3)(d) and 24(1), (2) and (4) of the AIFMD".
▪ ESMA/2014/1560 — "Advice — Investment-based crowdfunding".
▪ ESMA/2014/312 — "ESMA's technical advice to the European Commission on the information that competent authorities should provide to ESMA pursuant to Article 67(3) of the AIFMD".
▪ ESMA/2014/161 — "Draft implementing technical standards on notification — EuSEF".
▪ ESMA/2014/160 — "Draft implementing technical standards on notification — EuVECA".
▪ ESMA/2013/1339 — "Guidelines on reporting obligations under Articles 3(3)(d) and 24(1), (2) and (4) of the AIFMD".
▪ ESMA/2013/611 – "Guidelines on key concepts of the AIFMD".
▪ ESMA/2013/998 — "Guidelines on the model MoU concerning consultation, cooperation and the exchange of information related to the supervision of AIFMD entities".

- ESMA/2013/232 — "Guidelines on sound remuneration policies under the AIFMD".
- ESMA/2013/600 — "Guidelines on key concepts of the AIFMD".
- ESMA/2013/476 — "Peer Review — Money Market Fund Guidelines".
- ESMA/2013/201 — "Guidelines on sound remuneration policies under the AIFMD".
- ESMA/2013/413 — "Final report — Draft regulatory technical standards on types of AIFMs".

ESRB Recommendations and Reports

- ESRB (2014) – "Occasional Paper No 1: Money Market Funds in Europe and Financial Stability".
- ESRB/2012/1 – "Recommendation of the ESRB of 20 December 2012 on money market funds".

NATIONAL LEVEL (UK) – Laws, Regulations and Norms

Alternative Investment Funds

- Financial Services and Markets Act 2000 c. 8
  Secondary legislation:
  - SI 2001/1228 – Open-Ended Investment Companies Regulations 2001.
- Companies Act 2006 c.46.

London Stock Exchange (LSE)

- London Stock Exchange "Rule Book: Rules of the London Stock Exchange" (5 May 2015).

1.5.2 Securities and Foreign Exchange

EUROPEAN LEVEL – Laws, Regulations and Norms

Undertakings for Collective Investment in Transferable Securities (UCITS)

- Commission Regulation (EU) No 584/2010 "implementing Directive 2009/65/EC of the European Parliament and of the Council as regards the form and content of the standard notification letter and UCITS attestation, the use of electronic communication between competent authorities for the purpose of notification, and procedures for on-the-spot verifications and investigations and the exchange of information between competent authorities" (*Undertakings for Collective Investment in Transferable Securities Implementing Regulation No 2 (UCITS) V*) (1 July 2010).

- Commission Regulation (EU) No 583/2010 "implementing Directive 2009/65/EC of the European Parliament and of the Council as regards key investor information and conditions to be met when providing key investor information or the prospectus in a durable medium other than paper or by means of a website" (*Undertakings for Collective Investment in Transferable Securities Implementing Regulation No 1 (UCITS) V*) (1 July 2010).
- Directive 2009/65/EC on "the coordination of laws, regulations and administrative provisions relating to undertakings for collective investment in transferable securities (UCITS) (recast)" (*Undertakings for Collective Investment in Transferable Securities Directive (UCITS) V*) (13 July 2009).
  - [UK] SI 2013/1388 — Collective Investment in Transferable Securities (Contractual Scheme) Regulations 2013.
  - [UK] SI 2011/2859 – Regulated Covered Bonds (Amendment) Regulations 2011.

Amendments:

- Directive 2014/91/EU (23 July 2014) "amending Directive 2009/65/EC on the coordination of laws, regulations and administrative provisions relating to undertakings for collective investment in transferable securities (UCITS) as regards depositary functions, remuneration policies and sanctions" (*UCITS (Amendment) Directive (UCITS V)*) (23 July 2014).
- Commission Directive 2010/44/EU "implementing Directive 2009/65/EC of the European Parliament and of the Council as regards certain provisions concerning fund mergers, master-feeder structures and notification procedure" (*UCITS Implementing (No 2) Directive*) (1 July 2010).
- [UK] SI 2011/1613 – Undertakings for Collective Investment in Transferable Securities Regulations 2011.
- Commission Directive 2010/43/EU "implementing Directive 2009/65/EC of the European Parliament and of the Council as regards organisational requirements, conflicts of interest, conduct of business, risk management and content of the agreement between a depositary and a management company" (*UCITS Implementing (No 1) Directive*) (1 July 2010).
- Directive 2007/16/EC "implementing Council Directive 85/611/EEC on the coordination of laws, regulations and administrative provisions relating to undertakings for collective investment in transferable securities (UCITS) as regards the clarification of certain definitions" (*UCITS Definitions Clarification Directive*) (19 March 2007).
- Directive 2001/107/EC "amending Council Directive 85/611/EEC on the coordination of laws, regulations and administrative provisions relating to undertakings for collective investment in transferable securities (UCITS) with a view to regulating management companies and simplified prospectuses" (21 January 2002) and

Directive 2001/108/EC "amending Council Directive 85/611/EEC on the coordination of laws, regulations and administrative provisions relating to undertakings for collective investment in transferable securities (UCITS), with regard to investments of UCITS (UCITS III)" (21 January 2002).

- [UK] SI 2003/2066 – Collective Investment Schemes (Miscellaneous Amendments) Regulations 2003.

- Council Directive 85/611/EEC on "the coordination of laws, regulations and administrative provisions relating to undertakings for collective investment in transferable securities (UCITS)" (UCITS Directive) (20 December 1985).

Securities Settlement and Central Securities Depositories Regulation (CSDR)

- Regulation (EU) No 909/2014 on "improving securities settlement in the European Union and on central securities depositories and amending Directives 98/26/EC and 2014/65/EU and Regulation (EU) No 236/2012" (*Securities Settlement and Central Securities Depositories Regulation*) (23 July 2014).
  Secondary legislation:
  - [UK] SI 2015/347 — Financial Markets and Insolvency (Settlement Finality) (Amendment) Regulations 2015.
  - [UK] SI 2014/2879 — Central Securities Depositories Regulations 2014.

Trading and Short Selling Regulation

The SSR applies to people undertaking short selling of shares, sovereign debt, sovereign credit default swaps (CDS).

- Regulation (EU) No 236/2012 on "short selling and certain aspects of credit default swaps" (*Short Selling Regulation (SSR)*) (14 March 2012).
  Supplementing:
  - Commission delegated regulation (EU) No 918/2012 "supplementing Regulation (EU) No 236/2012 of the European Parliament and of the Council on short selling and certain aspects of credit default swaps with regard to definitions, the calculation of net short positions, covered sovereign credit default swaps, notification thresholds, liquidity thresholds for suspending restrictions, significant falls in the value of financial instruments and adverse events" (*Short Selling (Supplementary) Regulation*) (5 July 2012).
    Correcting legislation:
    - Commission Delegated Regulation (EU) 2015/97 "correcting Delegated Regulation (EU) No 918/2012 as regards the notification of significant net short positions in sovereign debt" (*Short Selling (Supplementary) (Amendment) Regulation*) (17 October 2014).

- Commission Delegated Regulation (EU) No 826/2012 "supplementing Regulation (EU) No 236/2012 of the European Parliament and of the Council with regard to regulatory technical standards on notification and disclosure requirements with regard to net short positions, the details of the information to be provided to the European Securities and Markets Authority in relation to net short positions and the method for calculating turnover to determine exempted shares" (Short Selling (*Regulatory Technical Standards) Regulation*) (29 June 2012).

EUROPEAN LEVEL – Standards, Frameworks and Guidance

Technical Standards for Short Selling (Regulation (EU) No 236/2012)

- Commission Implementing Regulation (EU) No 827/2012 "laying down implementing technical standards with regard to the means for public disclosure of net position in shares, the format of the information to be provided to the European Securities and Markets Authority in relation to net short positions, the types of agreements, arrangements and measures to adequately ensure that shares or sovereign debt instruments are available for settlement and the dates and period for the determination of the principal venue for a share according to Regulation (EU) No 236/2012 of the European Parliament and of the Council on short selling and certain aspects of credit default swaps" (*Short Selling (Implementing Technical Standards) Regulation*) (29 June 2012).
- Commission Delegated Regulation (EU) No 919/2012 "supplementing Regulation (EU) No 236/2012 of the European Parliament and of the Council on short selling and certain aspects of credit default swaps with regard to regulatory technical standards for the method of calculation of the fall in value for liquid shares and other financial instruments" (*Short Selling (Regulatory Technical Standards No 2) Regulation*) (5 July 2012).

ESMA Guidelines

- ESMA/2014/937 — "Guidelines for competent authorities and UCITS management companies".
- ESMA/2014/1417 — "Final Report on ESMA's technical advice to the European Commission on delegated acts required by the UCITS V Directive".
- ESMA/2014/294 — "Final report on the revision of the provisions on diversification of collateral in ESMA's Guidelines on ETFs [Exchange-Traded Funds] and other UCITS issues".
- ESMA/2013/74 — "Exemption for market making activities and primary market operations under Regulation (EU) 236/2012 of the European Parliament and the Council on short selling and certain aspects of Credit Default Swaps".

- ESMA/2013/158 — "Guidelines on the exemption for market making activities and primary market operations under Regulation (EU) 236/2012 of the European Parliament and the Council on short selling and certain aspects of Credit Default Swaps".
- ESMA/2013/765 — "Guidelines compliance table: Exemption for market making activities and primary market operations under Regulation (EU) 236/2012 of the European Parliament and the Council on short selling and certain aspects of Credit Default Swaps".
- ESMA/2012/832 — "Guidelines for competent authorities and UCITS management companies".
- ESMA/2012/474 — "Guidelines on ETFs and other UCITS issues".
- ESMA/2012/197 — "Guidelines on risk measurement and the calculation of global exposure for certain types of structured UCITS".
- ESMA/2011/112 — "Final Report: Guidelines to competent authorities and UCITS management companies on risk measurement and the calculation of global exposure for certain types of structured UCITS".

ESRB Recommendations and Reports on Securities

- ESRB (2014) – "Occasional Paper No. 6 — Securities financing transactions and the (re)use of collateral in Europe".
- ESRB (2013) – "Occasional Paper No. 2 — Towards a monitoring framework for securities financing transactions".

ESRB Recommendations and Reports on Foreign Exchange (FX) trading

- ESRB (2014) – "Response from the ESRB to the ESMA Consultation Paper on mandatory clearing for FX NDF".
- ESRB/2011/2 – "Recommendation on US dollar denominated funding of credit institutions".
- ESRB/2011/1 -"ESRB Recommendation on lending in foreign currencies – Follow-up Report – Overall assessment". ESRB/2011/1 – "Recommendation on lending in foreign currencies".

ESRB Recommendations and Reports on benchmarks

- ESRB (2014) – "Macro-prudential aspects of the reform of benchmark indices in response to a consultation by the European Commission on a possible framework for the regulation of the production and use of indices serving as benchmarks in financial and other contracts".

<u>NATIONAL LEVEL (UK) – Laws, Regulations and Norms</u>

Cross-reference: No Act of Parliament is directly applicable. See applicable UK Statutory Instruments ("[UK] SI") implementing EU law in the corresponding European Level sub-section.

- Companies Act 2006 c.46.
  Secondary legislation:
  - SI 2013/632 — Uncertificated Securities (Amendment) Regulations 2013.
- Companies Act 1989 c.40.
  Secondary legislation:
  - SI 2001/3755 – Uncertificated Securities Regulations 2001.

Short Selling

- Delegated Regulation (EU) No 236/2012 on "short selling and certain aspects of credit default swaps"
  - Supervisory approaches and practices under Article 29(2) of the ESMA Regulation.

FCA Handbook

- FCA Handbook: Collective Investment Schemes (COLL)
  - COLL 11 – Master-feeder arrangements under the UCITS Directive
  - COLL 12 – Management company and product passports under the UCITS Directive
  - COLL 12.3 – EEA UCITS management companies
- FCA Handbook – Short selling (FINMAR 2)

<u>NATIONAL LEVEL (UK) – Standards, Frameworks and Guidance</u>

- FCA (2012) "Factsheet No 006 – The Short Selling Regulation (SSR)".

1.5.3 Derivatives

This covers trading in over-the-counter (OTC, or off-exchange traded) derivatives or *via* centralised, formal exchanges such as the NYSE (New York Stock Exchange), LSE (London Stock Exchange). Derivatives include collateralised debt obligations (CDO), credit default swaps (CDS), forward contracts (forwards), futures contracts (futures), mortgage-backed securities (MBS), options and other swaps.

<u>EUROPEAN LEVEL – Laws, Regulations and Norms</u>

European Market Infrastructure Regulation (EMIR)

- Regulation (EU) No 648/2012 on "OTC derivatives, central counterparties and trade repositories" (*European Market Infrastructure Regulation (EMIR)*) (4 July 2012). *Amendments and Supplements:*
  - Commission Delegated Regulation (EU) No 667/2014 "supplementing Regulation (EU) No 648/2012 of the European Parliament and of the Council with regard to rules of procedure for penalties imposed on trade repositories by the European Securities and Markets Authority including rules on the right of defence and temporal provisions" (*EMIR (Penalties Imposed on Trade Repositories by ESMA) Regulation*) (13 March 2014).
  - Commission Implementing Regulation (EU) No 591/2014 "on the extension of the transitional periods related to own funds requirements for exposures to central counterparties in Regulation (EU) No 575/2013 and Regulation (EU) No 648/2012 of the European Parliament and of the Council" (*CRR and EMIR (Extension of Transitional Periods) Regulation*) (3 June 2014).
  - Commission Delegated Regulation (EU) No 1003/2013"supplementing Regulation (EU) No 648/2012 of the European Parliament and of the Council with regard to fees charged by the European Securities and Markets Authority to trade repositories" (*EMIR (Trade Repository Fees) Regulation*) (12 July 2013).
  - Commission Delegated Regulation (EU) No 1002/2013 "amending Regulation (EU) No 648/2012 of the European Parliament and of the Council on OTC derivatives, central counterparties and trade repositories with regard to the list of exempted entities" (*EMIR (List of Exempted Entities) (Amendment) Regulation*) (12 July 2013).

<u>EUROPEAN LEVEL (UK) – Standards, Frameworks and Guidance</u>

Technical Standards for European Market Infrastructure Regulation (EMIR) - OTC, CCP) (Regulation (EU) No 648/2012)

- Commission Implementing Regulation (EU) No 484/2014 "laying down implementing technical standards with regard to the hypothetical capital of a central counterparty according to Regulation (EU) No 648/2012 of the European Parliament and of the Council" (*EMIR (Hypothetical Capital of a Central Counterparty — Implementing Technical Standards) Regulation*) (12 May 2014).

- Commission Delegated Regulation (EU) No 285/2014 "supplementing Regulation (EU) No 648/2012 of the European Parliament and of the Council with regard to regulatory technical standards on direct, substantial and foreseeable effect of contracts within the Union and to prevent the evasion of rules and obligations" (*EMIR (OTC Derivative Contracts – Regulatory Technical Standards) Regulation*) (13 February 2014).
- Commission Delegated Regulation (EU) No 876/2013 "supplementing Regulation (EU) No 648/2012 of the European Parliament and of the Council with regard to regulatory technical standards on colleges for central counterparties" (*EMIR (Colleges for Central Counterparties — Regulatory Technical Standards) Regulation*) (28 May 2013).
- Commission Delegated Regulation (EU) No 153/2013 "supplementing Regulation (EU) No 648/2012 of the European Parliament and of the Council with regard to regulatory technical standards on requirements for central counterparties" (*EMIR (Requirements for Central Counterparties — Regulatory Technical Standards) Regulation*) (19 December 2012).
- Commission Delegated Regulation (EU) No 152/2013 "supplementing Regulation (EU) No 648/2012 of the European Parliament and of the Council with regard to regulatory technical standards on capital requirements for central counterparties" (*EMIR (Capital Requirements for Central Counterparties — Regulatory Technical Standards) Regulation*) (19 December 2012).
- Commission Delegated Regulation (EU) No 151/2013 "supplementing Regulation (EU) No 648/2012 of the European Parliament and of the Council on OTC derivatives, central counterparties and trade repositories, with regard to regulatory technical standards specifying the data to be published and made available by trade repositories and operational standards for aggregating, comparing and accessing the data" (*EMIR (Data to be Published and Made Available by Trade Repositories and Operational Standards for Aggregating, Comparing and Accessing the Data — Regulatory Technical Standards) Regulation*) (19 December 2012).
- Commission Delegated Regulation (EU) No 150/2013 "supplementing Regulation (EU) No 648/2012 of the European Parliament and of the Council on OTC derivatives, central counterparties and trade repositories with regard to regulatory technical standards specifying the details of the application for registration as a trade repository" (*EMIR (Application for Registration as a Trade Repository — Regulatory Technical Standards) Regulation*) (19 December 2012).
- Commission Delegated Regulation (EU) No 149/2013 "supplementing Regulation (EU) No 648/2012 of the European Parliament and of the Council with regard to regulatory technical standards on indirect clearing arrangements, the clearing obligation, the public register, access to a trading venue, non-financial counterparties,

and risk mitigation techniques for OTC derivatives contracts not cleared by a CCP" (*EMIR (Indirect Clearing Arrangements, the Clearing Obligation, the Public Register, Access to a Trading Venue, Non-Financial Counterparties, and Risk Mitigation Techniques for OTC Derivatives Contracts not Cleared by a CCP — Regulatory Technical Standards) Regulation*) (19 December 2012).

- Commission Delegated Regulation (EU) No 148/2013 "supplementing Regulation (EU) No 648/2012 of the European Parliament and of the Council on OTC derivatives, central counterparties and trade repositories with regard to regulatory technical standards on the minimum details of the data to be reported to trade repositories" (*EMIR (Minimum Details of the Data to be Reported to Trade Repositories — Regulatory Technical Standards) Regulation*) (19 December 2012).
- Commission Implementing Regulation (EU) No 1247/2012 "laying down implementing technical standards with regard to the format and frequency of trade reports to trade repositories according to Regulation (EU) No 648/2012 of the European Parliament and of the Council on OTC derivatives, central counterparties and trade repositories" (*EMIR Implementing Regulation — Regulatory Technical Standards) Regulation*) (19 December 2012).

ESMA Guidance and Recommendations related to EMIR and OTC

- ESMA/2014/1133 — "Guidelines and Recommendations regarding the implementation of the CPSS-IOSCO Principles for Financial Market Infrastructures in respect of Central Counterparties".
- ESMA/2014/1009 — "Guidelines and Recommendations regarding the implementation of the CPSS-IOSCO Principles for Financial Market Infrastructures in respect of Central Counterparties".
- ESMA/2014/1184 — "Final report on ESMA's draft technical standards on the Clearing Obligation for Interest Rate OTC Derivatives".
- ESMA/2013/1657 — "Draft technical standards under EMIR on contracts with a direct, substantial and foreseeable effect within the Union and non-evasion".
- ESMA/2013/1087 — "Draft implementing technical standards amending Commission Implementing Regulation (EU) No 1247/2012 laying down implementing technical standards with regard to the format and frequency of trade reports to trade repositories".

ESRB Recommendations and Reports related to EMIR and OTC

- ESRB (2014) – "ESRB/2012/3 — ESRB response on eligible collateral for central counterparties (art. 46 of EMIR)".
- ESRB (2014) – "ESRB/2012/2 — ESRB response on the use of OTC derivatives by non-financial corporations (art 10 of EMIR)".

- ESRB (2014) – "Response from the ESRB to the ESMA Consultation Paper on mandatory clearing for OTC credit derivatives".

NATIONAL LEVEL (UK) – Laws, Regulations and Norms

Cross-reference: For further information, see 1.5.2 "Securities and Foreign Exchange", Undertakings for Collective Investment in Transferable Securities (UCITS).

- UCITS Directive (Council Directive 85/611/EEC), UCITS III (Directive 2001/108/EC), Article 22(4) of the *third non-life insurance Directive* (Council Directive 92/49/EEC) and Article 24(4) of the *Consolidated Life Assurance Directive* (Directive 2002/83/EC).
  Secondary legislation:
  - SI 2008/1714 – Regulated Covered Bonds (Amendment) Regulations 2008.
  - SI 2008/346 – Regulated Covered Bonds Regulations 2008.

NATIONAL LEVEL (UK) – Standards, Frameworks and Guidance

- FCA Handbook: SUP 15A – Application and notifications under EMIR
- FCA Handbook: The Perimeter Guidance Manual (PERG)
  - PERG 13.4 – Financial Instruments

1.6 INSURANCE

Classes: Property insurance, Pecuniary insurance, Motor insurance, Liability insurance, Marine and aviation insurance, Combined/package policies and Health insurance.

EUROPEAN LEVEL – Laws, Regulations and Norms

- Directive 2009/138/EC "on the taking-up and pursuit of the business of Insurance and Reinsurance (Solvency II) (recast)" (*Insurance and Reinsurance Directive (Solvency II)*) (25 November 2009).
  Amendments and Supplements:
  - Commission Delegated Regulation (EU) 2015/35 "supplementing Directive 2009/138/EC of the European Parliament and of the Council on the taking-up and pursuit of the business of Insurance and Reinsurance (Solvency II)" (*Solvency II (Taking-Up and Pursuit of Business) Regulation*) (10 October 2014).
- [UK] SI 2015/575 — Solvency 2 Regulations 2015.
- Directive 2009/103/EC "relating to insurance against civil liability in respect of the use of motor vehicles, and the enforcement of the obligation to insure against such liability (codified version)" (Motor Insurance Directive) (16 September 2009).

- Directive 2006/43/EC on "statutory audits of annual accounts and consolidated accounts, amending Council Directives 78/660/EEC and 83/349/EEC and repealing Council Directive 84/253/EEC" (17 May 2006).
  - [UK] SI 2008/565 – Insurance Accounts Directive (Miscellaneous Insurance Undertakings) Regulations 2008.
  - [UK] SI 2013/2005 – Companies and Partnerships (Accounts and Audit) Regulations.
- Council Directive 2005/68/EC on "reinsurance and amending Council Directives 73/239/EEC, 92/49/EEC as well as Directives 98/78/EC and 2002/83/EC" (*Reinsurance Directive*) (16 November 2005). [Repealed with effect from 1 January 2016]
  - [UK] SI 2007/3255 – Financial Services and Markets Act 2000 (Reinsurance Directive) Regulations 2007.
  - [UK] SI 2000/3254 – The Financial Services and Markets Act 2000 (Reinsurance Directive) Order 2007.
  - [UK] SI 2007/3253 – Reinsurance Directive Regulations 2007.
- Directive 2002/92/EC on "insurance mediation" (*Insurance Mediation Directive (IMD)*) (9 December 2002).
- Directive 2002/83/EC "concerning life assurance" (*Consolidated Life Assurance Directive*) (5 November 2002). [Repealed with effect from 1 January 2016]
  - SI 2004/3379 – Life Assurance Consolidation Directive (Consequential Amendments) Regulations 2004.
- Directive 2001/17/EC on "the reorganisation and winding-up of insurance undertakings" (*Winding-Up Directive (Insurers)*) (19 March 2001). [Repealed with effect from 1 January 2016]
- Directive 98/78/EC on "the supplementary supervision of insurance and reinsurance undertakings in an insurance or reinsurance group" (*Insurance Groups Directive (IGD)*) (27 October 1998).
- Council Directive 92/96/EEC on "the coordination of laws, regulations and administrative provisions relating to direct life assurance and amending Directives 79/267/EEC and 90/619/EEC" (10 November 1992) (*third life assurance Directive*).
- Council Directive 92/49/EEC on "the coordination of laws, regulations and administrative provisions relating to direct insurance other than life assurance and amending Directives 73/239/EEC and 88/357/EEC (*third non-life insurance Directive*)" (18 June 1992).
- Council Directive 92/49/EEC on "the coordination of laws, regulations and administrative provisions relating to direct insurance other than life assurance and amending Directives 73/239/EEC and 88/357/EEC (third non-life insurance Directive)" (*Third Non-life Insurance Directive*) (18 June 1992). [Repealed with effect from 1 January 2016]

- ▪ [UK] SI 1994/1696 – Insurance Companies (Third Insurance Directives) Regulations 1994 (*the Third Directives Regulations*).
- Council Directive 91/674/EEC on "the annual accounts and consolidated accounts of insurance undertakings" (*Insurance Accounts Directive (IAD)*) (19 December 1991).
- Council Directive 90/619/EEC "on the coordination of laws, regulations and administrative provisions relating to direct life assurance, laying down provisions to facilitate the effective exercise of freedom to provide services and amending Directive 79/267/EEC" (8 November 1990).
- Council Directive 90/618/EEC "amending, particularly as regards motor vehicle liability insurance, Directive 73/239/EEC and Directive 88/357/EEC which concern the coordination of laws, regulations and administrative provisions relating to direct insurance other than life assurance" (*Motor Services Directive*) (8 November 1990).
- Second Council Directive 88/357/EEC on "the coordination of laws, regulations and administrative provisions relating to direct insurance other than life assurance and laying down provisions to facilitate the effective exercise of freedom to provide services and amending Directive 73/239/EEC" (*Second Non-Life Insurance Directive*) (22 June 1988). [Repealed with effect from 1 January 2016]
  - ▪ [UK] SI 1994/1516 – The Insurance Companies Regulations 1994.
- Council Directive 87/344/EEC on "the coordination of laws, regulations and administrative provisions relating to legal expenses insurance" (*Legal Expenses Insurance Directive*) (22 June 1987). [Repealed with effect from 1 January 2016]
- Council Directive 87/343/EEC "amending, as regards credit insurance and suretyship insurance, First Directive 73/239/EEC on the coordination of laws, regulations and administrative provisions relating to the taking-up and pursuit of the business of direct insurance other than life assurance" (22 June 1987).
- Council Directive 78/473/EEC on "the coordination of laws, regulations and administrative provisions relating to Community co-insurance" (*Community Co-Insurance Directive*) (30 May 1978). [Repealed with effect from 1 January 2016]
- Council Directive 73/239/EEC on "the coordination of laws, Regulations and administrative provisions relating to the taking-up and pursuit of the business of direct insurance other than life assurance" (*First Non-Life Insurance Directive*) (24 July 1973). [Repealed with effect from 1 January 2016]
- Council Directive 64/225/EEC on "the abolition of restrictions on freedom of establishment and freedom to provide services in respect of reinsurance and retrocession" (*Reinsurance Restrictions Abolition Directive*) (25 February 1964). [Repealed with effect from 1 January 2016]

EUROPEAN LEVEL – Standards, Frameworks and Guidance

Technical Standards Regulations for Solvency II (Directive 2009/138/EC)

- Commission Implementing Regulation (EU) 2015/500 "laying down implementing technical standards with regard to the procedures to be followed for the supervisory approval of the application of a matching adjustment in accordance with Directive 2009/138/EC of the European Parliament and of the Council" (*Solvency II (Supervisory Approval Procedures for the Application of a Matching Adjustment — Implementing Technical Standards) Regulation*). (24 March 2015).
- Commission Implementing Regulation (EU) 2015/499 "laying down implementing technical standards with regard to the procedures to be used for granting supervisory approval for the use of ancillary own-fund items in accordance with Directive 2009/138/EC of the European Parliament and of the Council" (*Solvency II (Supervisory Approval Procedures for the Use of Ancillary Own-Funds Items — Implementing Technical Standards) Regulation*) (24 March 2015).
- Commission Implementing Regulation (EU) 2015/498 "laying down implementing technical standards with regard to the supervisory approval procedure to use undertaking-specific parameters in accordance with Directive 2009/138/EC of the European Parliament and of the Council" (*Solvency II (Supervisory Approval Procedures for the Use of Undertaking-Specific Parameters — Implementing Technical Standards) Regulation*) (24 March 2015).
- Commission Implementing Regulation (EU) 2015/462 "laying down implementing technical standards with regard to the procedures for supervisory approval to establish special purpose vehicles, for the cooperation and exchange of information between supervisory authorities regarding special purpose vehicles as well as to set out formats and templates for information to be reported by special purpose vehicles in accordance with Directive 2009/138/EC of the European Parliament and of the Council" (*Solvency II (Special Purpose Vehicles — Supervisory Approval Procedures, Cooperation and Exchange of Information between Supervisory Authorities and Formats and Templates for Information to be Reported — ITS) Regulation*) (19 March 2015).
- Commission Implementing Regulation (EU) 2015/461 "laying down implementing technical standards with regard to the process to reach a joint decision on the application to use a group internal model in accordance with Directive 2009/138/EC of the European Parliament and of the Council" (*Solvency II (Joint Decision Process to Use a Group Internal Model — Implementing Technical Standards) Regulation*) (19 March 2015).
- Commission Implementing Regulation (EU) 2015/460 "laying down implementing technical standards with regard to the procedure concerning the approval of an internal model in accordance with Directive 2009/138/EC of the European Parliament and of the Council" (*Solvency II (Approval Procedure for an Internal Model — Implementing Technical Standard) Regulation*) (19 March 2015).

European Insurance and Occupational Pensions Authority (EIOPA) Guidelines and Reports

- EIOPA-BoS-14/167 — "Guidelines on ancillary own funds".
- EIOPA-BoS-14/173 — "Guidelines on application of outwards reinsurance arrangements to the non-life underwriting risk sub-module".
- EIOPA-BoS-14/175 — "Guidelines on application of the life underwriting risk module".
- EIOPA-BoS-14/168 — "Guidelines on classification of own funds".
- EIOPA-BoS-14/165 — "Guidelines on contract boundaries".
- EIOPA-BoS-14/181 — "Guidelines on group solvency".
- EIOPA-BoS-14/171 — "Guidelines on look-through approach".
- EIOPA-BoS-14/182 — Guidelines on the methodology for equivalence assessments by national supervisory authorities under Solvency II" (including "Technical Annex I — Equivalence assessment under Article 227 of Solvency II Directive" and "Technical Annex II — Equivalence assessment under Article 260 of the Solvency II Directive").
- EIOPA-258/12 – "Final Report on Public Consultation No 11/008 on the proposal for Guidelines on Own Risk and Solvency Assessment".
- EIOPA-260-2012 – "Final Report on Public Consultations No 11/009 and 11/011 on the Proposal for the Reporting and Disclosure Requirements".
- EIOPA-TFIGS-12/007 – "Report on the Role of Insurance Guarantee Schemes in the Winding-Up Procedures of Insolvent Insurance Undertakings in the EU/EEA".
- EIOPA 11/163 – "Report on Calibration of Risk Factors in the Standard Formula of Solvency II".
- EIOPA-TFIGS-11/007 – "Report on the Cross-Border Cooperation Mechanisms between Insurance Guarantee Schemes in the EU".
- EIOPA-TFQIS5-11/001) – "Report on the Fifth Quantitative Impact Study for Solvency II".

Insurance Guidance

- Communication COM(2013) 213 final "Green Paper: the insurance of natural and man-made disasters" (16 April 2013).

NATIONAL LEVEL (UK) – Laws, Regulations and Norms

Cross-reference: No Act of Parliament is directly applicable. See applicable UK Statutory Instruments ("[UK] SI") implementing EU law in the corresponding European Level sub-section.

For further information, see also 1.2.1 Authorisation and regulatory supervision: Prudential Regulatory Authority Handbook.

- Consumer Insurance (Disclosure and Representations) Act 2012 c. 6.
  Secondary legislation:
  - Consumer Insurance (Disclosure and Representations) Act 2012.
- Financial Services and Markets Act 2000 c. 8.
- Insurance Companies Act 1982 c. 50.

SUB-NATIONAL LEVEL – Laws, Regulations and Norms

Group Insurance Risk Profile: Insurance risk is defined as the risk of adverse developments in the timing, frequency and severity of claims for insured/underwritten events and in customer behaviour, leading to reductions in earnings and/or value.

- Group Insurance Risk Policy
- Insurance Anti-Money Laundering Policy
- Insurance Business Unit Insurance Risk policies
- Insurance Business Unit Reinsurance policies

1.7 PENSIONS

EUREOPAN LEVEL – Laws, Regulations and Norms

- Directive 2003/41/EC on "the activities and supervision of institutions for occupational retirement provision" (3 June 2003).

EUROPEAN LEVEL – Standards, Frameworks and Guidance

- Communication COM(2010) 365 "Green Paper: Towards adequate, sustainable and safe European pension systems" (7 July 2010).

Technical Standards for European Insurance and Occupational Pensions Authority (Directive 2003/41/EC)

- Commission Implementing Regulation (EU) No 643/2014 "laying down implementing technical standards with regard to the reporting of national provisions of prudential nature relevant to the field of occupational pension schemes according to Directive 2003/41/EC of the European Parliament and of the Council" (*IORP (Reporting of National Provisions of a Prudential Nature — Implementing Technical Standards) Regulation*) (16 June 2014).

EIOPA Guidelines and Reports

- EIOPA-BoS-14/266 — "EIOPA Report on Costs and charges of IORPs". (Institutions for Occupational Retirement Provision)

- EIOPA-BoS-14/169 — "Guidelines on ring-fenced funds" (including "Technical Annex — Simplifications for the calculation of the SCR as if there was no loss of diversification (Guideline 17)").
- EIOPA-BoS-11/039 – "Report on Pre-enrolment Information to Pension Plan Members".
- EIOPA-11/031 – "Report on Variable Annuities".
- EIOPA-BoS-13/010 – "Good practices on information provision for Defined Contribution (DC) schemes".

NATIONAL LEVEL (UK) – Laws, Regulations and Norms

- Pensions Act 2014 c. 19.

NATIONAL LEVEL (UK) – Standards, Frameworks and Guidance

- The Pension Regulator (2012) "Trustee knowledge and understanding" and (2012) "Introducing the refreshed Trustee toolkit".
- The Pension Advisory Service: Various guidance and forms are available on their website (http://www.pensionsadvisoryservice.org.uk/).

FCA Handbook

- FCA Handbook: Pensions supplementary provisions (COBS 19)
  - COBS 19.1 – Pension transfers and opt-outs (Preparing and providing a transfer analysis, Suitability)
  - COBS 19.2 – Personal pensions, FSAVCs [free-standing additional voluntary contribution] and AVCs [Additional voluntary contribution]
  - COBS 19.3 – Product disclosure to members of occupational pension schemes
  - COBS 19.4 – Open market options (Definitions, Contents of open market options statement, Signposting pensions guidance, Tax implications)
  - COBS 19.5 – Independent governance committees (IGCs)
  - COBS 19.6 – Restriction on charges in qualifying schemes (Application, Express agreement, Default arrangements: charging structures and restrictions, Compliance with the restrictions on charges, Consultancy charges)
  - COBS 19.7 – Retirement risk warnings (Definitions, Application, Purpose, Trigger: when does a firm have to follow the steps?, Step 1: determine whether the client has received guidance or regulated advice, Step 2: identify risk factors, Step 3: provide appropriate retirement risk warnings, Communicating the signpost and retirement risk warning, Record keeping)
  - COBS 19 Annex 1 – Retirement risk warnings - steps to take

PART II

Information and Communications Technology Laws and Regulations

It's hard to pay attention these days because of multiple effects of the information technology nowadays. You tend to develop a faster, speedier mind, but I don't think it's necessarily broader or smarter.
Robert Redford (1936-)

Computers are useless. They can only give you answers.
Pablo Picasso (1881-1973)

PART 2

ICT LAWS AND REGULATIONS

This Part of the Regulatory Compliance Matrix categorises laws, regulations and norms relevant to the Information and Communications Technology sector (as well as to the IT departments of companies in any sector), and maps it to the relevant standards, framework and guidance that may assist ICT companies and IT departments to comply with their legal and regulatory requirements. The ICT sector is a vast one, but at a minimum it covers mobile devices and services; computer manufacturers; software; semiconductors and electronics manufacturers; Internet and web-based services; data hosting and management; satellite communication networks and network providers; consumer electronics; and the newly emerging digital services.

Figure 3: Information and Communication Technologies Regulatory Compliance Matrix

	LAWS, REGULATIONS and NORMS	STANDARDS, FRAMEWORKS and GUIDANCE

· ICT SPECIFIC	1. Market regulation of the Information Society
	  1.1. Market liberalisation and regulation framework
	  1.2. The New Regulatory Framework
	  1.3. Trans-European Networks (TEN)
	2. Internet regulation
	  2.1. Safer Internet Use
	3. Telecommunications
	  3.1. Wireless policy
	  3.2. Access and interconnection
	  3.3. Satellites
	4. Digital media and content
		- Standards defined and guidance issued by international organisations
		- Standards defined by standardisation institutes and guidance issued by supervisory authorities at European level
		- Standards defined by standardisation institutes and guidance issued by regulatory agencies at national level
		- Publicly funded research yield
		- Technical standards defined by the ICT industry and industry associations
		- IT Platforms and Protocols
		- Other ICT-specific guidance

	LAWS, REGULATIONS and NORMS	STANDARDS, FRAMEWORKS and GUIDANCE

• ICT SPECIFIC	4.1. Digital interactive television
	4.2. Digital content
	5. Radio services and equipment
	   5.1. Radio interference
	   5.2. Compatibility
	   5.3. Radio equipment
	6. Audiovisual services
	   6.1. The audiovisual services industry
	7. Environment ("Green IT")
	   7.1. Green IT
	8. Other ICT-specific norms
	   8.1. Wireless and fixed line
	   8.2. Data storage and power management	

INFORMATION AND COMMUNICATIONS TECHNOLOGY – REGULATORY AUTHORITIES AND KEY INFLUENCERS

The following is a list of key ICT stakeholders which identifies and categorises the main stakeholders engaged in shaping ICT regulations, polices and standards. These stakeholders are described in greater detail and their importance assessed in *Industry Governance and Regulatory Compliance* (Guido Reinke, 2012). Appendix 6 (Stakeholder Directory) provides a more comprehensive list of stakeholders.

(1) Global Level – Authorities (non-US)

International Organisations

- **Relevant Specialized UN Agencies** [only ICT-relevant agencies are listed] are central to global efforts to solve problems challenging humanity. Cooperating in this effort are more than 30 affiliated organisations, known together as the UN system.
- **UN Conference on Trade and Development (UNCTAD)** has two divisions directly relevant to ICT affairs:
  - **Commission for Science and Technology for Development (CSTD)** is a subsidiary of the Economic and Social Council (ECOSOC). It provides the General Assembly and ECOSOC with high-level advice on relevant science and technology issues.
    [Website: http://unctad.org/cstd]

- **Investment, Technology and Enterprise Development (DITE)** analyses trends in foreign direct investment and their impact on development; helps countries to promote international investment and to understand the issues involved in international investment agreements; devises strategies for development of small and medium-sized enterprises; identifies policy options and implements capacity-building programmes to encourage the use of new technologies.
  [Website: http://unctad.org/dite]

- **International Telecommunications Union (ITU)** fosters international cooperation on telecommunications of all media, coordinates use of radio and TV frequencies, promotes safety measures and conducts research. Its membership represents a cross-section of the telecommunications and information technology industry, and includes 189 Member States and over 650 sector members. ITU is divided into three core sectors:
  - Radiocommunication Assembly (ITU-R)
  - Telecom Standardization Sector (ITU-T), and
  - Telecom Development (ITY-D).
  Reform calls for a common vision of the ITU's future as a public/private partnership, to preserve and strengthen its international credibility. The respective roles in this partnership must be better defined, so that both sides have rights and duties. The ITU's decision-making must reflect the modern, competitive telecommunications environment in which the private sector plays the leading role while the regulatory agencies act as an arbitrator for the wider public interest.
  [Website: http://www.itu.int]

- **United Nations Commission on International Trade Law (UNCITRAL)** is the core legal body of the UN system in the field of international trade law, it formulates modern, fair, and harmonized rules on commercial transactions.
  [Website: http://www.uncitral.org/uncitral/en]

- **Global Alliance for Information and Communication Technologies and Development (GAID)** was once a subgroup and is now a continuation of the Information and Communication Technologies (ICT) Task Force set up by Secretary-General Kofi Annan to find creative means to spread the benefits of the digital revolution and avert a two-tiered information society, it responds to the need for an inclusive global forum for cross-sectoral policy dialogue on the use of ICT for the achievement of internationally agreed development goals, notably reduction of poverty.
  [Website: http://www.un-gaid.org]

UN Special Interest Groups and Conferences

- **ICT for Development Platform (ICT4D Platform)** aims to enrich the political core of the World Summit on the Information Society (WSIS). The Platform brings together ICT4D specialists, best practices, innovations, and international experience and raises awareness of the importance of ICT for development.
  [Website: www.edwebproject.org/wsis03/ict4d.html]

- **UN Working Group on Internet Governance (WGIG)** was set up by the Declaration of Principles and Action Plan, its main activity is "to investigate and make proposals for action, as appropriate, on the governance of Internet by 2005". The WGIG was asked to present the result of its work in a report "for consideration and appropriate action for the second phase of the WSIS in Tunis 2005".
  [Website: http://www.wgig.org]

- **UN Conference on Trade and Development (UNCTAD)** deals with trade, commodities, investment, technology, enterprise development; macroeconomic policies, debt, development financing, transport, customs, and information technology.
  [Website: http://www.unctad.org]

- **United Nations Economic Commission for Europe (UNECE)** fosters sustainable economic growth among its 55 member countries, providing a forum for communication among States; brokes international legal instruments addressing trade, transport, the environment; and supplies statistics and economic and environmental analysis.
  [Website: http://www.unece.org]

- **United Nations Centre for Trade Facilitation and Electronic Business (UN/ CEFACT)** aims to better the ability of business, trade and administrative organizations from developed, developing and transitional economies to exchange products and relevant services effectively.
  [Website: http://www.unece.org/cefact]

- **UN Development Programme (UNDP)** is the UN's global development network, an organization advocating for change and connecting countries to knowledge, experience and resources.
  [Website: http://www.undp.org]

Other Fora

- **Global Business Dialogue on e-Society, formerly Global Business Dialogue on e-Commerce (GBDe)** is a CEO-led, worldwide business initiative established to help create a policy framework for development of a global online economy.
  [Websitehttp://www.gbd-e.org]

- **International Telecommunications User Group (INTUG)** is an international association of users of communication technology and applications founded in 1974. Its members include national user groups and individual members from major multinational enterprises, academia, law and other relevant industry sectors. [Website: http://intug.org]

- **Global Information Infrastructure Commission (GIIC)** fosters private-sector leadership and private- and public-sector cooperation in the development of information networks and services to advance global economic growth, education and quality of life. It is an independent, non-governmental initiative involving leaders from developing and industrialized countries. GIIC's goals are to:
  - strengthen the leadership role of the private sector in the development of a diverse, affordable and accessible information infrastructure
  - promote involvement of developing countries in the building and utilization of truly global and open information infrastructure
  - facilitate activities and identify policy options which foster effective applications of telecommunications, broadcasting and information technologies and services..

  [Website: http://www.giic.org]

- **World Information Technology and Services Alliance (WITSA)** is a consortium of 53 information technology (IT) industry associations from economies around the world. WITSA members represent over 90 percent of the world IT market. As the global voice of the IT industry, WITSA is dedicated to:
  - advocating policies that advance the industry's growth and development
  - facilitating international trade and investment in IT products and services
  - strengthening WITSA's national industry associations through the sharing of knowledge, experience, and critical information
  - providing members with a vast network of contacts in nearly every geographic region of the world
  - hosting the World Congress on IT, the premier industry-sponsored, global IT event
  - hosting the Global Public Policy Conference; and
  - hosting the Global Information Security Summit.

  Founded in 1978 and originally known as the World Computing Services Industry Association, it has increasingly assumed an active role in international public policy issues affecting the creation of a robust global information infrastructure, including advocacy for:
  - increasing competition through open markets and regulatory reform
  - protecting intellectual property
  - encouraging cross-industry and government cooperation to enhance

119

information security
- bridging the education and skills gap
- reducing tariff and non-tariff trade barriers to IT goods and services; and
- safeguarding the viability and continued growth of the Internet and electronic commerce.

[Website: http://www.witsa.org/v2]

- **International Telecommunications Satellite Organisation (INTELSAT)** is the world's largest commercial satellite communications services provider. On July 18, 2001 Intelsat became a private company, 37 years after being formed as an intergovernmental consortium owning and managing a constellation of communications satellites (Intelsats) to provide international broadcast services. [Website: http://www.intelsat.com]

Global Fora

- **World Radiocommunication Conferences (WRCs) of the ITU** are held every three to four years. It is the job of a WRC to review and, if necessary, revise the Radio Regulations, the international treaty governing the use of the radio-frequency spectrum as well as geostationary-satellite and non-geostationary-satellite orbits. The agenda of revisions is set by the ITU Council, taking into account recommendations made by previous WRCs.
[www.itu.int/en/ITU-R/conferences/wrc/Pages/default.aspx]

- **World Radiocommunications Conferences (WRCs) of the FCC** are organised by the US Federal Communications Commission (FCC) and periodically convened to consider the regulatory framework for managing the international use of radio-frequency spectrum in a rational and equitable manner.
[Website: http://www.fcc.gov/wrc-12]

- **World Summit on the Information Society (WSIS)**, held in two phases, with 175 countries participating, the first took place in Geneva, 10-12 December 2003, hosted by Switzerland, and the second in Tunis, 16-18 November 2005, hosted by Tunisia. Four documents were adopted:
- Geneva Declaration of Principles
- Geneva Plan of Action
- Tunis Commitment, and
- Tunis Agenda for the Information Society.
The ITU took the lead in organizing the Summit.
[Website: http://www.itu.int/wsis] [http://groups.itu.int/wsis-forum2012/Home.aspx]

- **ITU Telecom and ITU World Telecom** is part of the ITU (*q.v.*), it organizes events for the world's ICT community, providing a unique global networking

forum where great minds, companies and new technologies connect. One ITU Telecom event is held each year, with ITU World Telecom events held every three years.
[Website: http://www.itu.int/ITUTELECOM] [http://world2012.itu.int]

- **The Internet Governance Forum (IGF)** helps the UN Secretary-General carry out the WSIS mandate to convene a permanent forum for multi-stakeholder policy dialogue, through the UN ICT Task Force and non-governmental stakeholder participation.
[Website: http://www.intgovforum.org]

Scientific and Research Organisations

- **International Council for Science (ICSU)** is a non-governmental organization representing a global membership that includes 104 national scientific bodies and 29 international scientific unions. Through this extensive international network, it hosts discussions of issues relevant to international science policy and makes known the importance of international science for policy issues. It undertakes the following core activities:
  - Planning and coordinating interdisciplinary research to address major issues of relevance in both science and society
  - Actively advocating for freedom in the conduct of science, promoting equitable access to scientific data and information, and facilitating science education and capacity building
  - Acting as a focus for the exchange of ideas, the communication of scientific information and the development of scientific standards; and
  - Supporting in excess of 600 scientific conferences, congresses and symposia per year all around the world, as well as the production of a wide range of newsletters, handbooks, learned journals and proceedings.
[Website: http://www.icsu.org]

- **United Nations Educational, Scientific and Cultural Organization, Institute for Information Technologies in Education (UNESCO IITE)** contributes to the design and implementation of UNESCO programmes in regard to application of information and communication technologies in education.
[Website: http://www.unesco.org]

Standards Organisations (with strong industry participation)

- **Organization for the Advancement of Structured Information Standards (OASIS)** is an international consortium that drives the development, convergence, and adoption of e-business standards. The consortium produces more Web services standards than any other organization, including for security and e-business, and

assists standardization efforts in the public sector and for application-specific markets. Founded in 1993, OASIS counts more than 5,000 participants representing over 600 organizations in 100 countries.
[Website: http://www.oasis-open.org]

- **Institute of Electrical and Electronics Engineers – Standards Association (IEEE-SA)** is the leading developer of a broad range of global industry standards including: power and energy, biomedical and healthcare, information technology, telecommunications, transportation, nanotechnology and information assurance. IEEE has over 20,000 members from corporations, organizations, universities, and government agencies around the globe.
[Website: http://standards.ieee.org]

- **Internet Corporation for Assigned Names and Numbers (ICANN)** is responsible for technical coordination of the assignment of parameters in identifier spaces used on the Internet, including MIME media types, port numbers, private-enterprise numbers, and protocol numbers. It is also responsible for technical aspects of assigning top-level domains (including ccTLDs) within the Internet's domain name system, and for coordinating the IP-address allocation system operated in conjunction with Regional Internet Registries.
[Website: http://www.icann.org]

- **Wi-Fi Alliance, formerly Wireless Ethernet Compatibility Alliance** is an international non-profit that certifies the interoperability of wireless Local Area Network products based on the IEEE 802.11 specification. Currently the Wi-Fi Alliance has 205 members, and 915 products have received Wi-Fi certification since certification began in March of 2000. Its goal is to enhance user experience through product interoperability.
[Website: http://www.wi-fi.org]

- **Payment Card Industry (PCI) Security Standards Council** is a global forum for ongoing development, enhancement, storage, dissemination and implementation of security standards for account data protection, its mission is to enhance payment account data security by promoting broad adoption of the PCI Security Standards. It owns, develops and distributes the PCI Data Security Standard (DSS), and was founded by American Express, Discover Financial Services, JCB, MasterCard Worldwide, and Visa International.
[Website: https://www.pcisecuritystandards.org]

Task Forces, Working Groups, Workshops, Industry Committees

- **Internet Engineering Task Force (IETF)** is an international community of network designers, operators, vendors, and researchers concerned with the evolution of Internet architecture and its smooth operation. IETF has more than

60 working groups whose activities include anti-spam research, IPv6 development, and application- and network standard development.
[Website: http://www.ietf.org]

- **Internet Protocol version 6 Forum (IPv6 Forum)** is a consortium of Internet vendors, industry subject matter experts, and research and education networks, with a clear mission to advocate IPv6 by dramatically improving technology, market, and deployment user and industry awareness of IPv6, creating a secure New Generation Internet allowing world-wide equitable access to knowledge and technology. It is a non-profit organisation with head office in Luxembourg.
  [Website: http://www.ipv6forum.org]

- **World Wide Web Consortium (W3C)** pursues its mission through the creation of Web standards and guidelines, called W3C Recommendations, of which it has published more than ninety since 1994. It engages in education and outreach, develops software, hosts an open forum for discussion about the Web, and developed a Platform for Internet Content Selection (PICS), which enables labels to be associated with Internet content.
  [Website: http://www.w3.org]

- **Internet Systems Consortium (ISC)** is a non-profit corporation supporting the infrastructure of a universal-connect, self-organizing Internet, and the autonomy of its participants, by developing and maintaining core production quality software, protocols, and operations. ISC is the renowned producer and distributor of Critical Internet Infrastructure software. Its commercial quality open source software, including BIND and DHCP, is deployed by over 80% of Internet providers worldwide.
  [Website: http://www.isc.org]

- **G8 Digital Opportunity Task Force (G8 DOT Force)** was created by the G8 Heads of State at their Kyushu-Okinawa Summit in July 2000, it brought together 43 teams from government, the private sector, non-profit organizations, and international organisations. Representing developed and developing countries, its objective was to identify ways the digital revolution can benefit all the world's people, especially the poorest and most marginalized.
  [Website: http://www.g8.utoronto.ca/summit/2001genoa/dotforce1.html]

(2) European Level – Authorities

Specific Agencies

- **European Space Agency (ESA)** promotes the vision of Europe's future in space and of the benefits of space (*e.g.* satellites) for Europeans on the ground. It develops strategies to fulfil this vision, through collaborative projects in space science and technology.
  [Website: http://www.esa.int]

- **European Telecommunications Satellite Organisation (EUTELSAT)** sets certain standards and parameters in order to guarantee high quality reception and the safety of the overall system.
  [Website: http://news.eutelsat.com]

- **European Network and Information Security Agency (ENISA)** was founded under the authority of Regulation (EC) No 460/2004, its main role is to support the exchange of information and facilitate co-operation on issues of IT security in the Single Market. It aims to achieve a high level of security awareness amongst businesses; analyse risks; and follow up standardisation efforts in collaboration with suppliers.
  [Website: http://www.enisa.eu.int]

- **The European Registry of Internet Domain Names (EURid)** is a Belgian non-profit that the European Commission chose to operate the new .eu top level domain. It will establish 4 additional regional offices to support registries (Brussels, Stockholm, Pisa, Prague).
  [Website: http://www.eurid.eu]

EU Research

- **Joint Research Centre (JRC)** is an essential element of the European Research Area (ERA), the Institute for Prospective Technological Studies (IPTS), its subsidiary, carries out and supports scientific and technical research in areas such as Information Society technologies, cybersecurity, research policy, economic and technical change.
  [Website: http://www.jrc.cec.eu.int]

- **Innovation Relay Centres (IRC)** facilitates innovative technology transfer to and from European companies and research departments.
  [Website: irc.cordis.lu; http://www.innovationrelay.net]

- **CORDIS Technology Marketplace** connects people to technology, featuring research results and business opportunities related to emerging technologies.
  [Website: http://www.cordis.lu/marketplace] [http://www.cordis.lu/results]

- **Euro Info Centres (EIC)**, comprising more than 320 centres in 42 countries, inform, advise and assist businesses on all EU issues, including policies, legislation, and R&D programmes. Its Research & Development Working Group helps EICs increase their level of service in the field of R&D and innovation.
  [Website: europa.eu.int/europ./enterprise/networks/eic/eic.html]

- **European Business and Innovation Centre Network (EBN)** brings together 160 Business and Innovation Centres (BICs) and similar organisations, such as incubators, and innovation and entrepreneurship centres.
  [Website: http://www.ebn.be]

- **Intellectual Property Rights (IPR) Helpdesk** is the first-line assistance for IP issues.
  [Website: http://www.ipr-helpdesk.org]

- **European Institute of Innovation and Technology (EIT)** was set up in 2006 as a flagship research university for excellence in higher education, research and innovation.
  [Website: http://ec.europa.eu/education/policies/educ/eit/index_en.html]

- **EU Academies' Science Advisory Council (EASAC)** is a platform for the national Academies of Europe to work together to inject high-quality science into EU policy-making. EASAC's task is to build science into policy at the EU level by providing independent, expert, credible advice about the scientific aspects of public policy issues to those who make or influence policy for the European Union.
  [Website: http://www.easac.org]

European Independent Regulatory Authorities

- **European Data Protection Working Party (Article 29 Working Party)**, established by Article 29 of Directive 95/46/EC, is the independent EU Advisory Body on Data Protection and Privacy. Its tasks are laid down in of Directive 95/46/EC (Article 30) and Directive 2002/58/EC (article 15).
  [Website: http://ec.europa.eu/justice/policies/privacy/workinggroup/index_en.htm]
  [Website: http://ec.europa.eu/justice/data-protection/article-29/index_en.htm]

- **Body of European Regulators for Electronic Communications (BEREC)** (formerly the European Regulators Group (ERG)) was established by the Regulatory Framework Directive to assist the Commission in developing the Internal Market for electronic communications and services and in ensuring the consistent application of the regulatory framework.
  [Website: http://berec.europa.eu]

- **Radio Spectrum Policy Group (RSPG)** adopts opinions assisting and advising the Commission on radio spectrum policy issues; on co-ordination of policy approaches; and, where appropriate, on harmonisation with regard to the availability and efficient use of radio spectrum as necessary for the establishment and functioning of the internal market.
  [Website: http://rspg.groups.eu.int]

European Committees and Councils – Mediators (Collective European Fora – Connected to the EU Institutions)

- **Advisory Committees of Directorates General** within the Commission represent the ICT industry on all relevant committees. Its Communication & Information Resource Centre Administrator (CIRCA) coordinates the following committees:
  [Website: http://forum.europa.eu.int/Public/irc/infso/Home/main]

- **Communication Committee (COCOM)** was established under the new regulatory framework for electronic communications, in order to replace the ONP Committee and the Licensing Committee (instituted under the 1998 regulatory package for telecommunications). The committee assists the Commission in carrying out its executive powers under the new regulatory framework and the Regulation on the .eu Top Level Domain. [https://circabc.europa.eu/faces/jsp/extension/wai/login.jsp]

- **Radio Spectrum Committee (RSC)** was established under the Radio Spectrum Decision 676/2002/EC as part of the new regulatory framework for electronic communications, it assists the Commission in developing and adopting technical implementation measures aimed at ensuring harmonised conditions for the availability and efficient use of radio spectrum, as well as the availability of information related to the use of the radio spectrum. [Website: http://ec.europa.eu/information_society/policy/ecomm/radio_spectrum/eu_policy/rsc/index_en.htm]

- **Advisory Committee on the Implementation of Open Telecommunications Network Provision (ONP)** was established under the ONP Framework Directive 90/387/EC, it also deals with issues arising from the other ONP Directives (e.g. on Leased Lines, Voice Telephony and Interconnection). The ONP Committee meetings are attended by representatives of the Member States and the EEA countries as well as any candidate countries, including the independent national regulatory authorities. Exercising both advisory and regulatory functions, the Committee plays a key role in encouraging co-operation between Member States at the working level, helping them seek guidance and clarification from the Commission on particular Directives-implementation issues. The Committee is closely involved in preparing important elements of market regulation such as the Commission Recommendations on Interconnection, the annual Leased Line Report, and the implementation of the Regulation on Local Loop Unbundling. It has been superseded by Cocom.

- **Licensing Committee** was established under the Licensing Directive 97/13/EC, the Committee meetings are attended by representatives of the Member States and the EEA countries, including the independent national regulatory authorities. Exercising both advisory and regulatory functions, its principal task is to harmonise the conditions for licensing so as to establish a "one-stop shopping" procedure; as well as to discuss the need for harmonisation of spectrum. It has been superseded by Cocom.

- **Committee on Industry, Research and Energy (ITRE)** of the European Parliament is responsible for monitoring and reporting on the EU's industrial policy and the application of new technologies, including measures relating to SMEs; research policy, including the dissemination and exploitation of research findings; the activities of the Joint Research Centre; the information society and information technology, including the establishment and development of trans-European networks in the telecommunication infrastructure sector. It also coordinates European space policy, and as such, has ties with the European Space Agency. It has oversight duties on the Joint Research Centre and the Central Office for Nuclear Measurements, and similar projects.

[Website: http://www.europarl.europa.eu/committees/itre_home_en.htm]

(3) National Level (EU Member States) – Authorities

- **Regulators in Europe – eCommunications** – ICT Independent Regulatory Authorities (IRAs) exist in each EU Member-State; *e.g.*
  - in Germany the *Bundesnetzagentur*;
  - in the UK the *Office for Communication* (Ofcom);
  - in France the *Autorité de Régulation des Communications Électroniques et des Postes* (ARCEP).
- **Regulators in Europe – Data Protection / Privacy** – Data Protection/ Information Commissioners exist in each EU Member State; *e.g.*
  - in Germany *Der Bundesbeauftragte für den Datenschutz und die Informationsfreiheit*;
  - in the UK the *Information Commissioner*;
  - in France the Commission *Nationale de l'Informatique et des Libertés*.
- **Government departments and ministries of EU Member States** – *e.g.*
  - in Germany the *Bundesministerium für Wirtschaft und Technologie* (the Federal Ministry of Economics and Technology);
  - in the UK the Department for Business, Innovation and Skills (BIS);
  - in France the *Ministère du Redressement Productif* (Ministry of Productive Recovery).
- **National governmental supporting bodies and ministries of EU Member States** – *e.g.*
  - in the UK the Cabinet Office; Computer Crime Policy Team in the Home Office; and the House of Lords Science and Technology Committee.
- **Central Government programmes** – *e.g.*
  - in the UK the Serious Organised Crime Agency (SOCA); Critical National Infrastructure (CNI); the Computer Emergency Response Team (CERT); and the Serious and Organised Crime Agency (SOCA).
- **Standards Institutes & National Standardisation Bodies** – *e.g.*
  - in Germany the *Deutsches Institut für Normung* e.V. (DIN);

- in the UK British Standards Institution (BSI);
- in France the *Association Française de Normalisation* (AFNOR).

(4) National Level (UK) – Authorities

The Governmental Supporting Bodies, Central Government Departments and Ministries in the United Kingdom involved in shaping ICT policy and regulation are as follows:

- Cabinet Office (responsible for Information Assurance, 'Get Safe Online and ITsafe')
- Home Office, *e.g.* Computer Crime Policy Team
- Department for Business, Innovation and Skills (BIS); formerly Department for Business, Enterprise and Regulatory Reform (BERR) and before that the Department of Trade and Industry (DTI)
- House of Lords, Science and Technology Committee

2.1 MARKET REGULATION OF THE INFORMATION SOCIETY

2.1.1 Market liberalisation and regulation framework

GLOBAL LEVEL – Laws, Regulations and Norms

Not applicable: This is an EU regulatory initiative, hence applicable laws, regulations and norms exist only at European Level and below.

GLOBAL LEVEL – Standards, Frameworks and Guidance

- International Chamber of Commerce (2004): "Telecoms liberalization: An international business guide for policymakers" (Paris).
- OECD (2013) "Code of liberalisation of current invisible operations".
- OECD (2008) "OECD Codes of Liberalisation: User Guide".
- OECD (1998) "Business Statement on the Impact of Telecommunications Liberalisation on Electronic Commerce", made on the occasion of the OECD Ministerial Conference "A Borderless World: Realising the Potential of Global Electronic Commerce".

EUROPEAN LEVEL – Laws, Regulations and Norms

Liberalisation of the Market

- Directive 2002/77/EC on "competition in the markets for Electronic Communications Services" (*Liberalisation Directive*) (16 September 2002).

Regulation of the Framework

- Decision 2010/299/EU "repealing Decision 2002/627/EC establishing the European Regulators Group for Electronic Communications Networks and Services" (10 May 2010).

European Initiative and Policy Papers

- Directive 2004/38/EC on "the right of citizens of the Union and their family members to move and reside freely within the territory of the Member States" (*Citizen Rights Directive*) (29 April 2004).

EUROPEAN LEVEL – Standards, Frameworks and Guidance

European Information Society Framework

- Communication COM(2003) 567final "The role of eGovernment for Europe's future" (26 September 2003).
- Communication COM(98) 596 final "Green Paper on radio spectrum policy in the context of European Community policies such as telecommunications, broadcasting, transport, and R&D" (9 December 1998).
- Communication COM(97) 623 "Green Paper on the Convergence of the Telecommunications, Media and Information Technology Sectors, and the Implications for Regulation. Towards an Information Society Approach" (3 December 1997).
- Communication COM(96) 590 "Towards a European Numbering Environment: Green Paper on a numbering policy for telecommunications services in Europe" (20 November 1996).
- Communication COM(96) 389 "Green Paper: Living and Working in the Information Society: People First" (24 July 1996).
- Communication COM(96) 359 "Standardization and the Global Information Society: The European Approach" (24 July 1996).
- Communication COM(94) 682 "Green Paper on the Liberalisation of Telecommunications Infrastructure and Cable Television Networks - Part II - A Common Approach to the Provision of Infrastructure for Telecommunications in the European Union" (25 January 1995).
- Communication COM(94) 440 "Green Paper on the liberalisation of Telecommunications Infrastructure and Cable Television Networks: Part One - Principle and Timetable" (25 October 1994).
- Communication COM(94) 145 "Towards the Personal Communications Environment: Green Paper on a common approach in the field of mobile and personal Communications in the European Union" (April 1994).

- Recommendation (1994) "Europe and the global information society - Recommendations to the European Council" (Bangemann Report) (30 November 1994).
- Communication COM(87) 290 "Towards a Dynamic European Economy, Green Paper on the development of the common market for telecommunications services and equipment" (30 June 1987).

NATIONAL LEVEL (UK) – Laws, Regulations and Norms

- Digital Economy Act 2010 c. 24.
- [Electronic] Communications Act 2003 c. 21.
  Secondary legislation:
  - SI 2004/545 – Office of Communications Act 2002 (Commencement No. 3) and Communications Act 2003 (Commencement No. 2) (Amendment) Order 2004.
- Telecommunications Act 1984 c. 12.

NATIONAL LEVEL (UK) – Standards, Frameworks and Guidance

- Department for Culture, media and Sport (July 2013) "Connectivity, Content and Consumers: Britain's digital platform for growth".
- BS 8419-1:2005 "Interoperability between metadata systems used for learning, education and training. Code of practice for the development of application profiles".
- Ofcom (2005) "The Strategic Telecommunications Review".
- BS 8426:2003 "A code of practice for e-support in e-learning systems".

2.1.2 The New Regulatory Framework

GLOBAL LEVEL – Laws, Regulations and Norms

Not applicable: This is an EU regulatory initiative, hence applicable laws, regulations and norms exist only at European Level and below.

GLOBAL LEVEL – Standards, Frameworks and Guidance

Not applicable: This is an EU regulatory initiative, hence applicable laws, regulations and norms exist only at European Level and below.

EUROPEAN LEVEL – Laws, Regulations and Norms

The Harmonisation Directives (2009 updates)

- Directive 2009/140/EC "amending Directives 2002/21/EC on a common regulatory framework for electronic communications networks and services, 2002/19/EC on access to, and interconnection of, electronic communications networks and associated facilities, and 2002/20/EC on the authorisation of electronic communications networks and services" (*eCommunications Framework*)(25 November 2009).

- Directive 2009/136/EC "amending Directive 2002/22/EC on universal service and users' rights relating to electronic communications networks and services, Directive 2002/58/EC concerning the processing of personal data and the protection of privacy in the electronic communications sector, and Regulation (EC) No 2006/2004 on cooperation between national authorities responsible for the enforcement of consumer protection laws" (*EU Cookie* or *ePrivacy Directive*) (25 November 2009).

Electronic Communications Services

The Harmonisation Directives:

1. Directive 2002/21/EC on "a common regulatory framework for electronic communications infrastructure and associated services" (*Framework Directive*) (7 March 2002).
2. Directive 2002/19/EC on "access to, and interconnection of, electronic communications networks and associated facilities" (*Access Directive*) (7 March 2002).
3. Directive 2002/20/EC on "authorisation of electronic communications networks and services" (*Authorisation Directive*) (7 March 2002).
4. Directive 2002/22/EC on "Universal service and users' rights relating to electronic communications networks and services" (*Universal Service Directive*) (7 March 2002). Decision 2003/548/EC on "minimum set of leased lines with harmonised characteristics and associated standards referred to the Universal Services Directive" (23 July 2003).
5. Directive 2002/58/EC "concerning the procession of personal data and protection of privacy in the electronic communications sector" (*ePrivacy Directive*) (12 July 2002).

Framework-related Regulations

- Commission Regulation (EC) No 611/2013 "on the measures applicable to the notification of personal data breaches under Directive 2002/58/EC of the European Parliament and of the Council on privacy and electronic communications" (*Privacy and Electronic Communications (Notification of Personal Data Breaches) Regulation*) (24 June 2013).
- Regulation (EC) No 531/2012 on "roaming on public mobile communications networks within the Union" (13 June 2012).
- Regulation (EC) No 717/2007 on "roaming on public mobile telephone networks within the Community and amending Directive 2002/21/EC" (*Roaming Directive*) (27 June 2007).
- Communication COM(2004) 28 on "unsolicited commercial communications or 'spam'" (22 January 2004)

- Decision 676/2002/EC on "a regulatory framework for radio spectrum policy in the European Community" (*Radio Spectrum Decision*) (7 March 2002).
- Regulation (EC) No 2887/2000 on "unbundled access to the local loop" (18 December 2000).

Standards-setting procedures in support of harmonization

- Directive 98/34/EC "laying down a procedure for the provision of information in the field of technical standards and regulations and of rules on Information Society services" (22 June 1998).
- Directive 98/48/EC "amending Directive 98/34/EC laying down a procedure for the provision of information in the field of technical standards and regulations" (20 July 1998).

Telecoms Licences

- Directive 97/13/EC on "a common framework for general authorizations and individual licences in the field of telecommunications services" (10 April 1997).

EUROPEAN LEVEL – Standards, Frameworks and Guidance

NRA Framework Authority under the Harmonisation Directives

- Communication COM(2006) 28 final on "Market Reviews under the EU Regulatory Framework – Consolidating the internal market for electronic communications" (6 February 2006).
- Recommendation 2003/311/EC on "relevant product and services markets within the electronic communications sector susceptible to regulation in accordance with the Framework Directive" (11 February 2003). OJ L 114/45
- Recommendation 2003/497/EC on "relevant product and service markets within the electronic communications sector susceptible to ex ante regulation in accordance with Directive 2002/21/EC on a common regulatory framework for electronic communication networks and services" (11 February 2003).
- Recommendation 2003/561/EC on "notifications, time limits and consultations under art. 7 of the Framework Directive" (23 July 2003).
- European Commission's Information Society Directorate-General Commission Staff Working Document on "the Treatment of Voice over Internet Protocol (VoIP) under the EU Regulatory Framework" (14 June 2004).
- Notice (98/C 6/04) Status of voice communications on Internet under Community law and, in particular, pursuant to Directive 90/388/EEC (10 January 1998).

NATIONAL LEVEL (UK) – Laws, Regulations and Norms

- Communications Act 2003 c. 21. (Implementation of the EU Communications Directives on 25 July 2003).
  Secondary legislation:
  - SI 2014/1825 – The Communications Act 2003 (Disclosure of Information) Order 2014.
  - SI 2003/2155 – The Communications Act 2003 (Consequential Amendments) Order 2003.
- Electronic Communications Act 2000 c. 7.
  Secondary legislation:
  - SI 2000/1798 – Electronic Communications Act 2000 (Commencement No. 1) Order 2000.
  - SI 2000/3373 – The Companies Act 1985 (Electronic Communications) Order 2000.
- Telecommunications (Fraud) Act 1997 c. 4.
- Telecommunications Act 1984 c. 12.

NATIONAL LEVEL (UK) – Standards, Frameworks and Guidance

Ofcom Guidance

- Ofcom (September 2005) "Telecommunications Strategic review".
- Ofcom (23 June 2005) "telecommunications: A new regulatory approach".
- Ofcom (2011) "Electronic Communications Code".

Information Commissioners Office Guidance

- ICO (7/09/2011) "The Guide to Privacy and electronic communications".
- ICO (may 2012) "Guidance on the rules on use of cookies and similar technologies".
- ICO (17/07/2012) "Notification of personal data breaches".

2.1.3 Trans-European Networks (TEN)

The function of Trans-European Networks is to create a modern and effective infrastructure to link European regions and national networks. •Trans-European Telecommunications Networks (eTEN) have as their aim the deployment of telecommunication networks based services. They focus strongly on public services and are at the very heart of the initiative "eEurope -- An Information Society for All".

<u>EUROPEAN LEVEL – Laws, Regulations and Norms</u>

Trans-European [Telecommunications] Networks (TEN)

- Decision No 1336/97/EC "on a series of guidelines for trans-European telecommunications networks" (17 June 1997).
  Amending Acts:
  - Decision No 1376/2002/EC "amending Decision No 1336/97/EC on a series of guidelines for trans-European telecommunications networks" (12 July 2002).
- Decision No. 1692/96/EC "on Community guidelines for the development of the trans-European transport network" (23 July 1996).
- Consolidated versions of the Treaty on European Union and the Treaty on the Functioning of the European Union, Title XVI Trans-European Networks, Article 170 (ex Article 154 TEC) – Article 172 (ex Article 156 TEC).

<u>EUROPEAN LEVEL – Standards, Frameworks and Guidance</u>

- Report from the Commission to the Council, the European Parliament, the European Economic and Social Committee and the Committee of the Regions COM (2009) 5 final "on the implementation of the trans-european transport network guidelines 2004 – 2005: Pursuant to Article 18 of Decision 1692/96/EC" (20 January 2009).

2.2 INTERNET REGULATION

2.2.1 Safer Internet Use

<u>EUROPEAN LEVEL – Laws, Regulations and Norms</u>

Safer Internet Use is covered in other thematic sections of this Matrix, including information security, data protection and privacy rights, and electronic commerce.

The Internet: Safer Internet Use

- Decision No 854/2005/EC "establishing a multi-annual Programme on promoting safer use of the Internet and new online technologies" (11 May 2005).
- Decision No 1151/2003/EC "amending Decision No 276/1999/EC adopting a multiannual Community action plan on promoting safer use of the Internet by combating illegal and harmful content on global networks" (16 June 2003).
- Decision No 276/1999 "adopting a multiannual Community action plan on promoting safer use of the Internet by combating illegal and harmful content on global networks" (25 January 1999).

EUROPEAN LEVEL – Standards, Frameworks and Guidance

- Communication COM(2002)152 "Follow-up to the multiannual Community action plan on promoting safer use of the Internet by combating illegal and harmful content on global networks – Proposal for a Decision final amending Decision No 276/1999/EC adopting a multiannual Community action plan on promoting safer use of the Internet by combating illegal and harmful content on global networks" (22 March 2002).

New internet protocol

- Communication COM(2002) 96 final "Next Generation Internet – priorities for action in migrating to the new internet protocol Ipv6" (21 February 2002).

2.3 TELECOMMUNICATIONS

2.3.1 Wireless policy

GLOBAL LEVEL – Laws, Regulations and Norms

Radio Spectrum Policy

- The Radio Regulations incorporate the decisions of the World Radiocommunication Conferences, including all Appendices, Resolutions, Recommendations and ITU-R Recommendations incorporated by reference (http://www.itu.int/en/ITU-R/).

GLOBAL LEVEL – Standards, Frameworks and Guidance

Radio Spectrum Policy

- Standards defined by ITU Radiocommunication Sector (ITU-R).

EUROPEAN LEVEL – Laws, Regulations and Norms

Radio Spectrum Policy

- Directive 2006/28/EC "amending, for the purposes of their adoption to technical progress, Directive 72/245/EEC relating to the radio interference (electronic magnetic compatibility) of vehicles and amending Directive 70/156/EEC on the approximation of the laws of the Member States relating to the type-approval of motor vehicles and their trailers" (6 March 2006).

- Directive 2005/82/EC repealing Council Directive 90/544/EEC on "the frequency bands designated for the co-ordinated introduction of pan-European land-based public radio paging in the Community" (14 December 2005).
- Directive 2005/49/EC "amending, for the purposes of their adaptation to technical progress, Council Directive 72/245/EEC relating to the radio interference (electromagnetic compatibility) of vehicles and Council Directive 70/156/EEC on the approximation of the laws of the Member States relating to the type-approval of motor vehicles and their trailers" (25 July 2005).
- Decision 2005/513/EC on "the harmonised use of radio spectrum in the 5 GHz frequency band for the implementation of wireless access systems including radio local area networks (WAS/RLANs)" (11 July 2005).
- Decision 2005/50/EC on "the harmonisation of the 24GHz range radio spectrum band for the time-limited use by automotive short range radar equipment in the Community" (17 January 2005).
- Decision No 676/2002/EC on "a regulatory framework for radio spectrum policy in the European Community" (Radio Spectrum Decision).

Radio and Telecommunications Equipment Liberalisations

- Commission Decision on "the application of Article 3(3)(e) of Directive 1999/5/EC to radio equipment intended to participate in the Automatic Identification System (AIS)" (25 January 2005).
- Directive 1999/5/EC on "radio equipment and telecommunications terminal equipment and the mutual recognition of their conformity" (9 March 1999).
  Proposed Amendments:
  - Directive 2014/53/EU "on the harmonisation of the laws of the Member States relating to the making available on the market of radio equipment and repealing Directive 1999/5/EC" (16 April 2014).
- Agreement on mutual recognition between the European Community and the United States of America (18 May 1998).

Interfaces and technical design

- Directive 1999/5/EC on "radio equipment and telecommunications terminal equipment and the mutual recognition of their conformity" (9 March 1999).

EUROPEAN LEVEL – Standards, Frameworks and Guidance

Radio Spectrum Policy

- "Opinion on Digital Switchover" (document RSPG04-55).
- "Opinion on Multimedia Services" (document RSPG06-143).

- "Report and Final Opinion: Scientific use of Spectrum" (document RSPG06-144).
- "Final Opinion on EU Spectrum Policy Implications of the Digital Dividend" (document RSPG07-161).
- "Final Revised Opinion on WRC-07" (document RSPG07-162).

Third-Generation Mobile Communications

- Communication COM(2002) 301 final "Towards the Full Roll-Out of Third Generation Mobile Communications" (20 March 2002).
- Communication COM(2001) 141 final "The introduction of third generation mobile communication in the European Union: State of play and the way forward" (20 March 2001).

Radio and Telecommunications Equipment Liberalisation

- Decision No 31/2005 of the Joint Committee established under the Agreement on Mutual Recognition between the European Community and the United States of America of 14 February 2005 related to the listing of a Conformity Assessment Body under the Sectoral Annex on Telecommunication Equipment 2005/251/EC (22 March 2005).

Technical Standards that require licencing

- WCDMA 2100 with simultaneous voice and package data (PS max speed UL/DL 128/384kbps, CS max speed 64kbps).
- EGPRS, class B, multislot class 10 (UL/DL = 118.4/238.8kbps).
- GPRS, class B, multislot class 10.
- Speech codecs: FR, EFR, WCDMA, GSM AMR.

NATIONAL LEVEL (UK) – Laws, Regulations and Norms

- Wireless Telegraphy Act 2006 c. 36.

NATIONAL LEVEL (UK) – Standards, Frameworks and Guidance

Cross-reference: For further information, see 2.8.1 "Wireless and fixed line".

2.3.2 Access and interconnection

EUROPEAN LEVEL – Laws, Regulations and Norms

- Regulation (EC) No 2887/2000 on "unbundled access to the local loop" (30 December 2000).

EUROPEAN LEVEL – Standards, Frameworks and Guidance

Notice (2002/C 165/03) "Commission guidelines on market analysis and the assessment of significant market power under the Community regulatory framework for electronic communications networks and services" (11 July 2002).

2.3.3 Satellites

EUROPEAN LEVEL – Laws, Regulations and Norms

- Regulation (EC) No 683/2008 on "the further implementation of the European satellite navigation programmes (EGNOS and Galileo)" (9 July 2008).
- Regulation (EC) No 1943/2006 "amending Regulation (EC) No 876/2002 setting up the Galileo Joint Undertaking" (12 December 2006).
- Regulation (EC) No 876/2002 "on the establishment of Galileo Joint Undertaking" (21 May 2002).

EUROPEAN LEVEL – Standards, Frameworks and Guidance

- Communication COM(2006) 769 final on "Green Paper: Satellite Navigation Applications" (8 December 2006).
- Communication COM(2003) 17 final "Green Paper: European Space Policy" (21 January 2003).
- Communication COM(90) 490 final "Towards Europe-Wide Systems and Services – Green Paper on a common approach in the field of satellite communications in the European Community" (22 November 1990).

2.4 DIGITAL MEDIA AND CONTENT

2.4.1 Digital interactive television

EUROPEAN LEVEL – Laws, Regulations and Norms

- Directive 2007/65/EC "amending Council Directive 89/552/EEC on the coordination of certain provisions laid down by law, regulation or administrative action in Member States concerning the pursuit of television broadcasting activities" (11 December 2007).
- Directive 97/26/EC on "the coordination of certain provisions laid down by law, regulation or administrative action in Member States concerning the pursuit of television broadcasting activities" (30 June 1997).

- Directive 89/552/EC on "the coordination of certain provisions laid down by Law, Regulation or Administrative Action in Member States concerning the pursuit of television broadcasting activities" (Television without Frontiers Directive) (3 October 1989).

EUROPEAN LEVEL – Standards, Frameworks and Guidance

- Communication COM(2011) 427 "Green Paper on the online distribution of audiovisual works in the European Union: opportunities and challenges towards a digital single market" (13 July 2011).
- Notice (2004/C 102/02) "Commission interpretative communication on certain aspects of the provisions on televised advertising in the 'Television without frontiers' Directive" (28 April 2004).
- Communication COM(2003) 784 final on "the future of European regulatory audiovisual policy" (15 December 2005).

Technical Protocols

- Internet Protocol TV (IPTV). Industry standards (*e.g.* Microsoft's IPTV).
- Single Programme Transport Stream (SPTS).
- Formats for MPEG-2, MPEG-4 HD, MPEG-4 AVC, MPEG-7 (metadata) (Moving Picture Experts Group; ISO working group).
- Multimedia Home Platform (MHP) and set-top boxes (STB).
    - Video Networks.
    - Fibre-to-the-home (FTTH) technology.
    - Video-on-demand (VOD).
    - VGA camera.
    - Resolution "standards"; *e.g.*, 176x208 pixels, 640x460 pixels, 1600x1200 pixels, etc.
    - 3GPP video streaming.
    - Digital Video Broadcasting (DVB-SH).

NATIONAL LEVEL (UK) – Laws, Regulations and Norms

- Broadcasting Act 1996 c. 55 [esp. §§ 18-31].

NATIONAL LEVEL (UK) – Standards, Frameworks and Guidance

- Cabinet Office (March 2015) "Telecommunications and Digital Infrastructure Maps", second publication.
- Department for Culture, media and Sport (6 August 2014) "Digital Communications Infrastructure Strategy", consultation document.

2.4.2 Digital content

EUROPEAN LEVEL – Laws, Regulations and Norms

- Recommendation 2006/952/EC on "the protection of minors and human dignity and on the right of reply in relation to the competitiveness of the European audiovisual and on-line information services industry" (20 December 2006).
- Recommendation 2005/865/EC on "film heritage and the competitiveness of related industrial activities" (*Protection of film heritage of European significance*) (9 December 2005).
- Council of Europe "Additional Protocol to the Convention on Cybercrime, Concerning the Criminalisation of Acts of a Racist and Xenophobic Nature Committed through Computer Systems CETS No. 189" (28 January 2003).

EUROPEAN LEVEL – Standards, Frameworks and Guidance

- Communication COM(2010) 183 "Green Paper: Unlocking the potential of cultural and creative industries" (27 April 2010).
- Decision 456/2005/EC "establishing a multi-annual Community programme to make digital content in Europe more accessible, usable and exploitable" (of 9 March 2005).

NATIONAL LEVEL (UK) – Laws, Regulations and Norms

Obtaining, use and dissemination of illegal content is covered in the UK by the following:

- SI 2010/2128 – The Equality Act (Disability) Regulations 2010 (DDA).
- Coroners and Justice Act 2009 c. 25 [esp. Part 2 §§ 62-69].
- Criminal Justice and Immigration Act 2008 c. 4 [esp. Part 5 §§ 63-71].
- Sexual Offences Act 2003 c. 42 [esp. §§ 45-46].
- Criminal Justice and Police Act 2001 c. 16 [esp. § 42].
- Protection of Children Act 1999 c. 14.
- Protection from Harassment Act (PHA) 1997 c. 40.
- The Defamation Act 1996 c. 31.
- Disability Discrimination Act 1995 c. 50.
- Criminal Justice and Public Order Act 1994 c. 33 [esp. Part VII §§ 84-87].
- Criminal Justice Act 1988 c. 33 [esp. Part XI §§ 160, 160A & 161].
- Malicious Communications Act 1988 c. 27.
- Public Order Act 1986 c. 6.
- Civic Government (Scotland) Act 1982 c. 45 [esp. § 52].
- Protection of Children Act 1978 c. 37.
- Obscene Publications Act 1964 c. 74.

- Obscene Publications Act 1959 c. 66
- Children and Young Persons (Harmful Publications) Act, 1955 c. 28.
- Offences Against the Person Act 1861 c. 100 [esp. § 16].

<u>NATIONAL LEVEL (UK) – Standards, Frameworks and Guidance</u>

- Regulatory Policy Committee (25 July 2014) "Impact assessment opinion: Extending Copyright Exceptions for Educational Use"
- Intellectual Property Office (16 May 2014) "Artist's Resale Right".
- House of Lords (24 July 2012) "1st Report of Session 2012-13: Broadband for all – an alternative vision".
- BIS (2010) "Digital Radio" and "Vehicles sold with digital radios by 2013".
- ICO (2011) "Personal information online – code of practice"

<u>SUB-NATIONAL LEVEL – Laws, Regulations and Norms</u>

- Copyright Policy
- Policy on Business Conduct

<u>SUB-NATIONAL LEVEL – Standards, Frameworks and Guidance</u>

- European Charter for the Development and the Take-up of Film Online, agreed on 23 May 2006 at the Europe Day of the 59th Cannes Film Festival.
- OMA DRM 1.0 including forward lock for content protection, combined delivery, separate delivery, and super distribution.

2.5 RADIO SERVICES AND EQUIPMENT

2.5.1 Radio interference

<u>EUROPEAN LEVEL – Laws, Regulations and Norms</u>

Radio Interference (electromagnetic compatibility) of vehicles

- Directive 2009/19/EC on "amending, for the purposes of its adaptation to technical progress, Directive 72/245/EC relating to the radio interference (electromagnetic compatibility) of vehicles" (12 March 2009).
- Directive 2006/28/EC on "amending, for the purposes of their adaptation to technical progress, Directive 72/245/EEC relating to the radio interference (electromagnetic compatibility) of vehicles and Directive 70/156/EEC on the approximation of the laws of the Member States relating to the type-approval of motor vehicles and their trailers" (6 March 2006).

EUROPEAN LEVEL – Standards, Frameworks and Guidance

See 2.8.1 Wireless and fixed line, below.

2.5.2 Compatibility

GLOBAL LEVEL – Standards, Frameworks and Guidance

- ISO 33.100 "Electromagnetic compatibility (EMC)".
- ISO 33.100.10 "Emission".
- ISO 33.100.20 "Immunity".
- ISO 33.100.99 "Other aspects related to EMC".

EUROPEAN LEVEL – Laws, Regulations and Norms

Electromagnetic Compatibility

- Directive 2014/30/EU "on the harmonisation of the laws of the Member States relating to electromagnetic compatibility" (26 February 2014).
- Directive 2004/108/EC on "the approximation of the laws of the Member States relating to electromagnetic compatibility and repealing Directive 89/226/EEC" (*EMC Directive*) (15 December 2004).

EUROPEAN LEVEL – Standards, Frameworks and Guidance

- ETSI EN 301 489-34 V1.4.1 "Electromagnetic compatibility and Radio spectrum Matters (ERM); ElectroMagnetic Compatibility (EMC) standard for radio equipment and services; Part 34: Specific conditions for External Power Supply (EPS) for mobile phones" (28/02/2014).
- European Commission (8th February 2010) "Guide for the EMC Directive 2004/108/EC".
- Harmonised Standards by the European Standards Organisation (CEN, CENELEC, or ETSI) such as EN 55099:2009, EN 55099:2010 and EN 55088:2008.

NATIONAL LEVEL (UK) – Laws, Regulations and Norms

- The Electromagnetic Compatibility Regulations 2006.
  Secondary legislation:
  - SI 2006/3418 – The Electromagnetic Compatibility Regulations 2006.

NATIONAL LEVEL (UK) – Standards, Frameworks and Guidance

- Department for Business, Innovation & Skills (1 November 2012) "The Electromagnetic Compatibility Regulations 2006: Guidelines for the designation of Notified Bodies"

- DTI URN 06/2236 (December 2006) "Implementing the new Electromagnetic Compatibility (EMC) Directive in the United Kingdom DTI Response to the Public Consultation".
- BS EN 55011 "Industrial, scientific and medical equipment. Radio-frequency disturbance characteristics. Limits and methods of measurement".
- BS EN 55022 "Information technology equipment. Radio disturbance characteristics. Limits and methods of measurement".

2.5.3 Radio equipment

EUROPEAN LEVEL – Laws, Regulations and Norms

Radio Equipment intended to participate in the Automatic Identification System (AIS)

- Commission Decision on "the application of Article 3(3)(e) of Directive (1999/5/EC) to radio equipment intended to participate in the Automatic Identification System (AIS)" (25 January 2005).

EUROPEAN LEVEL – Standards, Frameworks and Guidance

Cross-reference: For further information, see 2.8.1 "Wireless and fixed line", below.

2.6 AUDIOVISUAL SERVICES

2.6.1 The audiovisual services industry

EUROPEAN LEVEL – Laws, Regulations and Norms

- Directive 2010/13/EU on "the coordination of certain provisions laid down by law, regulation or administrative action in Member States concerning the provision of audiovisual media services" (Audiovisual Media Services Directive) (10 March 2010).

EUROPEAN LEVEL – Standards, Frameworks and Guidance

- Communication COM(2013) 231, "Green Paper – Preparing for a Fully Converged Audiovisual World: Growth, Creation and Values" (24 April 2013).
- Technical media formats (decoding): MP3, AAC, Real Audio, WAV, Nokia Ring Tones, AMR, AMR-WB, AMR-NB, AU, MIDI, H.263, JPEG, JPEG2000, EXIF 2.2, GIF 87/89, PNG, BMP (W-BMP), MBM, MPEG-4, eAAC+.
- Decision No. 1718/2006/EC concerning "the implementation of a programme of support for the European audiovisual sector" (MEDIA 2007) (15 November 2006).

European Audiovisual Observatory

- Council of Europe Resolution (92) 70 establishing a European Audiovisual Observatory.

2.7 ENVIRONMENT ("GREEN IT")

2.7.1 Green IT

G:PBAL LEVEL – Laws, Regulations and Norms

Not applicable: This is an EU regulatory initiative, hence applicable laws, regulations and norms exist only at European Level and below.

GLOBAL LEVEL – Standards, Frameworks and Guidance

- ISO 14001:2004 "Environmental management systems -- Requirements with guidance for use".

EUROPEAN LEVEL – Laws, Regulations and Norms

Energy Efficiency

- Directive 2012/27/EU on "energy efficiency, amending Directives 2009/125/EC and 2010/30/EU and repealing Directives 2004/8/EC and 2006/32/EC (25 October 2012).
- Directive 2006/32/EC on energy end-use efficiency and energy services and repealing Council Directive 93/76/EEC" (5 April 2006).
- Directive 2004/8/EC on "the promotion of cogeneration based on a useful heat demand in the internal energy market and amending Directive 92/42/EEC" (11 February 2000).

Waste Electrical and Electronic Equipment (WEEE)

- Directive 2012/19/EU on "waste electrical and electronic equipment (WEEE)" (4 July 2012).
- Directive 2008/112/EC "amending Directives 76/768/EEC, 88/378/EEC, 1999/13/EC and Directives 2000/53/EC, 2002/96/EC and 2004/42/EC in order to adapt them to Regulation (EC) No 1272/2008 on classification, labelling and packaging of substances and mixtures" (16 December 2008).
- Directive 2003/108/EC "amending Directive 2002/96/EC on waste electrical and electronic equipment (WEEE)" (8 December 2003).

- ▪ [UK] SI 2007/3454 – The Waste Electrical and Electronic Equipment (Amendment) Regulations 2007.
- Directive 2002/96/EC on "waste electrical and electronic equipment (WEEE)" (27 January 2003).
  - ▪ [UK] SI 2006/3289 – The Waste Electrical and Electronic Equipment Regulations 2006.
- Directive 2002/95/EC on "the restriction of the use of certain hazardous substances in electrical and electronic equipment" (27 January 2003).

EUROPEAN LEVEL – Standards, Frameworks and Guidance

Waste Electrical and Electronic Equipment (WEEE)

- European Recycling Platform (ERP): Europe's leading WEEE compliance scheme.
- ISO14001:2004 "Environmental Management Standard" (replaces the old ISO14001:1996 standard).

Environment

- Communication COM(2013) 123 final "Green Paper: On a European Strategy on Plastic Waste in the Environment" (7 March 2013).
- Communication COM(2007) 140 "Green Paper on market-based instruments for environment and related policy purposes" (28 March 2007).

NATIONAL LEVEL (UK) – Laws, Regulations and Norms

Green Regulation

- Green Energy (Definition and Promotion) Act 2009 c. 19.
- Climate Change Act 2008 c.27.
- SI 2004/3391 – The Environmental Information Regulations 2004.

NATIONAL LEVEL (UK) – Standards, Frameworks and Guidance

Waste Electrical and Electronic Equipment

- UK Environment Agency "Waste electrical and electronic equipment: A guide to when electrical and electronic equipment is considered waste and the controls that apply" (March 2012).
- BSI BIP 2117 "The Waste Electrical and Electronic Equipment Directive. Requirements and Implementation" (July 2008).
- DEFRA (2005) "Code of practice on the discharge of the obligations of public authorities under the Environmental information regulations 2004 (SI 2004/3391)".

2.8 OTHER ICT-SPECIFIC NORMS

2.8.1 Wireless and fixed line

EUROPEAN LEVEL – Laws, Regulations and Norms

- Directive 1999/5/EC on "radio equipment and telecommunications terminal equipment and the mutual recognition of their conformity" (9 March 1999).

EUROPEAN LEVEL – Standards, Frameworks and Guidance

The following lists examples of standards especially applicable to ICT manufacturers:
Wireless Standards

- Universal Mobile Telecommunications Services (UMTS)
- UMTS High Speed Downlink Packet Access (HSDPA, speeds up to 3.5Mbps, Mobile Broadband)..
- General Packet Radio Services (GPRS) – 2.5G cellular technology.
- General System of Mobile Communications (GSM) – 2G cellular technology: 900/ 1800/ 1900 MHz GSM.
- EDGE (Enhanced Data Rates for Global Evolution) – emerging 3G technology, 3 times faster data transfer as with GSM/GPRS.
- Wideband Code-Division Multiple Access (WCDMA) – Europe's 3G cellular technology; WCDMA 2100 networks with simultaneous voice and package data (PS max speed UL/DL 128/384kbps, CS max speed 64kbps).
- EGPRS, class B, multislot class 10 (UL/DL = 118.4/238.8kbps).

Wireless protocols (incl. security)

- Virtual Private Networking (VPN) – to secure end-to-end communication.
- Private Mobile Networks (PMN), Private Mobile Exchange (PMX).
- Media Access Control (MAC).
- Visitor Based Network (VBN).
- Wireless Application Protocol (WAP).
- Wireless Encryption/Equivalent Privacy (WEP) protocol (Wlan standard, Institute of Electrical and Electronics Engineers, old standard).
- WiFi Protected Access (WPA and WPA2) security protocol (Wi-Fi Alliance).
- Radio Frequency Identification (RFID) Standard, RFID Security.
- Temporal key integrity protocol (TKIP).
- WI-Fi Protected Setup standard (WPS).
- Wireless Mark-up Language (WML).
- Wireless Fidelity (WiFi) – wireless local area networking technology Standards.

Emerging standards to address Internet security

- High-Speed Uplink Packet Access (HSUPA, 5.8Mbps).
- High Speed Downlink Packet Access (HSDPA, 14Mbps).
- 3G LTE (Long-Term Evolution) standard, a.k.a. Super 3G' (enhance the capabilities of 3G networks from 2009, 20Mbps).
- Very high bit-rate DSL (VDSL, xDSL technology providing data transmission, 20-50 Mbps).
- Worldwide Interoperability for Microwave Access (WiMax, up to 75Mbps).
- Fiber-to-the-X (FTTx, 10-100Mbps).

Frequency Spectrum

- 802.15 or XDA – Bluetooth. Ulta wide broadband (IEEE 802.15.3a, 2gbps within 4ms).
- 802.11a (54 MB sec, 5GHz band, 300 feet range, licensed spectrum)
- 802.11b (11 MB sec, 2.4GHz, 200 feet range, unlicensed spectrum)
- 802.11g (54 MB sec, 2.4 GHz, unlicensed spectrum)
- 802.11i (Forthcoming, security-hardened version of WiFi standard)
- 802.16 – WiMAX, wide-radius, high-bandwidth wireless coverage
- 802.1X - certificates or per-user passwords (IEEE protocol)
- 802.11n (wireless network broadband)
- WiMAX (Alvarion, Intel, 5GHz 802.n mesh and 2.4 GHz 902.11 access).
- Direct Sequence Spread Spectrum (DSSS) (complies with 802.11b).
- Remote Authentication Dial-In User Service (Radius).

Network connection

- X.25 Network connections between DTE and DCE, data link layer protocol (ITU-T standard).
- X.121 International Data Numbers (ITU-T standard).
- X.21 serial communications over synchronous digital lines [ITU-T standard).
- X.28 terminal-to-PAD interface [ITU-T standard].
- X.75 specification for signalling system between two PDNs (ITU-T standard).

Voice Features

- Speaking Independent Name Dialling (SIND).
- Stereo Handset HS-3.
- Stereo Handset HS-3.

Fixed line internet connection

- Fixed Broadband: ADSL2+, VDSL (speeds up to 55Mbps).

Network Cables

- Connectivity Cable (USB): CA-53
- USB 2.0 full speed via Pop-PortTM (Nokia standard) interface

2.8.2 Data storage and power management

EUROPEAN LEVEL – Laws, Regulations and Norms

Not applicable: Binding laws, regulations and norms do not exist for this domain.

EUROPEAN LEVEL – Standards, Frameworks and Guidance

Memory

- Multi Media Card (MMC), reduced size Mul; (RS-MMC).
- 64 MB Reduced Size Dual Voltage (1.8/3V) Multi Media Card (MMC).

Storage Devices/Interfaces

- Fibre Channel, Serial ATA (SATA), Serial Attached SCSI (SAS), parallel SCSI.
- DAS (Direct-Attached Storage) and FAS (Fabric-Attached Storage).
- Virtual Tape Libraries (VTL) – SAS/SCSI ((Small Computer System Interface) or ATA/SATA disk arrays.

Power Management

- General Battery Standards (IEC 60086-1 BS 387, ANSI C18.1M, ERR 1625).
- Lithium Standards (BS EN 60086-4:2000, IEC).
- Nickel Metal Hydride Standards, Nickel Cadium Standards, Lead Acid Standards, Photovoltaic Standards, Safty Standards, *etc*.
- Standards for chargers for mobile devices: *e.g.* Nokia AC-4, USB Type-C connector and IEEE P1823 (global standard for a "universal power adapter for mobile devices" (UPAMD)).

PART III

General Laws and Regulations – applicable to all organisations

If you have ten thousand regulations you destroy all respect for the law.
Winston Churchill (1874 - 1965)

Laws are like cobwebs, which may catch small flies, but let wasps and hornets break through.
Jonathan Swift (1667 – 1745)

We may brave human laws, but we cannot resist natural ones.
Jules Verne (1828 – 1905)

Moral values, and a culture and a religion, maintaining these values are far better than laws and regulations.
Swami Sivananda (1887 – 1963)

PART 3

GENERAL LAWS AND REGULATIONS

This last Part of the Regulatory Compliance Matrix categorises laws, regulations and norms generally applicable across all industry sectors, and maps it to relevant standards, frameworks and guidance to assist companies to comply with certain general legal and regulatory requirements. Many of the items presented in this Part apply not only to commercial organisations, but also to the public sector and charity organisations. Examples include finance and accounting rules, anti-bribery and corruption law, employment law, data protection, and intellectual property rights.

Figure 4: General Regulatory Compliance Matrix

	LAWS, REGULATIONS and NORMS	STANDARDS, FRAMEWORKS and GUIDANCE

GENERAL	1. Business regulation
	    1.1 Company law and associated responsibilities (incl. company formation)
	    1.2 Insolvency and Mergers & Acquisition
	    1.3 Corporate governance, accounting, audit and risk management
	    1.4 Disclosure of electronic documents with civil litigation and official investigations
	    1.5 Anti-bribery and corruption ("ABC")
	    1.6 Public procurement
	    1.7 Contract law and competition
	    1.8 Finance and taxation law
		- Standards defined and guidance issued by international organisations
		- Standards defined by standardisation institutes and guidance issued by supervisory authorities at European level
		- Standards defined by standardisation institutes and guidance issued by regulatory agencies at national level
		- Technical standards defined by industry and industry associations
		- Compliance frameworks developed within industry
		- Third-party compliance audits and attestations

GENERAL	2. Consumer protection and employment law 2.1. Consumer protection and Alternative Dispute Resolution 2.2 Work and employment 2.3 Health and Safety 3. Information security 3.1. Electronic signatures 3.2. Network security and security products (applications) 3.3. Cybercrime 3.4. Security for passports and visas	– Targeted industry self-governance initiatives – Other general guidance
	4. Data protection and privacy rights 4.1. General data protection and privacy 4.2 Records management and data retention 4.3. Pan-European data transfer 4.4. Access to information and investigations 5. Intellectual property rights 5.1. General 5.2. Copyright 5.3. Patents 5.4. Trade marks and designs 5.5. Legal protection of hardware 5.6. Legal protection of software 5.7. Domain names 6. Electronic commerce 6.1. e-Commerce regulation for applications and services 6.2. e-Government	

REGULATORY AUTHORITIES THAT REGULATE ALL INDUSTRY SECTORS AND KEY INFLUENCERS

(1) Global Level – Authorities (non-US)

- **International Organization for Standardization (ISO)** is a worldwide federation of national standards bodies and an independent, non-governmental membership organisation comprising 147 countries. Founded on 23 February 1947 and headquartered in Geneva, Switzerland, it is the world's largest developer of voluntary

international proprietary, industrial and commercial standards, and promotes standardisation with a view to facilitating the international exchange of goods and services. ISO has developed over 19,500 international standards to date.
[Website: http://www.iso.org,]
[ISO standards catalogue – Website: http://www.iso.org/iso/home/store/catalogue_tc]

- **Group of Eight (G8), formerly G-7 before Russia joined in 1994** is an international forum for the governments of Canada, France, Germany, Italy, Japan, Russia, the United Kingdom and the United States, which represent 65% of the world economy. Each year, Member States take turns at the G-8 presidency, setting its annual agenda and hosting the summit of the year. They agree on co-ordination of strategies, stimulation of research, information, knowledge exchange, security policy, etc.
  [Website: http://g8live.org]

- **Group of Twenty (G-20)**, comprising Argentina, Australia, Brazil, Canada, China, France, Germany, India, Indonesia, Italy, Japan, México, Russia, Saudi Arabia, South Africa, South Korea, Turkey, the United Kingdom, the United States, and the EU, is an informal forum that promotes an open and constructive dialogue between finance ministers and central bank governors of systemically significant industrial and emerging market economies. Representing around two-thirds of the world's population and 90% of world gross domestic product, the G-20 is uniquely placed to tackle issues of significance for the international economy and monetary system.
  [Website: http://www.g20.org]

- **World Economic Forum (WEF)** is an independent international organization committed to improving the state of the world, it provides a collaborative framework for world leaders to address global issues, engaging particularly its corporate members in global citizenship.
  [Website: http://www.weforum.org]

- **World Trade Organisation (WTO)** is the only international organization dealing with the rules of international trade, at its heart are the WTO agreements negotiated, signed and ratified by the bulk of the world's trading nations. Its goal is to help producers, exporters and importers of goods and services do business. It has 151 members, and is the successor to GATT (q.v.).
  [Website: http://www.wto.org]

- **Organisation for Economic Co-operation and Development (OECD)**, with 30 Member States sharing a commitment to democratic government and market economy, has relationships with 70 other countries. Its work covers economic and social issues from macroeconomics to trade, education, development, and science and innovation. Its Directorate for Science, Technology and Industry (STI) "provides governments with analytical basis for policy formulation and advice on the scientific,

technological and industrial environment and its relation to growth, employment and well-being", and its Statistics Directorate (STD) provides statistics on a comparable basis; develops international statistical standards; and co-ordinates statistical activities both within the Organisation and with other international agencies.
[Website: http://www.oecd.org]

- **Business and Industry Advisory Committee to the OECD (BIAC)** is an independent advisory committee officially recognised by the OECD as representative of the OECD business community, it advises the OECD on business issues. Its members are the major industrial and employers' organisations in the 30 OECD member countries. Its 34 standing committees and policy groups mirror all economic policy issues the OECD covers, as well as their impacts on members and, increasingly, on non-members like Russia and China. Every year over 1000 business representatives get actively involved in the work of the OECD through BIAC, whose main objectives are to:
  - influence OECD policies to reflect business priorities
  - influence government representatives participating in OECD committees; and
  - provide members with information on OECD policies and their implications for business.
  [Website: http://www.biac.org]

- **United Nations (UN)** was established in 1945 by 51 countries committed to keeping peace through international cooperation and collective security, today, nearly every nation in the world belongs to the UN: membership totals 191 countries. It has six main organs: General Assembly, Security Council, Economic and Social Council, Trusteeship Council and the Secretariat (all based at UN Headquarters in New York), and the International Court of Justice (at The Hague).
  [Website: http://www.un.org]

  - **General Assembly (GA; UNGA)** is the deliberative body of the United Nations, it comprises all United Nations member states and meets in regular yearly sessions.
    [Website: http://www.un.org/ga]

  - **Economic and Social Council (ECOSOC)** is the central forum for discussing international economic and social issues, and for recommending policy to member states and the UN.
    [Website: http://www.un.org/en/ecosoc]

International Organisations

- **World Intellectual Property Organization (WIPO)** promotes international protection of intellectual property and promotes cooperation on copyrights, trademarks, industrial designs and patents. It is dedicated to helping ensure that the

rights of creators and owners of intellectual property are protected worldwide, and that inventors and authors are recognized and rewarded for their ingenuity.
[Website: http://www.wipo.org]

- **United Nations Educational, Scientific and Cultural Organization (UNESCO)** promotes universal education and cultural development, protection of the world's natural and cultural heritage, international cooperation in science, press freedom and communication.
[Website: http://www.unesco.org]

Business Associations

- **International Chamber of Commerce (ICC)** is the voice of world business, championing the global economy as a force for economic growth, job creation and prosperity. Founded in 1919, it sets rules and standards, promotes prosperity through global trade, providing business expertise and advocating for international business. Dedicated to the expansion of cross-border trade, the ICC champions liberalisation of telecoms and the development of infrastructure that supports global online commerce.
[Website: http://www.iccwbo.org/]

- **The ICC Commission on e-Business, IT and Telecoms (EBITT)** comprises a group of experts on the public policy aspects of ICTs, divided into the following Task Forces: TF on Telecoms Policy, TF on Protection of Personal Data, TF on IT Services, TF on Jurisdiction and Applicable Law in e-Commerce, TF on Consumer Policy for e-Business, TF on Security and Authentication, TF on Electronic Contracting. Headquartered in Paris it has national committee staff in some 64 countries.
[Website: http://www.iccwbo.org]

- **World Chambers Network (WCN)** is a global virtual network of over 12,000 registered Chambers of Commerce & Industry and Boards of Trade, representing tens of millions of businesses worldwide, it provides an electronic platform for Chambers worldwide to participate in eCommerce.
[Website: http://www.worldchambers.com]

- **International Corporate Governance Network (ICGN)** is an unincorporated, non-profit association having 4 primary purposes: (1) to host an investor-led network for exchanging views and information about corporate governance issues internationally; (2) to examine corporate governance principles and practices; (3) to develop and promote adherence to corporate governance standards and guidelines; and (4) to promote good corporate governance. Membership is open to those committed to the development of good corporate governance.
[Website: http://www.icgn.org]

- **Global Corporate Governance Forum (GCGF)** is a multi-donor trust fund co-founded by the World Bank Group and the Organisation for Economic Co-operation and Development (OECD) to promote global, regional, and local initiatives to improve the institutional framework and practices of corporate governance. Its activities promote sustainable economic growth and poverty reduction within the framework of agreed international development targets. With input from the Private Sector Advisory Group (PSAG), its work program encompasses: (1) raising awareness and building consensus for implementation of reform through meetings, briefings, policy papers, and conferences; (2) supporting institution and capacity building, and giving technical assistance to implementation at the field level through training programmes, toolkits and other direct assistance; (3) supporting research fitted to the needs of developing countries to underpin reform efforts, and building sustainable networks for academics in developing countries; and (4) disseminating best-practices materials, publications and guidelines developed with leading global specialists and practitioners.
  [Website: http://www.gcgf.org/wps/wcm/connect/Topics_Ext_Content/IFC_External_Corporate_Site/Global+Corporate+Governance+Forum]

- **International Compliance Association (ICA)** is a professional non-profit furthering regulatory compliance and anti-money laundering best practices, it educates and supports compliance and anti-money laundering professionals globally through the provision of internationally recognised qualifications, information exchange, and training. It also sets standards of technical knowledge and professional competence.
  [Website: http://www.int-comp.org]

- **International Association of Privacy Professionals (IAPP)** is the world's largest privacy professionals association, it has 4000 business, government and academic members from 32 countries.
  [Website: https://www.privacyassociation.org]

- **Anti-Phishing Working Group (APWG)** is a global pan-industrial and law-enforcement association focused on eliminating the fraud and identity theft that results from phishing, pharming and email spoofing of all types.
  [Website: http://www.antiphising.org]

(2) Global Level – Authorities (US)

US Authorities and Associations

- **The Committee of Sponsoring Organizations of the 'Treadway Commission' (COSO)** is a voluntary, private-sector organization dedicated to improving the quality of financial reporting through business ethics, effective controls, and corporate governance.
  [Website: http://www.coso.org]

- **Privacy International (PI)** is a human rights watchdog on surveillance and privacy invasions by governments and corporations. Based in London with offices in Washington, PI has conducted campaigns and research throughout the world on issues from wiretapping and national security to ID cards, video surveillance, data matching, medical privacy, and freedom of information and expression.
  [Website: http://www.privacyinternational.org]

(3) European Level (EU Member States) – Authorities

European Standards Institutes

New Approach to Standardisation in the Internal Market: joins up the efforts of CEN, CENELEC and ETSI (the three European standards organisations) to the European Commission and EFTA. [http://www.newapproach.org]

- **Comité Européen de Normatisation (CEN) [European Committee for Standardisation]** aids voluntary technical harmonization in Europe, coordinate with worldwide bodies and its European partners.
  [Website: http://www.cenorm.be]

- **European Committee for Electronic Standardisation (CENELEC)** creates voluntary electro-technical standards for Europe, having been converted in 1973 to a non-profit under Belgian law. It was officially recognised as the European standards organisation in its field by the European Commission in Directive 83/189/EEC. Its members have been collaborating in the interests of European harmonisation since the late Fifties, maturing alongside the European Economic Community. CENELEC works with 35,000 technical experts from 22 European countries to publish standards for the European market.
  [Website: http://www.cenelec.org]

- **European Telecommunications Standards Institute (ETSI)** was founded in 1988 to collaborate internationally toward developing globally applicable standards meeting the needs of the telecommunication/ electronic communication community, while fulfilling its duty to support EU and EFTA regulation and initiatives. Membership by category as of 1 Feb 2003: manufacturers 51%, service providers and others 24%, network operators 14%, administrators 8%, users 3%. It has 786 members from 56 countries.
  [Website: http://www.etsi.org]

Supporting Standards-Setting Initiatives

- **Information Society Standardization System (CEN-ISSS)** provides market players with a comprehensive and integrated range of standardisation-oriented services and products, to contribute to the success of the Information Society in Europe.
  [Website: http://www.cenorm.be/isss]

- **International Electrotechnical Commission (IEC)** facilitates co-operation between the IEC and CENELEC as stipulated in what is known as 'the Dresden Agreement' of September 1996.
  [Website: http://www.iec.ch]

Consumer Associations

- **Association pour la Normalisation Européenne pour les Consommateurs (ANEC)/ European Association for the Co-ordination of Consumer Representation in Standardisation** is "the European consumer voice in standardisation" and defends consumer interests within the processes of standardisation and certification. ANEC was set up in 1985 by national consumer bodies from EU and EFTA Member States to coordinate consumer representation in response to the New Approach to governance. ANEC is governed by a General Assembly (ANEC/GA).
  [Website: http://www.anec.eu]

- **European Consumer Centres Network (ECC-Net)** provides information, advice and assistance on cross-border shopping in the EU, Norway and Iceland. It informs consumers of their rights under European and national consumer legislation; gives advice on how to deal with consumer complaints; provides direct assistance in resolving complaints in an amicable way with traders when purchasing abroad, whether during travel or on-line; and redirects users to an appropriate body if ECC-Net cannot help.
  [Website: http://ec.europa.eu/consumers/ecc/index_en.htm]

- **Bureau Européen des Unions de Consommateurs (BEUC)/ European Consumers' Organisation** is a federation of independent national consumer organisations from all of the Member States of the EU and other European countries. Their job is to influence, in the consumer interest, the development of EU policy, while promoting and defending the interests of all European consumers.
  [Website: http://www.beuc.org]

Chambers of Trade and Commerce of EU Member States

Consultation and advice are provided by Chambers of Trade and Commerce or by relevant industry associations:

- **Austria** –
  - Wirtschaftskammer Österreich (WKÖ) / Austrian Economic Chambers
    [Website: https://www.wko.at/]

- **Belgium** –
  - Federatie van Belgische Kamers van Koophandel / Fédération des Chambres de Commerce belges (Federation of Belgian Chambers of Commerce)
    [Website: http://www.belgianchambers.be/]

- **Bulgaria** –
  - Българската търговско промишлена палата (BCCI) / Bulgarian Chamber of Commerce and Industry
    [Website: http://www.bcci.bg/]

- **Croatia** –
  - Hrvatska Gospodarska Komora (HGK) / Croatian Chamber of Economy
    [Website: http://web.hgk.hr/]

- **Cyprus** –
  - Cyprus Chamber of Commerce and Industry (CCCI)
    [Website: http://www.ccci.org.cy/]

- **Czech Republic** –
  - Hospodářská Komora České Republiky (HK ČR) / Czech Chamber of Commerce
    [Website: http://www.komora.cz/]

- **Denmark** –
  - Dansk Erhverv / Danish Chamber of Commerce
    [Website: https://www.danskerhverv.dk/]

- **Estonia** –
  - Eesti Kaubandus-Tööstuskoda / Estonian Chamber of Commerce and Industry
    [Website: http://www.koda.ee/et]

- **Finland** –
  - Keskuskauppakamari / Finnish Chambers of Commerce (FinnCham)
    [Website: http://kauppakamari.fi/]

- **France** –
  - Assemblée des Chambres Françaises de Commerce et d'Industrie (ACFCI)
    [Website: http://www.acfci.cci.fr]

  - L'Union des Chambres de Commerce et d'Industrie Françaises à l'Etranger (UCCIFE)
    [Website: http://www.uccife.org/en]

- **Germany** –
  - Die deutschen Auslandshandelskammern (AHK) / German Chambers of Commerce
    [Website: http://www.ahk.de]

  - Deutscher Industrie- und Handelskammertag (DIHK) / Association of German Chambers of Industry and Commerce
    [Website: http://www.dihk.de]

- **Greece** –
  - Εμπορικό και Βιομηχανικό Επιμελητήριο Αθηνών (EBEA) / Athens Chamber of Commerce and Industry
    [Website: http://www.acci.gr/]

- **Hungary** –
  - Magyar Kereskedelmi és Iparkamara (MKIK) / Hungarian Chamber of Commerce and Industry
    [Website: http://www.mkik.hu/]

- **Ireland** –
  - Chambers Ireland / (Comhlachas Tráchtála na hÉireann)
    [Website: http://www.chambers.ie/]

- **Italy** –
  - Le Camere di Commercio d'Italia / The Chambers of Commerce of Italy
    [Website: http://www.camcom.gov.it/]

  - Unioncamere – l'Unione Italiana delle Camere di Commercio, Industria, Artigianato e Agricoltura / Italian Union of Chambers of Commerce, Industry, Handicrafts and Agriculture
    [Website: http://www.unioncamere.gov.it/]

- **Latvia** –
  - Latvijas Tirdzniecības un rūpniecības kamera (LTRK) / Latvian Chamber of Commerce and Industry
    [Website: http://www.chamber.lv/en]

- **Lithuania** –
  - Lietuvos Prekybos, Pramonės ir Amatų Rūmų Asociacija / Association of Lithuanian Chambers of Commerce, Industry and Crafts
    [Website: http://www.chambers.lt/]

- **Luxembourg** –
  - Chambre de Commerce Luxembourg
    [Website: http://www.cc.lu/]

- **Malta** –
  - The Malta Chamber of Commerce, Enterprise and Industry / (Il-Kamra Malta tal-Kummerċ, l-Intrapriża u l-Industrija)
    [Website: http://www.maltachamber.org.mt/]

- **Netherlands** –
  - Kamer van Koophandel (KvK)
    [Website: http://www.kvk.nl/]

- **Poland** –
  - Krajowa Izba Gospodarcza (KIG) / Polish Chamber of Commerce
    [Website: http://en.kig.pl/]

- **Portugal** –
  - Associação Industrial Português – Câmara de Comércio e Indústria (AIP-CCI)
    [Website: http://www.aip.pt/]

- **Romania** –
  - Camera de Comerţ şi Industrie a României (CCIR) / Romanian Chamber of Commerce and Industry
    [Website: http://ccir.ro/]

- **Slovakia** –
  - Slovenská Obchodná A Priemyselná Komora (SOPK) / Slovak Chamber of Commerce and Industry
    [Website: http://web.sopk.sk/]

- **Slovenia** –
  - Gospodarska zbornica Slovenije (GZS) / Chamber of Commerce and Industry of Slovenia
    [Website: http://www.gzs.si/]

- **Spain** –
  - Cámara de Comercio de España / Spanish Chamber of Commerce
    [Website: http://www.camara.es/]

- **Sweden** –
  - Sveriges Handelskamrar / The Swedish Chambers of Commerce
    [Website: http://www.sverigeshandelskamrar.se/]

- **United Kingdom** –
  - British Chambers of Commerce (BCC)
    [Website: http://www.britishchambers.org.uk]

  - Confederation of British Industry UK (CBI)
    [Website: http://www.cbi.org.uk]

Standards Institutes – National Standardisation Bodies

Every EU Member State has national standards organisations. The main ones are as follows:

- **Austria** –
  - Austrian Standards
    [Website: https://www.austrian-standards.at/]

- Österreichischer Verband für Elektrotechnik (ÖVE)
  [Website: http://www.ove.at]

- **Belgium** –
  - Bureau de Normalisation / Bureau voor Normalisatie (NBN)
    [Website: http://www.nbn.be]

  - Comité Electrotechnique Belge/ Belgisch Elektrotechnisch Comité (CEB/BEC)
    [Website: http://www.ceb-bec.be]

- **Bulgaria** –
  - Български Институт за Стандартизация (БИС) / Bulgarian Institute for Standardization (BDS)
    [Website: http://www.bds-bg.org/]

- **Croatia** –
  - Hrvatski Zavod za Norme (HZN)
    [Website: http://www.hzn.hr/]

- **Cyprus** –
  - Κυπριακος Οργανισμος Τυποποιησης (CYS) (Cyprus Organisation for Standardisation)
    [Website: http://www.cys.org.cy/]

- **Czech Republic** –
  - Úřad pro Technickou Normalizaci, Metrologii a Státní Zkušebnictví (ÚNMZ) / Czech Office for Standards, Metrology and Testing
    [Website: http://www.unmz.cz]

  - Czech Standards Institute (CNI)
    [Website: http://csni.cz/]

- **Denmark** –
  - Dansk Standard (DS)
    [Website: http://www.ds.dk]

  - Telestyrelsen / National Telecom Agency (NTA)
    [Website: http://www.itst.dk]

- **Estonia** –
  - Eesti Standardikeskus (EVS) / Estonian Centre for Standardisation
    [Website: http://www.evs.ee/]

- **Finland** –
  - Suomen Standardisoimisliitto SFS r.y. (SFS) / Finnish Standards Association
    [Website: http://www.sfs.fi]

- Suomen Sähköteknillinen Standardisoimisyhdistys r.y. (SESKO)/ Finnish Electrotechnical Standards Association
  [Website: http://www.sesko.fi]

- **France** –
  - Association Française de Normalisation (AFNOR)
    [Website: http://www.afnor.fr]

- **Germany** –
  - Deutsches Institut für Normung e.V. (DIN)
    [Website: http://www.din.de]

  - Deutsche Kommission Elektrotechnik Elektronik Informationstechnik im DIN und VDE (DKE)
    [Website: http://www.dke.de]

- **Greece** –
  - Ελληνικός Οργανισμός Τυποποίησης (ΕΛΟΤ)/ Hellenic Organization for Standardization (ELOT)
    [Website: http://www.elot.gr]

- **Hungary** –
  - Magyar Szabványügyi Testület (MSzT) / Hungarian Standards Institution
    [Website: http://www.mszt.hu/]

- **Ireland** –
  - National Standards Authority of Ireland (NSAI)/ Údarás um Chaighdeáin Náisiúnta na hÉireann
    [Website: http://www.nsai.ie]

  - Electro Technical Council of Ireland (ETCI)
    [Website: http://www.etci.ie]

- **Italy** –
  - Ente Nazionale Italiano di Normazione (UNI)
    [Website: http://www.uni.com]

  - Comitato Elettrotecnico Italiano (CEI)
    [Website: http://www.ceiweb.it]

- **Latvia** –
  - Latvijas Nacionālā standartizācijas institūcija (LVS) / Latvian Standard
    [Website: https://www.lvs.lv/]

- **Lithuania** –
  - Lietuvos Standartizacijos Departmentas (LST) / Lithuanian Standards Board
    [Website: http://www.lsd.lt/]

- **Luxembourg** –
  - Portail de Qualité (Qualité, Securité, Conformité)
    [Website: http://www.portail-qualite.public.lu/]

  - Institut Luxembourgeois de la Normalisation (ILNAS)
    [Website: http://www.ilnas.public.lu]

- **Malta** –
  - Malta Standards Authority (MSA)
    [Website: http://www.iso.org/iso/about/iso_members/iso_member_body.
    htm?member_id=1927]

- **Netherlands** –
  - Nederlands Normalisatie Instituut / Nederlands Elektrotechnisch Comité (NEN)
    [Website: http://www.nen.nl]

- **Poland** –
  - Polski Komitet Normalizacyjny (PKN) / Polish Committee for Standardization
    [Website: http://www.pkn.pl/]

- **Portugal** –
  - Instituto Português da Qualidade (IPQ)
    [Website: http://www.ipq.pt]

- **Romania** –
  - Asociația de Standardizare din România (ASRO) / Romanian Standards
    Association
    [Website: http://www.asro.ro/]

- **Slovakia** –
  - Úrad pre Normalizáciu, Metrológiu a Skúšobníctvo Slovenskej Republiky
    (ÚNMS SR) / Slovak Office of Standards, Metrology and Testing
    [Website: http://www.unms.sk/]

- **Slovenia** –
  - Slovenski Inštitut za Standardizacijo (SIST) / Slovenian Institute for
    Standardization
    [Website: http://www.sist.si/]

- **Spain** –
  - Asociación Española de Normalización y Certificación (AENOR) / Spanish
    Association for Standardisation and Certification
    [Website: http://www.aenor.es]

- **Sweden** –
  - Standardiseringen i Sverige (SIS) / Swedish Standards Institute
    [Website: http://www.sis.se]

  - Svenska Elstandard SEK
    [Website: http://www.elstandard.se]

  - Informationstekniska Standardiseringen (ITS)
    [Website: http://www.its.se]

- **United Kingdom** –
  - British Standards Institution (BSI)
    [Website: http://www.bsi-global.com]

Data Protection/ Privacy Regulatory Authorities

Every EU Member State has a national data protection regulatory authority. These are listed below.
[Website: http://ec.europa.eu/justice/data-protection/bodies/authorities/eu/index_en.htm]

- **Austria** –
  - Österreichische Datenschutzkommission
    [Website: http://www.dsb.gv.at/]

- **Belgium** –
  - Commission de la protection de la vie privée / Commissie voor de bescheming von de persoonlijke levensfeer / Commission for the protection of privacy
    [Website: http://www.privacycommission.be]

- **Bulgaria** –
  - Commission for Personal Data Protection
    [Website: https://www.cpdp.bg/]

- **Croatia** –
  - Croatian Personal Data Protection Agency
    [Website: http://www.azop.hr/]

- **Cyprus** –
  - Commissioner for Personal Data Protection
    [Website: http://www.dataprotection.gov.cy/]

- **Czech Republic** –
  - The Office for Personal Data Protection
    [Website: https://www.uoou.cz/]

- **Denmark** –
  - Datatilsynet
    [Website: http://www.datatilsynet.dk]

- **Estonia** –
  - Estonian Data Protection Inspectorate
    [Website: http://www.aki.ee/eng/]

- **Finland** –
  - Office of Data Protection – Ombudsman
    [Website: http://www.tietosuoja.fi]

- **France** –
  - Commission Nationale de l'Informatique et des Libertés
    [Website: http://www.cnil.fr]

- **Germany** –
  - Der Bundesbeauftragte für den Datenschutz und die Informationsfreiheit
    [Website: http://www.bfdi.bund.de]

- **Greece** –
  - Αρχη Προστασιας Δεδομενων Προσωπικου Χαρακτηρα / Hellenic Data Protection Authority
    [Website: http://www.dpa.gr]

- **Hungary** –
  - Data Protection Commissioner of Hungary
    [Website: http://www.naih.hu/]

- **Ireland** –
  - Data Protection Commissioner / An Coimisineir Cosanta Sonraí
    [Website: http://www.dataprotection.ie]

- **Italy** –
  - Garante per la Protezione dei Dati Personali
    [Website: http://www.garanteprivacy.it]

- **Latvia** –
  - Data State Inspectorate
    [Website: http://www.dvi.gov.lv/]

- **Lithuania** –
  - State Data Protection
    [Website: https://www.ada.lt/]

- **Luxembourg** –
  - Commission Nationale pour la Protection des Données
    [Website: http://www.cnpd.lu]

- **Malta** –
  - Office of the Data Protection Commissioner
    [Website: http://idpc.gov.mt/]

- **Netherlands** –
  - College Bescherming Persoonsgegevens (CBP) / Dutch Data Protection Authority
    [Website: http://www.cbpweb.nl]

- **Poland** –
  - The Bureau of the Inspector General for the Protection of Personal Data
    [Website: http://www.giodo.gov.pl/]

- **Portugal** –
  - Comissão Nacional de Protecção de Dados
    [Website: http://www.cnpd.pt]

- **Romania** –
  - The National Supervisory Authority for Personal Data Processing
    [Website: http://www.dataprotection.ro/]

- **Slovakia** –
  - Office for Personal Data Protection of the Slovak Republic
    [Website: http://www.dataprotection.gov.sk/]

- **Slovenia** –
  - Information Commissioner
    [Website: https://www.ip-rs.si/]

- **Spain** –
  - Agencia de Protección de Datos
    [Website: http://www.agpd.es]

- **Sweden** –
  - Datainspektionen
    [Website: http://www.datainspektionen.se]

- **United Kingdom** –
  - UK Information Commissioner – The Office of the Information Commissioner Executive Department (ICO)
    [Website: https://ico.org.uk/]

- Scotland – Scottish Information Commissioner
  [Website: http://www.itspublicknowledge.info/home/ScottishInformation Commissioner.aspx]

- Northern Ireland – Information Commissioner's Office
  [Website: https://ico.org.uk/about-the-ico/who-we-are/northern-ireland-office/]

(4) National Level (UK) – Authorities

Relevant national (UK) regulatory authorities are as follows:

Consumer Associations

- **Office of Fair Trading (OFT)**: protecting consumers by preventing abuse; empowering consumers by giving them access to information and redress; and promoting competitive and responsive supply.
  [Website: http://www.oft.gov.uk]

- **Citizens Advice Bureaux**: quasi-public bodies offering free, confidential, impartial and independent advice.
  [Website: https://www.citizensadvice.org.uk]

Information Security and Fraud Agencies

- **Centre for the Protection of National Infrastructure (CPNI)** protects national security by providing protective security advice. CPNI's advice covers physical security, personnel security, and cyber security/information assurance. It is a merger of the National Infrastructure Security Co-ordination Centre (NISCC) and the Critical National Infrastructure (CNI).
  [Website: http://www.cpni.gov.uk/]

- **Government Communications Headquarters (GCHQ)** ensures that the UK cyber network and infrastructure are safe and secure.
  [Website: http://www.gchq.gov.uk/]

- **Communications-Electronics Security Group (CESG)** protects the vital interests of the UK by providing advice and guidance to the UK government on the security of communications and electronic data, in partnership with industry and academia.
  [Website: https://www.cesg.gov.uk/]

- **Computer Emergency Response Team (CERT UK)** works with partners across industry, government and academia to enhance the UK's cyber resilience.
  [Website: https://www.cert.gov.uk/]

- **National Crime Agency (NCA)** (formerly the Serious Organised Crime Agency) leads UK law enforcement's fight to cut serious organised crime. NCA has national and international reach and the mandate and powers to work in partnership with other law enforcement organisations to bring the full weight of the law to bear on organised criminals.
  [Website: http://www.nationalcrimeagency.gov.uk/]

- **Serious Fraud Office (SFO)** is an independent government department operating under the superintendence of the Attorney General. Its purpose is to investigate and, if appropriate, prosecute those who commit serious or complex fraud, bribery or corruption and to pursue them and others for the proceeds of their crimes.
  [Website: http://www.sfo.gov.uk/]

3.1 BUSINESS REGULATION

3.1.1 Company law and associated responsibilities (incl. company formation)

GLOBAL LEVEL – Laws, Regulations and Norms (examples)

Not applicable: This is an EU regulatory initiative, hence applicable laws, regulations and norms exist only at European Level and below. Company set-up and registration is regulated at European Level and National Level.

GLOBAL LEVEL – Standards, Frameworks and Guidance (examples)

Company Guidance

- Trade Union Advisory Committee to the OECD (TUAC) (2012) "The OECD Guidelines for Multinational Enterprises: Recommendations for Responsible Business Conduct in a Global Context" (Paris).
- Annual reports on the OECD Guidelines for Multinational Enterprises
  - OECD (2014) "Responsible business conduct by sector".
  - OECD (2013) "Responsible business conduct in action".
  - OECD (2012) "Mediation and consensus building".
  - OECD (2011) "A new agenda for the future".
  - OECD (2010) "Corporate responsibility - Reinforcing a unique instrument".
  - OECD (2009) "Consumer empowerment".
  - OECD (2008) "Employment and industrial relations".
  - OECD (2007) "Corporate responsibility in the financial sector".
  - OECD (2006) "Conducting business in weak governance zones".
  - OECD (2005) "Corporate responsibility in the developing world".

- OECD (2004) "Encouraging the contribution of business to the environment".
- OECD (2003) "Enhancing the role of business in the fight against corruption".
- OECD (2002) "Responsible supply chain management".
- OECD (2001) "Global instruments for corporate responsibility".

EUROPEAN LEVEL – Laws, Regulations and Norms

EU company law

- Directive 2013/34/EU on "the annual financial statements, consolidated financial statements and related reports of certain types of undertakings, amending Directive 2006/43/EC of the European Parliament and of the Council and repealing Council Directives 78/660/EEC and 83/349/EEC" (*Company Law (Annual and Consolidated Financial Statements and Related Reports) Directive*) (26 June 2013).
  - [UK] SI 2013/3008 — Small Companies (Micro-Entities' Accounts) Regulations.
- Directive 2012/17/EU "amending Council Directive 89/666/EEC and Directives 2005/56/EC and 2009/101/EC of the European Parliament and of the Council as regards the interconnection of central, commercial and companies registers" (*Central, Commercial and Companies Registers (Interconnection) Directive*) (13 June 2012).
- Council Directive 2007/36/EC on "the exercise of certain rights of shareholders in listed companies" (*Shareholder Rights Directive*) (11 July 2007).
  Implementing legislation (in the UK):
  - [UK] SI 2009/1632 – Companies (Shareholders' Rights) Regulations 2009.
- Directive 2004/25/EC "on takeover bids" (*Takeovers Directive*) (21 April 2004).
- Directive 2009/102/EC "in the area of company law on single-member private limited liability companies (codified version)" (*Twelfth Company Law Directive*) (16 September 2009).
- Directive 89/666/EEC "concerning disclosure requirements in respect of branches opened in a Member State by certain types of company governed by the law of another State " (*Eleventh Company Law Directive*) (21 December 1989).
- Council Directive 82/891/EEC "based on Article 54 (3) (g) of the Treaty, concerning the division of public limited liability companies" (*Sixth Company Law Directive*) (17 December 1982).
- Directive 2012/30/EU on coordination of safeguards which, for the protection of the interests of members and others, are required by Member States of companies within the meaning of the second paragraph of Article 54 of the Treaty on the Functioning of the European Union, in respect of the formation of public limited liability companies and the maintenance and alteration of their capital, with a view to making such safeguards equivalent (Recast)" (*Second Company Law Directive*) (25 October 2012).

- Directive 2009/101/EC "on coordination of safeguards which, for the protection of the interests of members and third parties, are required by Member States of companies within the meaning of the second paragraph of Article 48 of the Treaty, with a view to making such safeguards equivalent (codified version)" (*First Company Law Directive (codified)*) (16 September 2009).
- Council Directive 68/151/EEC on "coordination of safeguards which, for the protection of the interests of members and others, are required by Member States of companies within the meaning of the second paragraph of Article 58 of the Treaty, with a view to making such safeguards equivalent throughout the Community" (First Company Law Directive) (9 March 1968).
- Council Regulation (EEC) No. 2137/85 "on the European Economic Interest Grouping (EEIG)" (25 July 1985).
  Secondary legislation:
  - [UK] SI 1989/191 – European Communities (European Economic Interest Groupings) Regulations.
    Amended by:
    - [UK] SI 2009/2403 and SI 1989/638 – European Economic Interest Grouping Regulations 1989.
    - [UK] SI 2014/2382 — European Economic Interest Grouping and European Public Limited-Liability Company (Amendment) Regulations 2014).
    - [UK] SI 2009/2399 – European Economic Interest Grouping (Amendment) Regulations 2009 [pursuant to the Companies Act 2006]).
- Council Directive 2001/86/EC "supplementing the Statute for a European company with regard to the involvement of employees" (*Employee Consultation Directive*) (8 October 2001).
  - [UK] SI 2009/2401 – European Public Limited-Liability Company (Employee Involvement) (Great Britain) Regulations 2009.
- Council Regulation (EC) No. 2157/2001 "on the Statute for a European company (SE)" (8 October 2001).
  - [UK] SI 2004/2326 – European Public Limited-Liability Company Regulations 2004.
- Council Regulation (EC) No. 1435/2003 on "the Statute for a European Cooperative Society (SCE)" (22 July 2003).
- Council Directive 2006/68/EC of 6 September 2006 amending Council Directive 77/91/EEC as regards the formation of public limited liability companies and the maintenance and alteration of their capital.
  - [UK] SI 2008/719 – Companies (Reduction of Capital) (Creditor Protection) Regulations 2008.

<u>EUROPEAN LEVEL – Standards, Frameworks and Guidance</u>

- Communication COM(2003) 27 "Green Paper: Entrepreneurship in Europe" (21 January 2003).

EBA Guidelines

- EBA/GL/2014/08 — "Guidelines on the remuneration benchmarking exercise".
- EBA/GL/2014/01 — "Guidelines on the applicable notional discount rate for variable remuneration".
- EBA/GL/2012/4 – Guidelines on the Remuneration Benchmarking Exercise

<u>NATIONAL LEVEL (UK) – Laws, Regulations and Norms</u>

Companies Regulation

- Charities Act 2011 c. 25.
- Companies Act 2006 c. 46 [*see also* Limited Liability Partnership Act 2000 c. 12]. *Secondary legislation:*
  - SI 2015/17 — Company, Limited Liability Partnership and Business (Names and Trading Disclosures) Regulations.
  - SI 2013/1947 Companies and Limited Liability Partnerships (Forms, etc.) Amendment Regulations 2013.
  - SI 2014/1602 — Companies (Striking Off) (Electronic Communications) Order 2014.
  - SI 2014/1557 — Companies Act 2006 (Interconnection of Registers) Order 2014.
  - SI 2013/3008 — Small Companies (Micro-Entities' Accounts) Regulations. *Pursuant to the Companies Act implementing EU law:*
  - Council Dire"[UK] SI 2013/1672 ctive 2013/34/EU of 26 June 2013 (*Company Law (Annual and Consolidated Financial Statements and Related Reports) Directive*).
  - SI 2013/1973 — Companies (Receipt of Accounts and Reports) Regulations 2013.
  - SI 2013/2005 – Companies and Partnerships (Accounts and Audit) Regulations. *Pursuant to the Companies Act's implementing the following EU laws:*
    - Council Directive 90/605/EEC of 8 November 1990 (amending *the Fourth and Seventh Company Law (Accounting) Directive*).
    - Council Directive 2009/110/EC of 16th September 2009 (*the Electronic Money Directive*).
    - Council Directive 2006/43/EC of 17 May 2006.

- SI 2013/1970 — Companies Act 2006 (Strategic Report and Directors' Report) Regulations 2013.
- SI 2013/999 — Companies Act 2006 (Amendment of Part 18) Regulations 2013.
- SI 2013/600 — Companies Act 2006 (Amendment of Part 25) Regulations 2013.
- SI 2010/2537 – Companies Act 2006 (Transfer of Audit Working Papers to Third Countries) Regulations 2010.
- SI 2009/2436 – Unregistered Companies Regulations 2009.
- SI 2009/1917 – Overseas Companies (Execution of Documents and Registration of Charges) Regulations 2009.
- SI 2009/1804 – Limited Liability Partnerships (Application of Companies Act 2006) Regulations (as amended by SI 2014/3140 and by SI 2013/618).
- SI 2009/1803 – Registrar of Companies and Applications for Striking Off Regulations 2009.
- SI 2009/1801 – Overseas Companies Regulations 2009.
- SI 2009/1378 – Companies Act 2006 (Extension of Takeover Panel Provisions) (Isle of Man) Order 2009.
- SI 2009/1085 – Company and Business Names (Miscellaneous Provisions) Regulations 2009.
- SI 2009/388 – Companies (Shares and Share Capital) Order 2009.
- SI 2009/214 – Companies (Disclosure of Address) Regulations 2009.
- SI 2008/3014 – Companies (Registration) Regulations 2008.
- SI 2008/495 – Companies (Trading Disclosures) Regulations 2008.
- SI 2008/410 Large and Medium-sized Companies and Groups (Accounts and Reports) Regulations (as amended by SI 2013/1981).
- SI 2008/409 Small Companies and Groups (Accounts and Directors' Report) Regulations.
- SI 2008/373 The Companies (Revision of Defective Accounts and Reports) Regulations 2008 (as amended by SI 2013/2224).
- SI 2006/1644 – Companies (Disclosure of Information) (Designated Authorities) Order 2006.

- Companies (Audit, Investigations and Community Enterprise) Act 2004 c. 27.
  Secondary legislation:
  - SI 2004/3322(C. 154) – The Companies (Audit, Investigations and Community Enterprise) Act 2004 (Commencement) and Companies Act 1989 (Commencement No. 18) Order 2004.
  - SI 2005/1788 – The Community Interest Company Regulations 2005 (as amended by SI 2014/2483 and SI 2012/2335 and SI 2009/1942).
- Enterprise Act 2002 c. 40.

Secondary legislation:

- SI 2014/534 – Enterprise Act 2002 (Merger Fees and Determination of Turnover) (Amendment) Order 2014.
- SI 2014/533 — Enterprise Act 2002 (Mergers) (Interim Measures: Financial Penalties) (Determination of Control and Turnover) Order 2014.
- SI 2013/478 — Enterprise Act 2002 (Part 8) (Designation of the Financial Conduct Authority as a Designated Enforcer) Order 2013.
- SI 2003/1593 – The Enterprise Act 2002 (Consumer Protection) (Part 8 Domestic Infringements) Order 2003.
- Limited Liability Partnerships Act 2000 c. 12.
  Secondary legislation:
  - SI 2008/1913 – Large and Medium-sized Limited Liability Partnerships (Accounts) Regulations 2008.
  - SI 2001/1090 – Limited Liability Partnerships Regulations 2001.
- Company and Business Names (Chamber of Commerce, Etc.) Act 1999 c. 19.
- Companies Act 1989 c. 40.
- Company Directors Disqualification Act 1986 c. 46.
  Secondary legislation:
  - SI 2009/2471 – Companies (Disqualification Orders) Regulations 2009.
- Companies Consolidation (Consequential Provisions) Act 1985 c. 9.
- Business Names Act 1985 c. 7.
- Powers of Attorney Act 1971 c. 27.
- Companies Act 1948 c. 38.

NATIONAL LEVEL (UK) – Standards, Frameworks and Guidance

Company registration

- Companies House (December 2012) "Incorporation and Names".
- Companies House (November 2012) "Life of a Company – Part 1 Annual Requirements".
- Companies House (December 2012) "Life of a Company – Part 2 Event Driven Filings".
- Companies House (October 2012) "Limited Liability Partnership Incorporation and Names".
- Companies House (May 2012) European Economic Interest Groupings.
- Charity Commission (2012) "Charity requirements and guidance".

SUB-NATIONAL LEVEL – Laws, Regulations and Norms

Governance Principle: Governance risk is defined as the risk that the Group's organisational infrastructure fails to provide robust oversight of decision making and the control mechanisms to ensure strategies and management instructions are implemented effectively.

- Governance Policy (Board and Organisation)
- Disposals, Mergers, Acquisitions and Joint Ventures Policy
- Ethics Policy
- Environmental Policy
- Change Management Policy

3.1.2 Insolvency and Mergers & Acquisitions

<u>EUROPEAN LEVEL – Laws, Regulations and Norms</u>

Mergers & Acquisitions

- Council Directive 2011/35/EU concerning "mergers of public limited liability companies" (*Third Company Law Directive*) (5 April 2011).
- Council Directive 2009/109/EC "amending Council Directives 77/91/EEC, 78/855/EEC and 82/891/EEC, and Directive 2005/56/EC as regards reporting and documentation requirements in the case of mergers and divisions" (*Company Law (Amendment No 2) Directive*) (16 September 2009).
  - [UK] SI 2011/1606 – Companies (Reporting Requirements in Mergers and Divisions) Regulations 2011.
- Council Directive 2007/44/EC "amending Council Directive 92/49/EEC and Directives 2002/83/EC, 2004/39/EC, 2005/68/EC and 2006/48/EC as regards procedural rules and evaluation criteria for the prudential assessment of acquisitions and increase of holdings in the financial sector" (*Acquisitions Directive*) (5 September 2007) [Repealed with effect from 3 January 2017]
- Council Directive 2005/56/EC "on cross-border mergers of limited liability companies" (*Cross-Border Mergers Directive*) (26 October 2005).
  - [UK] SI 2007/2974 Companies (Cross-Border Mergers) Regulations (as amended by SI 2015/180).
- Council Regulation (EC) No 139/2004 on "the control of concentrations between undertakings" (*the EC Merger Regulation*)" (20 January 2004).
  - Commission Implementing Regulation (EU) No 1269/2013 "amending Regulation (EC) No 802/2004 implementing Council Regulation (EC) No 139/2004 on the control of concentrations between undertakings" (5 December 2013).
  - Commission Regulation (EC) No 802/2004 "implementing Council Regulation (EC) No 139/2004 on the control of concentrations between undertakings" (EC Merger (Implementing) Regulation) (7 April 2004).

- [UK] SI 2004/1079 – EC Merger Control (Consequential Amendments) Regulations 2004.

Insolvency

- Directive 2006/123/EC "on services in the internal market" (12 December 2006).
  - [UK] Provision of Services (Insolvency Practitioners) Regulations 2009.
- Council Directive 2003/58/EC "amending Council Directive 68/151/EEC as regards disclosure requirements in respect of insolvency" (15 July 2003).
  - [UK] SI 2008/1897 – Companies (Trading Disclosures) (Insolvency) Regulations 2008.
- Council Directive 2001/24/EC on the reorganisation and winding up of credit institutions" (*the Winding-up Directive (Banks)*) (4 April 2001).
- Council Regulation (EC) No 1346/2000 on "insolvency proceedings" (*Insolvency Regulation*). (29 May 2000).
  Amendments:
  - Council Implementing Regulation (EU) No 663/2014 "replacing Annexes A, B and C to Regulation (EC) No 1346/2000 on insolvency proceedings" (*Insolvency (Amendment) Regulation*) (5 June 2014).
  - Council Implementing Regulation (EU) No 583/2011 amending the lists of insolvency proceedings, winding-up proceedings and liquidators in Annexes A, B and C to Regulation (EC) No 1346/2000 on insolvency proceedings and codifying Annexes A, B and C to that Regulation" (*Insolvency (Amendment) Regulation*) (9 June 2011).
  - Council Implementing Regulation (EU) No 210/2010 " amending the lists of insolvency proceedings, winding-up proceedings and liquidators in Annexes A, B and C to Regulation (EC) No 1346/2000 on insolvency proceedings and codifying Annexes A, B and C to that Regulation" (*Insolvency (Amendment) Regulation*) (25 February 2010).
  - Council Regulation (EC) No 788/2008 "amending the lists of insolvency proceedings and winding-up proceedings in Annexes A and B to Regulation (EC) No 1346/2000 on insolvency proceedings and codifying Annexes A, B and C to that Regulation" (*Insolvency Lists Revision Regulation IV*) (24 July 2008).
  - Council Regulation (EC) No 681/2007 "amending the lists of insolvency proceedings, winding-up proceedings and liquidators in Annexes A, B and C to Regulation (EC) No 1346/2000 on insolvency proceedings" (*Insolvency Lists Revision Regulation III*) (13 June 2007).
  - Council Regulation (EC) No 694/2006 "amending the lists of insolvency proceedings, winding-up proceedings and liquidators in Annexes A, B and C to Regulation (EC) No 1346/2000 on insolvency proceedings" (*Insolvency Lists Revision Regulation II*) (27 April 2006).
  - Council Regulation (EC) No 603/2005 "amending the lists of insolvency proceedings, winding-up proceedings and liquidators in Annexes A, B and C to

Regulation (EC) No 1346/2000 on insolvency proceedings Document: OJ 2005 L100/1" (*Insolvency Lists Revision Regulation I*) (12 April 2005).

EUROPEAN LEVEL – Standards, Frameworks and Guidance

- Communication COM(2014) 449 final "White Paper: Towards more effective EU merger control" (9 July 2014).
- European Commission, Competition Handbooks "EU Competition Law: Rules Applicable to Merger Control" (1 April 2010).
- Communication from the Commission to the Council COM/2009/0281 final "Report on the functioning of Regulation No 139/2004" (18 June 2009).
- Communication COM(96) 19 "Community Merger Control – Green Paper on the review of the merger regulation" (31 January 1996).

NATIONAL LEVEL (UK) – Laws, Regulations and Norms

Mergers & Acquisitions

- City Code on Takeovers and Mergers (20 May 2013)
  - SI 2008/3073 – Takeover Code (Concert Parties) Regulations 2008.
- Enterprise Act 2002 c. 40.
  Secondary legislation:
  - SI 2004/1079 – EC Merger Control (Consequential Amendments) Regulations 2004.
  - SI 2014/533 – Enterprise Act 2002 (Mergers) (Interim Measures: Financial Penalties) (Determination of Control and Turnover) Order.

Insolvency

- Financial Services and Markets Act 2000 c. 8 [see ss. 286, 428(3)].
  Secondary legislation:
  - SI 2009/853 – The Financial Markets and Insolvency Regulations 2009.
  - SI 1991/880 – The Financial Markets and Insolvency Regulations 1991.
- Insolvency Act 2000 c. 39.
  Secondary legislation:
  - SI 2006/1030 – Cross-Border Insolvency Regulations 2006.
- Companies Act 1989 c. 40 [see ss. 155 (4) (5), 158 (4) (5), 185, 186 (1), 187 (3)].
- Insolvency Act 1986 c. 45.
  Secondary legislation:
  - SI 2015/391 Insolvency Practitioners (Amendment) Regulations 2015.
  - SI 2014/817 – Insolvency (Commencement of Proceedings) and Insolvency Rules 1986 (Amendment) Rules 2014.
  - SI 2009/356 – Bank Insolvency (England and Wales) Rules 2009.

- SI 2014/583 – Insolvency Proceedings (Fees) (Amendment) Order 2014.
- SI 2006/3107 – Banks (Former Authorised Institutions) (Insolvency) Order 2006.
- SI 2005/524 – Insolvency Practitioners Regulations 2005.
- SI 1994/2507 – Insolvency Regulations 1994.
- SI 1986/2123 – Co-operation of Insolvency Courts (Designation of Relevant Countries and Territories) Order 1986.

SUB-NATIONAL – Laws, Regulations and Norms

- Disposals, Mergers, Acquisitions and Joint Ventures Policy.

3.1.3 Corporate governance, accounting, audit and risk management

GLOBAL LEVEL – Laws, Regulations and Norms

- Sarbanes-Oxley Act (2002) "to rebuild public trust in corporate business and reporting practices", 15 USC Chapter 98 §§ 7201-7266, Public Law 107-204 (30 July 2002), Senate and House of Representatives of the United States of America.
  Important sections:
  - Title I – Public Company Accountancy Oversight Board (PCAOB) (incl. inspections, accounting standards)
  - Title II – Auditor independence (incl. mandatory rotating of registered public accountancy firms)
  - Title III – Corporate responsibility
  - Title IV – Enhanced Financial Disclosure (incl. SEC 404 Management assessment of internal controls)
  - Title VIII – Corporate and criminal fraud accountability
  - Title X – Corporate tax returns
  - Title XI – Corporate fraud and accountability

- The Dodd–Frank Wall Street Reform and Consumer Protection Act, Public Law 111–203; commonly referred to as "Dodd-Frank" (5 January 2010), Senate and House of Representatives of the United States of America.
  Important sections:
  - Title I – Financial Stability (incl. SEC 165 Enhanced supervisions and prudential standards/ capital requirements and resolution planning)
  - Title II – Orderly Liquidation Authority
  - Title IV – Hedge Funds Registration
  - Title V – Insurance

- Title VI – Regulation of Bank and Savings Associations (§ 619 Volcker Rule/ securitisation)
- Title VII – Wall Street Transparency and Accountability (incl. OTC derivatives; swaps)
- Title VIII – Payment, Clearing, and Settlement Supervision
- Title IX – Investor Protections (incl. Regulatory enforcement, Credit Rating Agencies, corporate governance, market abuse, compensation/ whistleblowing)
- Title X – Consumer financial protections (incl. penalties and enforcement powers)
- Title XIII – Mortgage reform

GLOBAL LEVEL – Standards, Frameworks and Guidance (examples)

Corporate Governance

- OECD (2004) "Principles of Corporate Governance" (supersedes the OECD Principles of 1999, endorsed by the member states at the OECD Council meeting at ministerial level on 26-27 May 1999).

Accountancy and Audit

- Public Company Accounting Oversight Board (PCAOB) Rules approved by the US Securities and Exchange Commission (SEC).
- American Institute of CPAs (AICPA): SSAE No 16 for Service Auditors ("Reporting on Controls at a Service Organization") and Clarified Auditing Standard for User Organizations ("Audit Considerations Relating to an Entity Using a Service Organization"). (supersedes SAS70, Standards on Services Organisations).
- Generally Accepted Accounting Principles (GAAP).
  The Accounting Standards Board (ASB) issues standards called Financial Reporting Standards (FRS). The ASB is part of the Financial Reporting Council (FRC), an independent regulator funded by a levy on listed companies.
- International Financial Reporting Standards (IFRS).
  European law requiring that all listed European companies report under International Financial Reporting Standards (IFRSs) since 2005. In the UK, companies which are not listed have the option to report either under IFRSs or under UK GAAP.
- International Accounting Standards Committee (IASC, 2001) "Guidelines for International Financial Reporting Standards".
- Institute of Chartered Accountants in England and Wales (ICAEW), Faculty of Information Technology: FIT 1/94 "Audit Information Systems".
- ICAEW, Audit and Assurance Faculty: AAF 1/06 "Assurance reports on internal controls of services organisations made available to third parties" (supersedes FRAG 21/94) International Accounting Standards (IAS) of the International Accounting Standards Board (IASB) and the International Financial Reporting Standards (IFRS) Foundation.
- ISO 19011:2011 – "Guidelines for auditing management systems"

Compliance, Quality & Risk Management

- ISO 9001:2015 "Quality Management".
- ISO 9001:2008 "Quality management systems -- Requirements".
- ISO 19600:2014 "Compliance management systems — Guidelines".
- ISO 10002:2014 "Quality management — Customer satisfaction — Guidelines for complaints handling in organizations"
- Financial Stability Board (18 November 2013) "Principles for an Effective Risk Appetite Framework".
- ISO 10018:2012 "Quality management -- Guidelines on people involvement and competence".
- ISO 26000:2010 "Guidance on social responsibility"
- IEC 31010:2009 "Risk management -- Risk assessment techniques".
- ISO 31000:2009 "Risk management — Principles and guidelines"
- ISO 9004:2009 "Managing for the sustained success of an organization -- A quality management approach".
- ISO Guide 73:2009 "Risk management — Vocabulary"
- ISO/IEC 38500:2008 "Corporate governance of information technology".
- ISO 9001:2008 "Quality management systems — Requirements".
- ISO 10014:2006 "Quality management -- Guidelines for realizing financial and economic benefits".
- ISO 10019:2005 "Guidelines for the selection of quality management system consultants and use of their services".
- ISO 10005:2005 "Quality management systems -- Guidelines for quality plans".
- ISO 9000:2005 "Quality management systems -- Fundamentals and vocabulary".
- ISO 14001:2004 "Environmental management systems — Requirements with guidance for use"
- ISO 10006:2003: "Quality management systems -- Guidelines for quality management in projects".

EUROPEAN LEVEL – Laws, Regulations and Norms

Accountancy and Audit

- Council Regulation (EU) No 537/2014 on "specific requirements regarding statutory audit of public-interest entities and repealing Commission Decision 2005/909/EC" (*Statutory Audit of Public-Interest Entities (Specific Requirements) Regulation*) (16 April 2014).
- Council Directive 2014/56/EU amending Directive 2006/43/EC on statutory audits of annual accounts and consolidated accounts" (*Statutory Audit (Amendment) Directive*) (16 April 2014).

- Decision No 716/2009/EC establishing a Community programme to support specific activities in the field of financial services, financial reporting and auditing" (16 September 2009).
- Council Directive 2008/30/EC amending Directive 2006/43/EC on "statutory audits of annual accounts and consolidated accounts, as regards the implementing powers conferred on the Commission" (*Statutory Audit (Amendment) Implementing Powers Directive*) (11 March 2008).
- Council Directive 2007/63/EC "amending Council Directives 78/855/EEC and 82/891/EEC as regards the requirement of an independent expert's report on the occasion of merger or division of public limited liability companies" (*Company Law Independent Reports Directive*) (13 November 2007).
- Council Directive 2006/46/EC "amending Council Directives 78/660/EEC on the annual accounts of certain types of companies, 83/349/EEC on consolidated accounts, 86/635/EEC on the annual accounts and consolidated accounts of banks and other financial institutions and 91/674/EEC on the annual accounts and consolidated accounts of insurance undertakings" (*Company Reporting Directive*) (14 June 2006).
- Council Directive 2006/43/EC on "statutory audits of annual accounts and consolidated accounts, amending Council Directives 78/660/EEC and 83/349/EEC and repealing Council Directive 84/253/EEC" (*8th Company Law Directive on statutory audit*) (17 May 2006).
    - [UK] SI 2013/2005 – Companies and Partnerships (Accounts and Audit) Regulations 2013.
    - [UK] SI 2007/3494 – Statutory Auditors and Third Country Auditors Regulations 2007.
    - Commission Implementing Decision 2013/280/EU of 11 June 2013 on the adequacy of the competent authorities of the United States of America pursuant to Directive 2006/43/EC.
    - [UK] SI 2013/1672 – Statutory Auditors and Third Country Auditors Regulations 2013, s. 13.
- Council Directive 2003/51/EC amending Directives 78/660/EEC, 83/349/EEC, 86/635/EEC and 91/674/EEC on the annual and consolidated accounts of certain types of companies, banks and other financial institutions and insurance undertakings (*Accounts Modernisation Directive*) (18 June 2003).
- Directive 2001/65/EC "amending Directives 78/660/EEC, 83/349/EEC and 86/635/EEC as regards the valuation rules for the annual and consolidated accounts of certain types of companies as well as of banks and other financial institutions" (*Fair Value Directive*) (27 September 2001).
- Council Directive 90/605/EEC "amending Council Directive 78/660/EEC on annual accounts ("*the Fourth Company Law (Accounting) Directive*") and Council

Directive 83/349/EEC on consolidated accounts (*"the Seventh Company Law (Accounting) Directive"*)" (8 November 1990).
- [UK] SI 2013/2005 – Companies and Partnerships (Accounts and Audit) Regulations 2013.
- Council Regulation No 1606/2002 on "the application of international accounting standards" (19 July 2002).
- Regulation (2137/85/EC) on "the European Economic Interest Grouping (EEIG)" (25 July 1985).

EUROPEAN LEVEL – Standards, Frameworks and Guidance

- Communication COM(2011) 164 "Green Paper: The EU corporate governance framework" (5 April 2011).
- Communication COM(2010) 561 "Green Paper: Audit Policy: Lessons from the Crisis" (13 October 2010).
- Commission Recommendation 2008/362 on "external quality assurance for statutory auditors and audit firms auditing public interest entities" (6 May 2008).
- Communication COM(2003) 286 "Reinforcing the statutory audit in the European Union" (21 May 2003).
- "Winter Report": Report of the High Level Group of Company experts (2002) on "A modern regulatory framework for company law in Europe" (Brussels).
- Recommendation (2002) "Statutory auditors' independence in the EU: a set of fundamental principles" (16 June 2002).
- Recommendation (2000) "Quality assurance for the statutory auditor in the EU".
- Communication COM(1998) 143/03 "on the statutory audit in the European Union: the way forward" (8 May 1998).
- Communication COM(96) 338 "Green Paper: The Role, the Position and the Liability of Statutory Auditors within the European Union" (24 July 1996).

ESMA Guidance

- ESMA/2014/643 — "Review on the application of accounting requirements for business combinations in IFRS financial statements".
- ESMA/2014/551 — "Activities of the IFRS Enforcers in Europe in 2013".
- ESMA/2013/1664 — "Review of Accounting Practices — Comparability of IFRS Financial Statements of Financial Institutions in Europe".
- ESMA/2013/1022 — "Activity Report of the IFRS Enforcement activities in Europe in 2012".
- ESMA/2013/2 — "European enforcers review of impairment of goodwill and other intangible assets in the IFRS financial statements".

EBA Guidelines

- EBA/GL/2014/03 — "Guidelines on disclosure of encumbered and unencumbered assets".

Compliance, Quality & Risk Management

Not applicable: Binding laws, regulations and norms exist only at other Levels of governance.

EUROPEAN LEVEL – Standards, Frameworks and Guidance

Corporate Governance

- Communication COM(2001) 428 final "European governance: a White Paper" (25 July 2001).

EU corporate governance and auditing

- Guidelines of the European Group of Auditors' Oversight Bodies (EGAOB) and Public Interest Oversight Board (PIOB).
- COSO (The Committee of Sponsoring Organizations of the Treadway Commission): 1. COSO Internal Control – Integrated Framework, and 2. COSO Enterprise Risk-Management Framework.
- COBIT Framework (Control Objectives for Information and related Technology), IT Governance Institute, ISACA.
- ITIL (IT Infrastructure Library, Office of Government Commerce/OGC). ITIL Configuration management database.
- CICA CoCo [Criteria of Control] Framework.
- International Chamber of Commerce (ICC) (2010) "Incoterms 2010 – International Commercial Terms: ICC rules for the use of domestic and international trade terms".
- International Chamber of Commerce (ICC) (2000) "Incoterms 2000 – International Commercial Terms: standard trade definitions for international sales contracts.
- Standards of the International Auditing Practices Committee (IAPC) and the International Accounting Standards Committee (IASC).
- "Guidelines on Auditing Quality" of EuroSAI (29 October 2004).

General Practice Guidance

- PRINCE (Project In Controlled Environment), Office of Government Commerce/ OGC.
- MSP (Management Successful Programmes); Office of Government Commerce/ OGC.

- Capability Maturity Model Integration (CMMI), Software Engineering Institute.
- Project Management Body of Knowledge (PMBOK).

NATIONAL LEVEL (UK) – Laws, Regulations and Norms

Accountancy and Audit regulation

- Local Audit and Accountability Act 2014 [see Schedule 5 and Companies Act, Part 42]
- Companies Act 2006, Part 42: statutory auditors.
  Secondary legislation:
  - SI 2014/2009 – Local Audit (Delegation of Functions) and Statutory Audit (Delegation of Functions) Order.
  - SI 2013/3008 – Small Companies (Micro-Entities' Accounts) Regulations 2013.
  - SI 2013/2005 – Companies and Partnerships (Accounts and Audit) Regulations 2013.
  - SI 2013/1672 – Statutory Auditors and Third Country Auditors Regulations 2013.
  - SI 2011/1487 – Companies Act 2006 (Annual Returns) Regulations 2011.
  - SI 2009/1581 – Companies Act 2006 (Accounts, Reports and Audit) Regulations 2009.
  - SI 2008/410 – Large and Medium-sized Companies and Groups (Accounts and Reports) Regulations 2008.
  - SI 2008/409 – Small Companies and Groups (Accounts and Directors' Report) Regulations 2008.
- Companies (Audit, Investigations and Community Enterprise) Act 2004 c. 27.
- Limited Liability Partnerships Act 2000 c. 12.
  Secondary legislation:
  - SI 2013/2005 – Companies and Partnerships (Accounts and Audit) Regulations 2013.
  - SI 2008/1911 – Limited Liability Partnerships (Accounts and Audit) (Application of Companies Act 2006) Regulations 2008.
  - SI 2008/1912 – Small Limited Liability Partnerships (Accounts) Regulations 2008.
  - SI 2007/3494 – Statutory Auditors and Third Country Auditors Regulations 2007.

NANTIONAL LEVEL (UK) – Standards, Frameworks and Guidance

Corporate Governance

- The Financial Reporting Council (2010) "The UK Corporate Governance Code" (The Combined Code).

- Higgs Report: "Review of the role and effectiveness of non-executive directors" (January 2003).
- Institute of Chartered Accountants in England & Wales (September 1999): The Turnbull Report – "Internal Control: Guidance for Directors on the Combined Code".
- London Stock Exchange, Confederation of British Industry, Institute of Directors, Consultative Committee of Accountancy Bodies, National Association of Pension Funds, Association of British Insurers (January 1998): Hampel Committee, Final Report on Corporate Governance. (The Hampel Report)
- Confederation of British Industry (17 July 1995): Greenbury Report on Directors' Remuneration.
- ICAEW (December 1994): Rutteman Report on Internal Control and Financial Reporting: Guidance for directors of listed companies registered in the UK.
- Financial Reporting Council and London Stock Exchange (December 1992): Cadbury Report on Financial Aspects of Corporate Governance.

3.1.4 Disclosure of electronic documents within civil litigation and official investigations

Note: This is a UK and United States regulatory initiative, hence applicable laws, regulations and norms exist only at National Level. However, as the collection of electronic documents is likely to involve other jurisdictions, this initiative has implications at Global and at European Levels.

NATIONAL LEVEL (UK) – Laws, Regulations and Norms

Disclosure within civil litigations (in England and Wales)

- Civil Procedure Rules
- Crime and Courts Act 2013 c. 22.
  Secondary legislation:
  - SI 2015/230 — Crime and Courts Act 2013 (Consequential Amendments) Order 2015.

Disclosure of Electronic Documents

- Ministry of Justice "Part 31 – Disclosure and Inspection of documents" (10 Sep 2013).
  Supplements:
  - Ministry of Justice "Practice Direction 31A – Disclosure and Inspection. This Practice Direction supplements CPR Part 31."
  - Ministry of Justice "Practice Direction 31B – Disclosure of electronic documents. This Practice Direction supplements CPR Part 31."

<u>NATIONAL LEVEL (UK) – Standards, Frameworks and Guidance</u>

Further guidance is available from the following agencies:

- CPS Crown Prosecution Service
- DoJ US Department of Justice
- DPA Deferred Prosecution Agreement
- ECU Economic Crime Unit
- NCA National Crime Agency
- SFO Serious Fraud Office
- SOCA Serious Organised Crime Agency

3.1.5 Anti-bribery and corruption ("ABC")

Cross-reference: For further information, see also 1.3.1 "Financial Crime: Anti-Money Laundering, sanctions and terrorism".

<u>GLOBAL LEVEL – Laws, Regulations and Norms</u>

Not applicable: Binding laws, regulations and norms exist only at other Levels of governance.

United States

- The Currency and Foreign Transactions Reporting Act of 1970 (legislative framework which is commonly referred to as the "Bank Secrecy Act" or "BSA").
- Patriot Act 2001, Title III.
- Trading with the Enemy Act 1917. (trade with countries deemed to be hostile)
- The Foreign & Corrupt Practices Act (FCPA) 1977.

<u>GLOBAL LEVEL – Standards, Frameworks and Guidance</u>

United Nations Guidance

- UN Global Compact "A Guide for Anti-Corruption Risk Assessment" (2013).
- UN Global Compact "Business Against Corruption: A Framework for Action - Implementation of the 10th UN Global Compact Principle Against Corruption" (2011).
- UN Global Compact "RESIST: Resisting Extortion and Solicitation in International Transactions"(2011).
- UN Global Compact "Global Compact Self Assessment Tool (Management and Anti-Corruption tabs)" (2010).
- UN Global Compact "Reporting Guidance on the 10th Principle Against Corruption" (2009).

- UN Office on Drugs and Crime "Technical Guide to the United Nations Convention against Corruption" (2009).
- UN "Convention against Corruption (UNCAC)" (14 December 2005): United Nations, Treaty Series, vol. 2349, p. 41; Doc. A/58/422.

OECD Guidance

- OECD "Anti-Corruption Ethics and Compliance Handbook for Business", with assistance from the OECD, UNODC, and World Bank. (2013).
- OCED's Guidelines for MultiNational Enterprises (Chapter VII - Combatting Bribery, Bribe Solicitation and Extortion) (2011).
- OECD "Good Practice Guidance on Internal Controls, Ethics and Compliance" (2010).
- OECD Recommendation of the Council on Tax Measures for Further Combating Bribery of Foreign Public Officials in International Business Transactions (25 May 2009).
- OECD Recommendation of the Council for Further Combating Bribery of Foreign Public Officials in International Business Transactions (Adopted by the Council on 25 May 2009 and 26 November 2009), including Annex 1 (Good Practice Guidance on Implementing Specific Articles of the Convention on Combating Bribery of Foreign Public Officials in International Business Transactions) and Annex II (Good practice guidance on internal controls, ethics, and compliance).
- OECD "Guidelines for Multinational Enterprises – Section VII" (2008).
- OECD Convention on Combating Bribery of Foreign Public Officials in International Business Transactions (Adopted by the Negotiating Conference on 21 November 1997).
- OECD Recommendation on Anti-Corruption Proposals for Aid-Funded Procurement: Follow-up report (May 1997).
- OECD Recommendation of the Council on Bribery and Officially Supported Export Credits (14 December 2006).

Transparency International (TI) Guidance

- TI "Countering Small Bribes - principles and good practice guidance for dealing with small bribes including facilitation payments" (2014).
- TI "Diagnosing bribery risk - guidance for the conduct of effective bribery risk assessment" (2013).
- TI "Business Principles for Countering Bribery", 3rd edition (2013).
- TI "Assurance framework for corporate anti-bribery programmes" (2012).
- TI "The 2010 UK Bribery Act Adequate Procedures Guidance on good practice procedures for corporate anti-bribery programmes" (2010).
- TI "Transparency International - ABC anti-bribery checklist" (2009).

- TI "TI's Business Principles for Countering Bribery: Transparency Internationsl Self-Evaluation Tool" (2009).
- TI "TI's Business Principles for Countering Bribery - Small and Medium Enterprise (SME) Edition" (2008).

International Standards Orgainsiations

- ISO 37001 Anti-bribery management system (2016).
- ISO/PC 278 Anti-bribery management systems.
- ISO/WD 37001 Anti-bribery management systems (2014-10-01).
- ISO 26000 social responsibility standard (2010).

International Chamber of Commerce

- ICC "ICC Rules on Combatting Corruption" (2011).
- ICC "Guidelines on Agents, Intermediaries and Other Third Parties" (2010).
- ICC Fighting Corruption - International Corporate Integrity Handbook (2008).
- ICC "Guidelines on Whistleblowing" (2007).

Oher International Organisations

- World Economic Forum "Partnering Against Corruption: Global Principles for Countering Corruption", an initiative of the World Economic Forum in partnership with Transparency International and the Basel Institute on Governance (2014).
- World Forum on Governance "Prague declaration on governance and anti-corruption" (2012).
- Institute of Business Ethics (IBE) "Business Ethics Briefing: The Ethics of Gifts & Hospitality" (2012).
- Good Corporation "Framework on bribery and corruption" (2012).
- The Wolfsberg Group (consists a number of leading international banks) "Wolfsberg Anti-corruption guidelines" (2011).
- Trace International "Trace Due Diligence Guidebook: Doing Business with Intermediaries Internationally" (2010).
- The World Bank "World Bank Group Integrity Compliance Guidelines" (2010).
- International Corporate Governance Network (ICGN) "ICGN Statement and Guidance on Anti-corruption Practices" (2009).
- Association of general counsel and company secretaries of the FTSE 100 (GC100) "Anti corruption compliance – guidance for assessing whether adequate procedures are in place to combat bribery and corruption" (2009).
- FTSE Group "FTSE4Good Countering Bribery Criteria" (2005).

United States

- US Department of Justice (DOJ)/ U.S. Securities and Exchange Commission (SEC) "FCPA A Resource Guide to the U.S. Foreign Corrupt Practices Act" (2012).

EUROPEAN LEVEL – Laws, Regulations and Norms

Cross-reference: For further information, see 1.3.1 "Financial Crime: Anti-Money Laundering, sanctions and Terrorism".

EUROPEAN LEVEL – Standards, Frameworks and Guidance

EU Anti-Fraud and Anti-Corruption initiatives

- Communication COM(2011) 327 "Green Paper: Strengthening mutual trust in the European judicial area – A Green Paper on the application of EU criminal justice legislation in the field of detention" (14 June 2011).
- Amsterdam European Council 2000/C 124/01: "The prevention and control of organised crime: a European Union strategy for the beginning of the new millennium" (27 March 2000).
- Brussels European Council 97/C 251/01: "Action plan to combat organized crime" (28 April 1997).

Guidance

Some guidance, including tools, information exchange and FAQs are provided by the following European organisations:

- The European Anti-Fraud Office (OLAF)
  [Website: http://ec.europa.eu/anti_fraud/index_en.htm]

- The European Union's Judicial Cooperation Unit (EUROJUST)
  [Website: http://www.eurojust.europa.eu]

- The European Police Office (Europol)
  [Website: https://www.europol.europa.eu/]

- Various Council Regulations for specific (payment) sanctions; *e.g.* Council Regulation (EU) No 388/2012 of 19 April 2012 amending Council Regulation (EC) No 428/2009 setting up a Community regime for the control of exports, transfer, brokering and transit of dual-use items.

NATIONAL LEVEL (UK) – Laws, Regulations and Norms

- Crime and Courts Act 2013 c. 22.

- Bribery Act 2010 c. 23.
  Secondary legislation:
  - Civil Recovery Order (CRO)
- Fraud Act 2006 c. 35.
- Criminal Justice Act 2003 c. 44.
- Proceeds of Crime Act 2002 c. 29 (POCA), Part 7.
  Secondary legislation:
  - SI 2009/975 – Proceeds of Crime Act 2002 (References to Financial Investigators) Order 2009.
  - SI 2008/946 – Proceeds of Crime Act 2002 (Investigations in England, Wales and Northern Ireland: Code of Practice) Order 2008.
  - SI 2008/1978 – Proceeds of Crime Act 2002 (Investigative Powers of Prosecutors in England, Wales and Northern Ireland: Code of Practice) Order 2008.
  - SI 2008/1909 – Proceeds of Crime Act 2002 (Disclosure of Information) Order 2008.
  - SI 2007/3287 – Proceeds of Crime Act 2002 (Business in the Regulated Sector and Supervisory Authorities) Order 2007.
  - SI 2006/1070 – Proceeds of Crime Act 2002 (Money Laundering: Exceptions to Overseas Conduct Defence) Order 2006.
  - SI 2003/171 – Proceeds of Crime Act 2002 (Failure to Disclose Money Laundering: Specified Training) Order 2003.
- Civil Contingencies Act 2004 c. 36.
- Courts Act 2003 c. 39.
- Anti-terrorism, Crime and Security Act 2001 c. 24.
- Public Interest Disclosure Act 1998 c. 23.
- Civil Evidence Act 1995 c. 38.
- Contempt of Court Act 1981 c. 49.
- Criminal Law Act 1977 c. 45 (CLA)
- Theft Act 1968 c. 60.
- Criminal Justice Act 1967 c. 80 (CJA)
- The Trading with the Enemy Act 1939 c. 89.
- Prevention of Corruption Act 1906 c. 34 (PCA)

NATIONAL LEVEL (UK) – Standards, Frameworks and Guidance

- Ministry of Justice "Guidance about procedures which relevant commercial organisations can put into place to prevent persons associated with them from bribing (section 9 of the Bribery Act 2010)".
- BS 10500 Anti-bribery management system (2015).
- British Bankers' Association (BBA) "Anti-Bribery and Corruption Guidance – Practical guidance for the banking sector in complying with the Bribery Act 2010 and meeting FCA obligations" (2014).

- BS 10500 Specification for an anti-bribery management system (ABMS) (2011).
- UK Ministry of Justice (2011) "The Bribery Act 2010 Guidance about procedures which relevant commercial organisations can put in place to prevent persons associated with them from bribing".
- UK Ministry of Justice (2010) "The Bribery Act 2010: Quick Start Guide".
- Transparency International "The 2010 UK Bribery Act Adequate Procedures – Guidance on Good Practice Procedures for Corporate Anti-Bribery Programmes" (2010).
- Serious Fraud Office (SFO) "Approach of the Serious Fraud Office to dealing with overseas corruption" (2009).

SUB-NATIONAL LEVEL – Laws, Regulations and Norms

Group Regulatory Risk Principle

Regulatory risk is defined as the risk that the Group is exposed to fines, censure, or legal or enforcement action due to failing to comply with applicable laws, regulations, codes of conduct or legal obligations.

- Compliance, Conflicts of Interest and Market Abuse Policy
- Cross Border Policy
- Legal Risk Management Policy
- Sanctions Policy
- Anti-money laundering Process
- Anti-Bribery Policy
- Whistleblowing Policy

3.1.6 Public procurement

GLOBAL LEVEL – Laws, Regulations and Norms

- UNCITRAL Model Law on Public Procurement (1 July 2011).
- Agreement on Government Procurement (GPA) (15 April 1994) [a WTO Uruguay Round agreement] 1915 UNTS 103.

GLOBAL LEVEL – Standards, Frameworks and Guidance

- ICC "Task Force on Public Procurement" [Website: http://www.iccwbo.org/ about-icc/policy-commissions/commercial-law-and-practice/task-force-on-public-procurement/].
- United Nations Environment Programme (UNEP) "Sustainable Public Procurement Programme" [Website: http://www.unep.org/10yfp/Programmes/Programme ConsultationandCurrentStatus/ Sustainablepublicprocurement/tabid/106267/].

- United Nations Office on Drugs and Crime (UNODC) (2013) "Good practices in ensuring compliance with article 9 of the United Nations Convention against Corruption: Guidebook on anti-corruption in public procurement and the management of public finances".
- OECD (2009) "OECD Principles for Integrity in Public Procurement".
- Chartered Institute of Purchasing & Supply (CIPS) (2013) "Ethical and Sustainable Procurement".

EUROPEAN LEVEL – Laws, Regulations and Norms

- Directive 2014/24/EU "on public procurement and repealing Directive 2004/18/EC" (*EU Procurement Directive (Public Sector)*) (26 February 2014).
  - [UK] SI 2015/102 – The Public Contracts Regulations 2015.
- Directive 2014/23/EU "on the award of concession contracts" (*EU Procurement Directive (Concessions)*) (26 February 2014).
- Directive 2014/25/EU "on procurement by entities operating in the water, energy, transport and postal services sectors and repealing Directive 2004/17/EC" (*EU Procurement Directive (Utilities)*) (26 February 2014).
- Directive 2009/81/EC on "the coordination of procedures for the award of certain works contracts, supply contracts and service contracts in the field of defence and security" (13 July 2009).
  - [UK] SI 2011/1848 – Defence and Security Public Contracts Regulations 2011 ("the DSPCR")
- Directive 2007/66/EC "amending Council Directives 89/665/EEC and 92/13/EEC with regard to improving the effectiveness of review procedures concerning the award of public contracts" (11 December 2007).
- Commission Regulation (EC) No 1564/2005 "establishing standard forms for the publication of notices in the framework of public procurement procedures pursuant to Directives 2004/17/EC and 2004/18/EC of the European Parliament and of the Council" (7 September 2005).
- Directive 2004/18/EC on "the coordination of procedures for the award of public works contracts, public supply contracts and public service contracts" (*European Procurement Directive*) (31 March 2004).
  - [UK] SI 2011/2053 – The Public Procurement (Miscellaneous Amendments) 2011.
  - [UK] SI 2006/5 – The Public Contracts Regulations 2006 ("the PCR") (as amended by SI 2009/2992).
  - [UK] SI 2006/1 – Public Contracts (Scotland) Regulations 2006 ("the Scottish PCR")
- Directive 2004/17/EC of the European Parliament and Council of 31st March 2004 coordinating the procurement procedures of entities operating in the water, energy, transport and postal services sectors.

- [UK] SI 2006/6 – Utilities Contracts Regulations 2006 ("the UCR") (as amended by SI 2009/3100).
- [UK] SI 2006/2 – Utilities Contracts (Scotland) Regulations 2006 ("the Scottish UCR").

- Directive 97/52/EEC "amending Directives 92/50/EEC, 93/36/EEC and 93/37/EEC concerning the coordination of procedures for the award of public service contracts, public supply contracts and public works contracts respectively" (13 October 1997).
- Directive 92/13/EEC "coordinating the laws, regulations and administrative provisions relating to the application of Community rules on the procurement procedures of entities operating in the water, energy, transport and telecommunications sectors" (25 February 1992).
- Directive 89/665/EEC on "the coordination of the laws, regulations and administrative provisions relating to the application of review procedures to the award of public supply and public works contracts" (21 December 1989).
- Council Decision 87/95/EEC on "standardization in the field of information technology and telecommunications" (22 December 1986).

EUROPEAN LEVEL – Standards, Frameworks and Guidance

- Communication COM(2011) 15 "Green Paper on the modernisation of EU public procurement policy – Towards a more efficient European Procurement Market" (27 January 2011).
- Communication COM(2010) 571 "Green Paper on expanding the use of e-Procurement in the EU" (10 October 2010).
- Communication COM(96) 583 "Green Paper – Public procurement in the European Union: Exploring the Way Forward" (27 November 1996).

NATIONAL LEVEL (UK) – Laws, Regulations and Norms

Cross-reference: No Act of Parliament is directly applicable. See applicable UK Statutory Instruments ("[UK] SI") implementing EU law in the corresponding European Level sub-section.

NATIONAL LEVEL (UK) – Standards, Frameworks and Guidance

- Cabinet Office and Crown Commercial Service (27 May 2015) "Information on implementing the 2014 EU Procurement Directives and training materials for procurement professionals".

3.1.7 Contract law and competition

GLOBAL LEVEL – Laws, Regulations and Norms

Not applicable: Binding laws, regulations and norms exist only at other Levels of governance.

GLOBAL LEVEL – Standards, Frameworks and Guidance

International Chamber of Commerce Guidance

- ICC (2012) "Model Contracts and Clauses".
- ICC (2011) "ICC Model International Franchising Contract".
- ICC (2011) "ICC Model Subcontract".
- ICC (2011) "ICC Legal Handbook on Global Sourcing Contracts".
- International Chamber of Commerce (ICC) (2010) "Incoterms 2010 – International Commercial Terms: ICC rules for the use of domestic and international trade terms".
- ICC (2002) "Model Commercial Agency Contract".
- International Chamber of Commerce (ICC) (2000) "Incoterms 2000 – International Commercial Terms: standard trade definitions for international sales contracts.

EUROPEAN LEVEL – Laws, Regulations and Norms

- Directive 2001/115/EC "amending Directive 77/388/EEC with a view to simplifying, modernising and harmonising the conditions laid down for invoicing in respect of value added tax" (*Electronic Invoicing Directive*) (20 December 2001).
- Directive 2000/31/EC on "certain legal aspects of information society services, in particular electronic commerce, in the Internal Market" (*E-Commerce Directive (ECD)*) (8 June 2000).
- Directive 1997/7/EC on "the Protection of Consumers in respect of Distance Contracts" (*Distance Selling Directive*) (20 May 1997).
- Council Directive 93/13/EEC "on unfair terms in consumer contracts" (*Unfair Contract Terms Directive*) (5 April 1993).

Competition encourages companies to offer consumers goods and services at the most favourable terms.

Antitrust regulation

- Commission Regulation (EC) No 773/2004 "relating to the conduct of proceedings by the Commission pursuant to Articles 81 and 82 of the EC Treaty" (7 April 2004).
- Council Regulation (EC) No 1/2003 "on the implementation of the rules on competition laid down in Articles 81 and 82 of the Treaty" (*the Antitrust regulation*) (16 December 2002).

Antitrust rules

- Article 101 of the Treaty on the Functioning of the European Union (TFEU) (25/03/1957; Rome) [This prohibits agreements between two or more independent market operators which restrict competition. The most flagrant example of illegal conduct infringing Article 101 is the creation of a cartel between competitors, which may involve price-fixing and/or market sharing].
- Article 102 of the Treaty on the Functioning of the European Union (TFEU) (25/03/1957; Rome) [This prohibits firms that hold a dominant position on a given market to abuse that position, for example by charging unfair prices, by limiting production, or by refusing to innovate to the prejudice of consumers].

EUROPEAN LEVEL – Standards, Frameworks and Guidance

- Communication (COM(2014) 453 "Ten Years of Antitrust Enforcement under Regulation 1/2003: Achievements and Future Perspectives" (9 July 2014).
- Communication COM(2013) 37 "Green Paper" On unfair trading practices in the business-to-business food and non-food supply chain in Europe" (13 January 2013).
- Communication COM(2010) 348 "Green Paper on policy options for progress towards a European Contract Law for consumers and businesses" (1 July 2010).
- Communication COM(2005) 672 "Green Paper: Damages actions for breach of the EC antitrust rules" (19 December 2005).
- Communication COM(2001) 398 on "European Contract Law" (11 July 2001).
- Standards for interoperability of e-invoice systems (*e.g.* sharing electronic files between companies, complying with Member States' different book-keeping standards):
    - Electronic data interchange (EDI) standards: ANSI X12, EDIFACT, ODETTE.
    - Comma-Separated Values (CSV) file: *e.g.* Request for Comments (RFC) standard.
- Communication COM(96) 721 "Green Paper on Vertical Restraints in EU Competition Policy" (22 January 1997).

NATIONAL LEVEL (UK) – Laws, Regulations and Norms

Cross-reference: For further information, see 3.1.1 "Company law and associated responsibilities (incl. company formation)".

- Companies Act 2006 c. 46.
- Competition Act 1998 c. 41.
    Secondary legislation:
    - SI 2014/536 – Competition Act 1998 (Concurrency) Regulations 2014
    - SI 2000/263 – Competition Act 1998 (Notification of Excluded Agreements and Appealable Decisions) Regulations 2000.

- Sale and Supply of Goods Act 1994 c. 35.
- Supply of Goods and Services Act 1982 c. 29.
- Sale of Goods Act 1979 c. 54.
- Unfair Contract Terms Act 1977 c. 50.
- Misrepresentation Act 1967 c. 7.

NATIONAL LEVEL (UK) – Standards, Frameworks and Guidance

- The Corporate Responsibility Coalition (2007), "The Companies Act 2006: Director's Duties Guidance".
- DTI (June 2007), "Companies Act 2006: Duties of company director – Ministerial statements".
- Institute of Chartered Secretaries & Administrators (2007), "ICSA Guidance on Directors' General Duties".

3.1.8 Finance and taxation law

GLOBAL LEVEL – Laws, Regulations and Norms

In general, taxation is under the authority of States, so that virtually no binding norms exist at the Global Level of governance; nevertheless, some nation-states have so much influence on others, particularly the US, that it is worth while including them in this Matrix.

United States

- Foreign Account Tax Compliance Act (FATCA) (October 27, 2009).

GLOBAL LEVEL – Standards, Frameworks and Guidance

- OCDE (2004) "Guidance Note – Compliance Risk Management: Managing and Improving Tax Compliance" (Forum on Tax Administration, Compliance Sub-group; Committee on Fiscal Affairs, Paris).

EUROPEAN LEVEL – Laws, Regulations and Norms

Tax Regulation

Value added Tax (VAT): "The common system of VAT applies to the production and distribution of goods and services bought and sold for consumption within the European Union (EU). To ensure that the tax is neutral in impact, irrespective of the number of transactions, taxable persons for VAT may deduct from their VAT account the amount of tax which they have paid to other taxable persons." (Europa website: http://europa.eu/ legislation_summaries/taxation/l31057_en.htm).

The EU VAT agreements are only temporary, as Member States are unwillingly to cede their sovereign powers of taxation to the EU. Most EU tax agreements aims to harmonize the Single Market for a competitive e-Commerce tax regime.

- Council Directive 2006/58/EC "amending Council Directive 2002/38/EC as regards the period of application of the VAT arrangements applicable to radio and television broadcasting services and certain electronically supplied services" (27 June 2006).
- Directive 2002/38/EC "amending temporarily Directive 77/388/EEC as regards the value added tax arrangements applicable to radio and television broadcasting services and certain electronically supplied services" (7 May 2002).
- Directive 1999/59/EC "amending Directive 77/388/EEC as regards the value added tax arrangements applicable to telecommunications services" (17 June 1999).
  - Directive 77/388/EEC on "the harmonization of the laws of the Member States relating to turnover taxes - Common system of value added tax: uniform basis of assessment" (*Sixth VAT Directive*) (17 May 1977).

Other EU Tax Regulation

- Council Directive 2008/7/EC "concerning indirect taxes on the raising of capital" (*Capital Duty Directive*) (12 February 2008).
- Council Directive 2003/49/EC on "a common system of taxation applicable to interest and royalty payments made between associated companies of different Member States" (*Interest and Royalties Directive*) (3 June 2003).
- Commission Regulation (EC) No 995/2001 "implementing Regulation (EC) No 2516/2000 of the European Parliament and of the Council modifying the common principles of the European system of national and regional accounts in the Community (ESA 95) as concerns taxes and social contributions" (22 May 2001).

EUROPEAN LEVEL – Standards, Frameworks and Guidance

As taxation is considered by Member States to be within their exclusive competence, guidance is primarily available from Member States national tax offices.

- Communication COM(2010) 695 "Green Paper on the future of VAT – Towards a simpler, more robust and efficient VAT system" (1 December 2010).
- Communication COM(2000) 349 on "administrative cooperation in the field of indirect taxation (VAT), as regards the VAT arrangements applicable to certain services supplied by electronic means" (7 June 2000).
- Communication COM(1998) 374 on "Electronic Commerce and Indirect Taxation" (17 June 1998).

EIOPA Guidelines and Reports

- EIOPA-BoS-14/177 — "Guidelines on loss-absorbing capacity of technical provisions and deferred taxes".

EBA Guidelines

- EBA/GL/2014/07 — "Guidelines on the data collection exercise regarding high earners".
- EBA/GL/2012/5 – "Guidelines on the Data Collection Exercise regarding High Earners".

NATIONAL LEVEL (UK) – Laws, Regulations and Norms

- Finance Act 2013 c. 29.
  Secondary legislation:
  - SI 2013/1962 – International Tax Compliance (United States of America) Regulations 2013.
- Income Tax (Earnings and Pensions) Act 2003 c.1.
- The Finance Act 1999 c.16, The Finance Act 2002 c. 23 and the Finance Act 2003 c. 14.
  Secondary legislation:
  - SI 2003/2682 – The Income Tax (Pay As You Earn) Regulations 2003 (as amended by SI 2013/521).
  - The Income Tax (Pay As You Earn) (Amendment) Regulations 2013.
- Finance Act 1998 c. 36.
- Value Added Tax Act 1994 c. 23.
- Taxes Management Act 1970 c. 9.

NATIONAL LEVEL (UK) – Standards, Frameworks and Guidance

Guidance and forms are available online at Gov.uk [Website: https://www.gov.uk/business-tax/vat].

- HM Revenue & Customs (July 2014) "VAT: exports, dispatches and supplying goods abroad".
- HM Revenue & Customs (1 January 2007) "Business tax – collection: VAT, Business tax, Tax agent and adviser guidance and Dealing with HMRC". This publication covers:
  - Registration, deregistration, change of details, transfer of VAT number, insolvency
  - VAT Returns, payments and corrections
  - International trade and excise
  - International visits and VAT refunds

- VAT accounting schemes
- Option to tax land and buildings
- Forms for individuals, local authorities and other non-business customers
- VAT for motor dealers

<u>SUB-NATIONAL LEVEL – Laws, Regulations and Norms</u>

- Tax Policy

3.2 CONSUMER PROTECTION AND EMPLOYMENT LAW

3.2.1 Consumer protection and Alternative Dispute Resolution

<u>GLOBAL LEVEL – Laws, Regulations and Norms</u>

Not applicable: Binding laws, regulations and norms exist only at other Levels of governance.

<u>GLOBAL LEVEL – Standards, Frameworks and Guidance</u>

International Guidelines

- UN (1985) "United Nations Guidelines for Consumer Protection".
- OECD "Guidelines for Consumer Protection in the Context of Electronic Commerce" (9 December 1999).

ISO standards

- ISO 10003:2007 "Quality management -- Customer satisfaction -- Guidelines for dispute resolution external to organizations".
- ISO 10001:2007 "Quality management -- Customer satisfaction -- Guidelines for codes of conduct for organizations".
- ISO 10004:2012 "Quality management -- Customer satisfaction -- Guidelines for monitoring and measuring".

<u>EUROPEAN LEVEL – Laws, Regulations and Norms</u>

Consumer Protection

- Council Directive 2005/29/EC "concerning unfair business-to-consumer commercial practices in the internal market and amending Council Directive 84/450/EEC, Directives 97/7/EC, 98/27/EC and 2002/65/EC of the European Parliament and of the Council and Regulation (EC) No 2006/2004 of the European

Parliament and of the Council (*Unfair Commercial Practices Directive*)" (UCP) (11 May 2005).

- [UK] SI 2008/1277 – The Consumer Protection from Unfair Trading Regulations 2008.

- Council Directive 2002/65/EC on "distance marketing of financial services and amending Council Directive 90/619/EEC and Directives 97/7/EC and 98/27/EC" (23 September 2002).

- [UK] SI 2004/2095 – Financial Services (Distance Marketing) Regulation 2004.

- Council Directive 98/27/EC on "injunctions for the protection of consumers' interests" (Injunctions Directive) (19 May 1998).

- Council Directive 97/7/EC on "the Protection of Consumers in respect of Distance Contracts" (Distance Selling Directive) (20 May 1997).

- [UK] SI 2000/2334 – Consumer Protection (Distance Selling) Regulations 2000.

- Council Directive 93/13/EEC on "unfair terms in consumer contracts" (5 April 1993).

- [UK] SI 1999/2083 – Unfair Terms in Consumer Contracts Regulations 1999 (UTCCRs).

- Council Directive 85/577/EEC "to protect the consumer in respect of contracts negotiated away from business premises" (20 December 1985).

- [UK] SI 2008/1816 – Cancellation of Contracts made in a Consumer's Home or Place of Work etc Regulations 2008.

- Council Directive 85/374/EEC on "the approximation of the laws, regulations and administrative provisions of the Member States concerning liability for defective products" (Product Liability Directive) (25 July 1985).

EUROPEAN LEVEL – Standards, Frameworks and Guidance

- Communication COM(2008) 794 final "Green Paper on Consumer Collective Redress" (27 November 2008).

- Communication COM(2002) 196 "Green Paper on alternative dispute resolution in civil and commercial law"(19 April 2002).

- Communication COM(2001) 531 final "Green Paper on European Union Consumer Protection" (2 October 2001).

- Recommendation (2001) 310 on "Principles for out-of-court bodies involved in the consensual resolution of consumer disputes" (4 April 2001).

- Communication COM(1999) 396 "Green Paper: Liability for defective products" (28 July 1999).

- Communication COM(98) 50 final "Globalisation and the Information Society: The Need For Strengthened International Coordination" (14 February 1998).

- Guidance on contract law from international organisations such as the International Chamber of Commerce.

- The European Social Charter (signed by the members of the Council of Europe in Turin, 18 October 1961) provides a framework for social rights in order to improve the standard of living and social well-being. It was intended to fill a gap left by the Convention for the Protection of Human Rights and Fundamental Freedoms, which essentially covers only civil and political rights.

NATIONAL LEVEL (UK) – Laws, Regulations and Norms

- Trade Descriptions Act 1968 c. 29.
- Electronic Communications Act 2000 c. 7.
  Secondary legislation:
    - SI 2001/2778 – The Unsolicited Goods and Services Act 1971 (Electronic Communications) Order 2001.
    - SI 2004/3236 – Consumer Credit Act 1974 (Electronic Communications) Order 2004.

NATIONAL LEVEL (UK) – Standards, Frameworks and Guidance

- Office of Fair Trading (OFT)/ Department for Business enterprise & Regulatory Reform (BERR) (May 2008) "Consumer Protection from unfair trading GUIDANCE on the UK Regulations (May 2008) implementing the Unfair Commercial Practices Directive".
- Office of Fair Trading (OFT) (2008) "Business to business promotions and comparative advertisements - A quick guide to the Business Protection from Misleading Marketing Regulations 2008".
- DTI Consumer White Paper "Modern Markets: Confident Consumers" (1999).

3.2.2 Work and employment

GLOBAL LEVEL – Laws, Regulations and Norms

Not applicable: This is an EU regulatory initiative, hence applicable laws, regulations and norms exist only at European Level and below.

GLOBAL LEVEL – Standards, Frameworks and Guidance

- OECD (2004) "Career Guidance and Public Policy: Building the GAP".
- OECD (3 September 2014) "OECD Employment Outlook 2014".

EUROPEAN LEVEL – Laws, Regulations and Norms

- Treaty of Rome, Article 141 (equal pay) ["as applied in a number of recent cases before the European Court of Justice and the domestic courts"]

- [UK] SI 2003/1656 – The Equal Pay Act 1970 (Amendment) Regulations 2003.
- Directive 2003/88/EC on "certain aspects of the organisation of working time" (*2003 Working Time Directive*) (4 November 2003).
- Council Directive 2001/23/EC on "the approximation of the laws of the Member States relating to the safeguarding of employees' rights in the event of transfers of undertakings, businesses or parts of undertakings or businesses" (*Transfers of Undertakings Directive*) (12 March 2001).
  - [UK] SI 2006/246 – The Transfer of Undertakings (Protection of Employment) Regulations 2006 (TUPE Regulations).
- Council Directive 2000/78/EC "establishing a general framework for equal treatment in employment and occupation" (*Employment Equality Framework Directive*) (27 November 2000).
  - [UK] SI 2006/1031 – The Employment Equality (Age) Regulations 2006.
- Council Directive 1998/59/EC on "the approximation of the laws of the Member States relating to collective redundancies" (*Collective Redundancies Directive*) (20 July 1998).
  - [UK] SI 2014/16 – The Collective Redundancies and Transfer of Undertakings (Protection of Employment) (Amendment) Regulations 2014.
- Directive 89/391/EEC on "the introduction of measures to encourage improvements in the safety and health of workers at work" (*European Framework Directive on Safety and Health at Work*) (12 June 1989).

EUROPEAN LEVEL – Standards, Frameworks and Guidance

General employment law are mostly defined at national level.

- Communication COM(2011) 367 "Green Paper: Modernising the Professional Qualifications Directive" (26 June 2011).
- Communication COM(2006) 708 "Green Paper: Modernising labour law to meet the challenges of the 21st century" (22 December 2006).

NATIONAL LEVEL (UK) – Laws, Regulations and Norms

- Immigration Act 2014 c. 22.
  Secondary legislation:
  - SI 2014/3086 — Immigration Act 2014 (Bank Accounts) (Prohibition on Opening Current Accounts for Disqualified Persons) Order 2014.
  - SI 2014/3085 — Immigration Act 2014 (Bank Accounts) Regulations 2014 (as amended by SI 2014/3074).
- Equality Act 2010 c. 15.
- Corporate Manslaughter and Corporate Homicide Act 2007 c. 19.
- Race Relations (Amendment) Act 2000 c. 34.
- National Minimum Wage Act 1998 c. 39.

Secondary legislation:
- SI 1999/584 – National Minimum Wage Regulations 1999.
- Disability Discrimination Act 1995 c. 50 (DDA).
- Social Security (Incapacity for Work) Act 1994 c. 18.
- Social Security Contributions and Benefits Act 1992 c. 4.
  Secondary legislation:
  - SI 2006/799 – The Statutory Sick Pay (General) Amendment Regulations 2006.
  - SI 2002/2822 – The Statutory Paternity Pay and Statutory Adoption Pay (General) Regulations 2002. .
- Social Security Administration Act 1992 c. 5.
- Trade Union and Labour Relations (Consolidation) Act 1992 c. 52.
  Secondary legislation:
  - SI 2014/16 – The Collective Redundancies and Transfer of Undertakings (Protection of Employment) (Amendment) Regulations 2014.
- Social Security Act 1986 c. 50.
  Secondary legislation:
  - SI 1986/1960 – The Statutory Maternity Pay (General) Regulations 1986.
- Social Security and Housing Benefits Act 1982 c. 24.
  Secondary legislation:
  - SI 1982/894 – The Statutory Sick Pay (General) Regulations 1982.
- Race Relations Act 1976 c. 74.
- Sex Discrimination Act 1975 c. 65.
- Employers' Liability (Compulsory Insurance) Act 1969 c. 57.
  Secondary legislation:
  - SI 1998/2573 – The Employers' Liability (Compulsory Insurance) Regulations 1998.

NATIONAL LEVEL (UK) – Standards, Frameworks and Guidance

Guidance produced by the Equality Commission for Northern Ireland (ECNI)

- Equality and Human Rights Commission (2011) "Equality Act 2010 Statutory Code of Practice: Employment Statutory Code of Practice".
- Equality and Human Rights Commission "Quick-start guide to providing equal pay".
- ECNI (2002) "Employment Practice Data Protection Code".
- ECNI (February 1999) "Code of Practice on Equal Pay".

Information Commissioner's Office

- ICO (June 2005) The Employment Practice Code".
- ICO (June 2005) "The Employment Practice Code – Supplementary Guidance".
- ICO (November 2011) "Quick guide to the employment practice code – Ideal for the small business".

- ICO (July 2010) "Personal information online code of practice".
- ICO (May 2011) "Data sharing code of practice".
- ICO (December 2012) "Subject access requests and employment references".
- ICO (2008) "CCTV code of practice".
- ICO (2008) "Data Protection Good Practice Note: Disclosure of employee information under TUPE".

Various central government departments

- BIS (2014): "Guidance on the Transfer of Undertakings (Protection of Employment) Regulations 2006 - for employers, employees and representatives".
- BIS (2014): "Employment rights on the transfer of an undertaking: a guide to the 2006 TUPE Regulations (as amended by the Collective Redundancies and Transfer of Undertakings (Protection of Employment) (Amendment) Regulations 2014)".
- Home Office (June 2013) "Surveillance Camera Code of Practice".
- Health and Safety Executive (April 2012) "Reporting of Injuries, Diseases and Dangerous Occurrences Regulations 1995".
- HM Revenue & Customs (March 2012): "Employer Helpbook for Statutory Maternity Pay".
- HM Revenue & Customs (online):"Statutory Sick Pay: an overview".

SUB-NATIONAL LEVEL – Laws, Regulations and Norms

Group People Risk Principle

People risk is defined as the risk that the Group fails to lead, manage and enable colleagues to deliver to customers, shareholders and regulators leading to reductions in earnings and/or value.

- Remuneration Policy
- Talent & Development Policy
- Employment Policy
- Recruitment Pre-Employment Vetting Policy
- Whistleblowing Policy

3.2.3 Health and Safety

GLOBAL LEVEL – Laws, Regulations and Norms

Not applicable: This is an EU regulatory initiative, hence applicable laws, regulations and norms exist only at European Level and below.

GLOBAL LEVEL – Standards, Frameworks and Guidance

International Labour Standards on Occupational Safety and Health

International Labour Organisation (ILO): The ILO has adopted more than 40 standards specifically dealing with occupational safety and health, as well as over 40 Codes of Practice. Nearly half of ILO instruments deal directly or indirectly with occupational safety and health issues [Website: http://www.ilo.org/].

Fundamental principles of occupational safety and health:

- C187 - Promotional Framework for Occupational Safety and Health Convention, 2006 (No. 187) "Convention concerning the promotional framework for occupational safety and health" Geneva, 95th ILC session (15 Jun 2006).
- C161 - Occupational Health Services Convention, 1985 (No. 161) "Convention concerning Occupational Health Services" Geneva, 71st ILC session (25 Jun 1985).
- C155 - Occupational Safety and Health Convention, 1981 (No. 155) "Convention concerning Occupational Safety and Health and the Working Environment" Geneva, 67th ILC session (22 Jun 1981).

EUROPEAN LEVEL – Laws, Regulations and Norms

- Directive 2009/148/EC on "the protection of workers from the risks related to exposure to asbestos at work" (30 November 2009).
- Directive 2009/104/EC concerning "the minimum safety and health requirements for the use of work equipment by workers at work (second individual Directive within the meaning of Article 16(1) of Directive 89/391/EEC)" (16 September 2009).
- Directive 2008/46/EC amending Directive 2004/40/EC on "minimum health and safety requirements regarding the exposure of workers to the risks arising from physical agents (electromagnetic fields) (18th individual Directive within the meaning of Article 16(1) of Directive 89/391/EEC) (23 April 2008).
- Council Directive 96/29/Euratom "laying down basic safety standards for the protection of the health of workers and the general public against the dangers arising from ionizing radiation" (13 May 1996).
  - [UK] SI 1999/3232 – The Ionising Radiations Regulations 1999.
- Council Directive 90/270/EEC "on the minimum safety and health requirements for work with display screen equipment (fifth individual Directive within the meaning of Article 16 (1) of Directive 89/391/EEC)" (*Health and Safety at Work – Display Screen Equipment Directive*) (29 May 1990).
  - Council Directive 90/269/EEC "on the minimum health and safety requirements for the manual handling of loads where there is a risk particularly of back injury to workers (fourth individual Directive within the meaning of Article 16 (1) of Directive 89/391/EEC)" (*Health and Safety at Work – Manual Handling of Loads Directive*) (29 May 1990).

- Council Directive 89/656/EEC "on the minimum health and safety requirements for the use by workers of personal protective equipment at the workplace (third individual directive within the meaning of Article 16 (1) of Directive 89/391/EEC)" (*Health and Safety at Work – Personal Protective Equipment Directive*) (30 November 1989).
- Council Directive 89/655/EEC "concerning the minimum safety and health requirements for the use of work equipment by workers at work (second individual Directive within the meaning of Article 16 (1) of Directive 89/391/EEC)" (*Health and Safety at Work – Workplace Equipment Directive*) (30 November 1989).
- Council Directive 89/654/EEC "concerning the minimum safety and health requirements for the workplace (first individual directive within the meaning of Article 16 (1) of Directive 89/391/EEC)" (*Health and Safety at Work – Workplace Directive*) (30 November 1989).
- Council Directive 89/391/EEC "on the introduction of measures to encourage improvements in the safety and health of workers at work" (*Health and Safety at Work – Framework Directive*) (12 June 1989).
- Directive 89/391/EEC on "the introduction of measures to encourage improvements in the safety and health of workers at work" (12 June 1989).
  - [UK] SI 2005/1541 – The Regulatory Reform (Fire Safety) Order 2005.
  - [UK] SI 1999/3242 – Management of Health and Safety at Work Regulations 1999.

EUROPEAN LEVEL – Standards, Frameworks and Guidance

- Communication COM(2008) 725 "Green Paper on the European Workforce for Health" (10 December 2008).
- Communication COM(2014) 332 final "EU Occupational Safety and Health (OSH) Strategic Framework 2014-2020" (6 June 2014).
- Communication COM(2014) 0219 final "Green Paper on mobile Health (mHealth)" (10 April 2014).
- Communication COM(2004) 0062 final "on the practical implementation of the provisions of the Health and Safety at Work Directives 89/391 (Framework), 89/654 (Workplaces), 89/655 (Work Equipment), 89/656 (Personal Protective Equipment), 90/269 (Manual Handling of Loads) and 90/270 (Display Screen Equipment)" (*Communication on the practical implementation of directives on health and safety at work*)

European Agency for Safety and Health (EU-OSHA)

- EU-OSHA "Healthy Workplaces Good Practice Awards 2014-2015" (15 April 2015).
- EU-OSHA "exposure to carcinogens and work-related cancer: a review of assessment methods" (15 December 2014).

- EU-OSHA "Calculating the cost of work-related stress and psychosocial risks" (27 June 2014).
- EU-OSHA "Estimating the cost of accidents and ill-health at work: A review of methodologies" (12 May 2014).
- EU-OSHA "Summary - Priorities for occupational safety and health research in Europe for the years 2013–2020" (21 March 2014).
- EU-OSHA "Executive Summary - Analysis of the determinants of workplace occupational safety and health practice in a selection of EU Member States" (16 September 2013).
- EU-OSHA "Worker participation in Occupational Safety and Health – a practical guide" (17 April 2012).
- EU-OSHA "Report - Occupational safety and health and economic performance in small and medium-sized enterprises: a review" (7 July 2009).

NATIONAL LEVEL (UK) – Laws, Regulations and Norms

- Employment Protection Act c. 71.
  Secondary legislation:
  - SI 2002/2677 – The Control of Substances Hazardous to Health Regulations 2002.
- Health and Safety at Work etc Act 1974 c. 37.
  Secondary legislation:
  - SI 2012/632 – The Control of Asbestos at Work Regulations 2012.
  - SI 2007/320 – The Construction (Design and Management) Regulations 2007.
  - SI 2004/3386 – The Control of Substances Hazardous to Health (Amendment) (COSHH) Regulations 2004.
  - SI 2003/2457 – Management of Health and Safety at Work and Fire Precautions (Workplace) (Amendment) Regulations 2003.
  - SI 2002/2676 – The Control of Lead at Work Regulations 2002.
  - SI 2002/2174 – The Health and Safety (Miscellaneous Amendments) Regulations 2002.
  - SI 1998/2306 – The Provision and Use of Work Equipment Regulations 1998.
  - SI 1996/1656 – The Work in Compressed Air Regulations 1996.
  - SI 1995/3163 – The Reporting of Injuries, Diseases and Dangerous Occurrences Regulations (RIDDOR) 1995 [also implements Offshore Safety Act 1992 c. 15 and Railways Act 1993 c. 43].
  - SI 1992/3004 – The Workplace (Health, Safety and Welfare) Regulations 1992.
  - SI 1992/3002 – Workplace (Health Safety and Welfare) Regulations 1992 [esp. §§ 5 & 11].
  - SI 1992/2793 – The Manual Handling Operations Regulations 1992.
  - SI 1992/2792 – Health and Safety (Display Equipment) Regulations 1992.
  - SI 1989/635 – The Electricity at Work Regulations 1989.

- SI 1991/917 – Health and Safety (First Aid) Regulations 1981.
- Fire Precautions Act 1971 c.40.
  Secondary legislation:
  - The Fire Precautions (Workplace) Regulations 1997.

NATIONAL LEVEL (UK) – Standards, Frameworks and Guidance

- HSE (September 2012) "Health and Safety Law: What you need to know".
- HSE (2012) "Working with substances hazardous to health: A brief guide to COSHH".
- HSE (June 2006) "Working with VDUs".
- HSE (2003) "The law on VDUs: An easy guide: Making sure your office complies with the Health and Safety (Display Screen Equipment) Regulations 1992 (as amended in 2002)".
- HSE (2003) "The law on VDUs: An easy guide: Making sure your office complies with the Health and Safety (Display Screen Equipment) Regulations 1992 (as amended in 2002)".
- HSE (June 2011) "Five steps to risk assessment".
- HSE (April 2012) "Advice on non-licensed work with asbestos".
- HSE (April 2012) "What to do if you uncover or damage materials that may contain asbestos".
- HSE (xxx) "Asbestos licence assessment, amendment and revocation guide (ALAARG)".
- HSE (2002) "A guide to the Work in Compressed Air Regulations 1996".
- HSE (2003) "The law on VDUs: An easy guide: Making sure your office complies with the Health and Safety (Display Screen Equipment) Regulations 1992 (as amended in 2002)".
- HSE (2011) "Health and safety made simple - The basics for your business".
- HSE (2009)The Health and Safety (First-Aid) Regulations 1981 - Approved Code of Practice and guidance".

3.3 INFORMATION SECURITY

3.3.1 Electronic signatures

GLOBAL LEVEL – Laws, Regulations and Norms

- Model Law on Electronic Signatures (UNCITRAL 2001).
  Secondary legislation:
  - Uniform Rules on electronic signatures and certification authorities by the United Nations Commission on International Trade Law (UNCITRAL)

<u>GLOBAL LEVEL – Standards, Frameworks and Guidance</u>

- UNCITRAL (Working Group on Electronic Commerce) Draft "Uniform Rules on Electronic Signatures" (12 November 98).
- IETF (Internet Engineering Task Force) Internet-3125 "Electronic Signature Policies" (March 2001.

ITU standards

- X.400 standard for "electronic mail transfer (ITU-T standard)".
- X.509 Public key certificate [ITU standard].
- X.500 standard for "distributed maintenance of files and directories (ITU-T standard)".
- Lightweight Directory Access Protocol (LDAP) standard [for reading X.500 directories].

<u>EUROPEAN LEVEL – Laws, Regulations and Norms</u>

- Commission Decision 2003/511/EC on "the publication of reference numbers of generally recognised standards for electronic signature products in accordance with Directive 1999/93/EC etc." (14 July 2003).
- Directive 1999/93/EC on "a Community Framework for Electronic Signatures" (13 December 1999).
  Annexe I: Requirements for qualified certificates
  Annexe II: Requirements for CSPs issuing qualified certificates
  Annexe III: Requirements for secure signature-creation devices
  Annexe IV: Recommendations for secure signature verification
  - [UK] SI 2002/318 – Electronic Signatures Regulations 2002.
- Commission Decision 2000/709/EC on "the minimum criteria to be taken into account by Member States when designating bodies in accordance with Article 3(4) of Directive 1999/93/EC of the European Parliament and of the Council on a Community framework for electronic signatures (6 November 2000).
- Council Decision 1999/468/EC "laying down the procedures for the exercise of implementing powers conferred on the Commission" (28 June 1999).

<u>EUROPEAN LEVEL – Standards, Frameworks and Guidance</u>

Guidance

- Communication COM(2006) 120 final "Report on the operation of Directive 1999/93/EC on a Community framework for electronic signatures" (15 March 2006).
- Communication COM(97)503 "Ensuring Security and Trust in Electronic Communication: Towards A European Framework for Digital Signatures and Encryption" (8 October 1997).

Electronic Signature Standards – European Commission

- Official recognition of EESSI (European Electronic Signature Standardisation Initiative) standards in OJ, 14.07.03 – Qualified Signatures, Qualified Certificates.

European Telecommunications Standard Institute (ETSI)

- ETSI TS 101 733 "Electronic Signature Formats" for usage of X.509.
- ETSI TS 101 456 "security management and policy requirements".

Encryption Technologies - Industry Standards

- SSL-128B (Secure Sockets Layer), AES (Advanced Encryption Standard), DES (Data Encryption Standard), 3DES, RC4, RSA (Redundant Acronym Syndrome), Hashing (MD5, SHA).
- Secure VPNs with IP Security Protocols (Ipsec).

NATIONAL LEVEL (UK) – Laws, Regulations and Norms

- Electronic Communications Act 2000 c. 7.
- Council Directive 2000/31/EC on "certain legal aspects of information society services, in particular electronic commerce, in the Internal Market" (*Electronic Commerce Directive*) (8 June 2000).

NATIONAL LEVEL (UK) – Standards, Frameworks and Guidance

National Standards

- Self Regulatory body and standards for trust services tScheme (www.tscheme.org. uk).
- Alliance for Electronic Business (tScheme) "HMG Public Key Infrastructure - High Level Processes and Procedures".

3.3.2 Network security and security products (applications)

GLOBAL LEVEL – Laws, Regulations and Norms

- United Nations Convention on the Use of Electronic Communications in International Contracts (2005).

GLOBAL LEVEL – Standards, Frameworks and Guidance

ISO Standards – Information security

- ISO/IEC 27040:2015 "Information technology -- Security techniques -- Storage security".
- ISO/IEC 27036-3:2013 "Information technology -- Security techniques -- Information security for supplier relationships -- Part 3: Guidelines for information and communication technology supply chain security".
- ISO/IEC 27033-1:2009 "Information technology -- Security techniques -- Network security -- Part 1: Overview and concepts".
- ISO/IEC 27013:2012 "Information technology -- Security techniques -- Guidance on the integrated implementation of ISO/IEC 27001 and ISO/IEC 20000-1".
- ISO/IEC 27006:2011 "Information technology -- Security techniques -- Requirements for bodies providing audit and certification of information security management systems".
- ISO/IEC 27005:2011 "Information technology -- Security techniques -- Information security risk management".
- ISO/IEC 27003:2010 "Information technology -- Security techniques -- Information security management system implementation guidance".
- ISO/IEC 27002:2013 "Information technology -- Security techniques -- Code of practice for information security controls".
- ISO/IEC 27001:2013 "Information Security Management System - Requirements. (Replacing BS7799-2).
- ISO/IEC TR 20000-10:2013 "Information technology -- Service management -- Part 10: Concepts and terminology".
- ISO/IEC 20000-2:2012 "Information technology -- Service management -- Part 2: Guidance on the application of service management systems".
- ISO/IEC 18045:2008 "Information technology -- Security techniques -- Methodology for IT security evaluation".

Other global standards

- OECD (2002) "OECD Guidelines for the Security of Information Systems and Networks: Towards a Culture of Security" (25 July 2002).
- OECD "Guidelines for Cryptographic Policy" (27 March 1997).
- BIAC and ICC "Information Security Assurance for Executives – An international business companion to the 2002 OECD Guidelines for the security of networks and information systems: Towards a culture of security" (November 2003).
- Information Security Forum (ISF) "Standard of Good Practice for Information Security" (2011).

- US Federal Information Processing Standards (FIPS):
  FIPS 140-1 level2/3/4 "Crypto Module Evaluation",
  FIPS 186-1 "Standard for DSA",
  FIPS 180-1 "Standard for SHA-1",
  FIPS 46-3 "Standard for 3-DES".
- ITSEC (Information Technology Security Evaluation Criteria) E1, E2, E3, E4, E5 and E6 (ratings)
- US National Institute of Standards and Technology "Advanced Encryption Standard" (AES).

EUROPEAN LEVEL – Laws, Regulations and Norms

Network Security

- Council Framework Decision 2005/222/JHA on "attacks against information systems" (24 February 2005).

Encryption

- N/A no specific encryption law exist within the EU.

Standardised and secured system of registries

- Regulation No 2216/2004/EC for "a standardised and secured system of registries pursuant to Directive 2003/87/EC of the European Parliament and of the Council and Decision No 280/2004/EC" (21 December 2004).

EUROPEAN LEVEL – Standards, Frameworks and Guidance

- Communication COM(2006) 688 on "Fighting spam, spyware and malicious software" (15 November 2006).
- Communication COM(2006) 251 "A strategy for a Secure Information Society – "Dialogue, partnership and empowerment"" (31 May 2006).
- Council Resolution 2003/C 48/01 on "a European approach towards a culture of Network and Information Security" (18 February 2003).

NATIONAL LAW (UK) – Laws, Regulations and Norms

- [Electronic] Communications Act 2003 c. 21.
- Mobile Telephone (Re-Programming) Act 2002 c. 31.
- Private Security Industry Act 2001 c. 12 [Schedule 2].
- Computer Misuse Act 1990 c. 18.
- Official Secrets Act 1989 c. 6.

<u>NATIONAL LEVEL (UK) – Standards, Frameworks and Guidance</u>

British Standard Institute (BSI)

- BS 25999 "Business Continuity Management" (1:2006 Code of Practice, 2:2007 Specification).
- BS 60950-1:2006 "Requirements for ensuring safety of IT equipment".

International Organization for Standardization (ISO)

- ISO/IEC 15408-1:2005 "Information technology -- Security techniques".
- ISO/IEC 15408-1:2009 "Information technology -- Security techniques -- Evaluation criteria for IT security -- Part 1: Introduction and general model".
- ISO/IEC 15408-2:2008 "Information technology -- Security techniques -- Evaluation criteria for IT security -- Part 2: Security functional components".
- ISO/IEC 15408-3:2008 "Information technology -- Security techniques -- Evaluation criteria for IT security -- Part 3: Security assurance components".
- ISO/IEC TR 15443-1:2012 "Information technology -- Security techniques -- Security assurance framework -- Part 1: Introduction and concepts".
- ISO/IEC TR 15446:2009 "Information technology -- Security techniques -- Guide for the production of Protection Profiles and Security Targets".
- ISO/IEC 18028:2006 "Information technology -- Security techniques".
- ISO/IEC 18028-4:2005 "Information technology -- Security techniques -- IT network security -- Part 4: Securing remote access".
- ISO/IEC 18045:2008 "Information technology -- Security techniques -- Methodology for IT security evaluation".
- ISO/IEC TR 19791:2010 "Information technology -- Security techniques -- Security assessment of operational systems".
- ISO/IEC 29128:2011 "Information technology -- Security techniques -- Verification of cryptographic protocols".

ISO – Business Continuity

- ISO/IEC 27031:2011 "Information technology -- Security techniques -- Guidelines for information and communication technology readiness for business continuity".

<u>SUB-NATIONAL LEVEL – Laws, Regulations and Norms</u>

- Information Security Policy
- Internet Usage Policy
- Email Usage Policy
- Physical and People Security (Physical Access) Policy

3.3.3 Cybercrime

<u>GLOBAL LEVEL – Laws, Regulations and Norms</u>

Not applicable: This is an EU regulatory initiative, hence applicable laws, regulations and norms exist only at European Level and below.

<u>GLOBAL LEVEL – Standards, Frameworks and Guidance</u>

US Cyber strategy

- National Institute of Standards and Technology (12 February 2014) "Framework for Improving Critical Infrastructure Cybersecurity".
- The White House Washington (February 2015) "National Security Strategy".
- The White House Washington (12 February 2013) "President's Executive Order on Drawing up a Strategy for Improving Critical Infrastructure Cybersecurity".
- The White House Washington (February 2003) "The National Strategy to Secure Cyberspace".
- Department of Defense Strategy for Operating in Cyberspace (July 2011) "The Five strategic initiatives".
- The White House Washington (May 2011) "International Strategy for Cyberspace. Prosperity, Security, and Openness in a Networked World".
- The White House Washington (2009) "Cyberspace Policy Review: Assuring a Trusted and Resilient Information and Communications Infrastructure".

<u>EUROPEAN LEVEL – Laws, Regulations and Norms</u>

Cybercrime

- Joint Commission to the European Parliament, the Council, the European Economic and Social Committee and the Committee of the Regions, High Representative of the European Union for Foreign Affairs and Security Policy JOIN (2013)" Cybersecurity Strategy of the European Union: An Open, Safe and Secure Cyberspace" (7 February 2013).
- Council Framework Decision 2005/222/JHA on "attacks against information systems" (24 February 2005).
- Council of Europe Convention on Cybercrime CETS No 185 (23 November 2001).

<u>EUROPEAN LEVEL – Standards, Frameworks and Guidance</u>

- Proposal for a Directive COM(2013)48 "concerning measures to ensure a high common level of network and information security across the Union" (7 February 2013).

NATIONAL LEVEL (UK) – Laws, Regulations and Norms

- Intelligence Services Act 1994 c. 13.
- Computer Misuse Act 1990 c. 18.
- Police and Justice Act 2006 Part 5 c. 48.
- Police and Justice Act 2006 (Commencement No 9) Order 2008 No 2503 c. 107.
- Serious Crime Act 2007 c. 27
- Police and Justice Act 2006 c. 48 [esp. §§ 35-40].
- Serious Organised Crime and Police Act 2005 c. 15.
- Police and Criminal Evidence Act 1984 c. 60.

NATIONAL LEVEL (UK) – Standards, Frameworks and Guidance

- CESG, Cabinet Office, Centre for the Protection of National Infrastructure and Department for Business, Innovation & Skills (16 January 2015) "Cyber security guidance for business: 10 Steps".
- GCHQ (16 Jan 2015) "10 Steps to Cyber Security".
- Department for Business Innovation & Skills ref BIS/15/37 (January 2015) "FTSE 350 Cyber Governance Health Check Summary".
- HM Government (January 2015) "Cyber essentials Scheme – Assurance Framework".
- GCHQ, CERT-UK (2015) "Common Cyber Attacks: Reducing the Impact".
- HM Government (January 2015) "FTSE 350 Cyber Governance Health Check Tracker Report".
- HM Government, Department for Business, Innovation and Skills (June 2014) "Cyber Essentials Scheme: Requirements for basic technical protection from cyber attacks".
- Department for Business, Innovation and Skills (BIS) (2012) "Cyber Risk Management: A Board Level responsibility".
- CESG (2012) "Executive Companion: 10 Steps to Cyber Security".
- Cabinet Office, Written Ministerial Statement (25 November 2011) "Minister for the Cabinet Office and Paymaster General: The UK Cyber Security Strategy: Protecting and Promoting the UK in a Digital World".
- Cabinet Office (November 2011) "The UK Cyber Security Strategy: Protecting and promoting the UK in a digital world".
- HM Government (October 2010) "A Strong Britain in an Age of Uncertainty: The National Security Strategy".

3.3.4 Security for passports and visas

<u>GLOBAL LEVEL – Laws, Regulations and Norms</u>

Not applicable: Binding laws, regulations and norms exist only at other Levels of governance.

<u>GLOBAL LEVEL – Standards, Frameworks and Guidance</u>

ISO Biometrics Standards

- ISO/IEC 19784-1:2006 "Information technology – Biometric application programming interface – Part 1: BioAPI specification".
- ISO/IEC 19784-1:2006/Amd 3:2010 "Support for interchange of certificates and security assertions, and other security aspects".
- ISO/IEC 19784-2:2007 "Information technology – Biometric application programming interface – Part 2: Biometric archive function provider interface".
- ISO/IEC 19784-4:2011 "Information technology – Biometric application programming interface – Part 4: Biometric sensor function provider interface".
- ISO/IEC 19785-1:2006 "Information technology – Common Biometric Exchange Formats Framework – Part 1: Data element specification".
- ISO/IEC 19785-2:2006 "Information technology – Common Biometric Exchange Formats Framework – Part 2: Procedures for the operation of the Biometric Registration Authority".
- ISO/IEC 19785-3:2007 "Information technology – Common Biometric Exchange Formats Framework – Part 3: Patron format specifications".
- ISO/IEC 19785-4:2010 "Information technology – Common Biometric Exchange Formats Framework – Part 4: Security block format specifications".
- ISO/IEC 19794-1:2011 "Information technology – Biometric data interchange formats – Part 1: Framework".
- ISO/IEC 19794-2:2005 "Information technology – Biometric data interchange formats – Part 2: Finger minutiae data".
- ISO/IEC 19794-3:2006 "Information technology – Biometric data interchange formats – Part 3: Finger pattern spectral data".
- ISO/IEC 19794-4:2005 "Information technology – Biometric data interchange formats – Part 4: Finger image data".
- ISO/IEC 19794-6:2005 "Information technology – Biometric data interchange formats – Part 6: Iris image data".
- ISO/IEC 19794-7:2014 "Information technology – Biometric data interchange formats – Part 7: Signature/sign time series data".
- ISO/IEC 19795-1:2006 "Information technology – Biometric performance testing and reporting – Part 1: Principles and framework".

- ISO/IEC 19795-2:2007 "Information technology – Biometric performance testing and reporting –Part 2: Testing methodologies for technology and scenario evaluation".
- ISO/IEC TR 19795-3:2007 "Information technology – Biometric performance testing and reporting – Part 3: Modality-specific testing".
- ISO/IEC 19795-4:2008 "Information technology – Biometric performance testing and reporting – Part 4: Interoperability performance testing".
- ISO/IEC 19795-5:2011 "Information technology – Biometric performance testing and reporting – Part 5: Access control scenario and grading scheme".
- ISO/IEC 19795-6:2012 "Information technology – Biometric performance testing and reporting – Part 6: Testing methodologies for operational evaluation".
- ISO/IEC 19795-7:2011 "Information technology – Biometric performance testing and reporting – Part 7: Testing of on-card biometric comparison algorithms".
- ISO/IEC 29794-1:2009 "Information technology – Biometric sample quality – Part 1: Framework".
- ISO/IEC WD 29794-4 "Information technology – Biometric sample quality – Part 4: Finger image data".
- ISO/IEC TR 29794-5:2010 "Information technology – Biometric sample quality – Part 5: Face image data".
- ISO/IEC FDIS 29794-6 "Information technology – Biometric sample quality – Part 6: Iris image data".

EUROPEAN LEVEL – Laws, Regulations and Norms

Standards for security features and biometrics in passports

- Council Regulation No 2252/2004 on "standards for security features and biometrics in passports and travel documents issued by Member States" (13 December 2004).

Visa Information

- Council Decision 2004/512/EC "establishing the Visa Information System (VIS)" (8 June 2004).

EUROPEAN LEVEL – Standards, Frameworks and Guidance

Cross-reference: For further information, see Global Level.

NATIONAL LEVEL (UK) – Laws, Regulations and Norms

Not applicable: This is an EU regulatory initiative, hence applicable laws, regulations and norms exist only at European Level and below.

<u>NATIONAL LEVEL (UK) – Standards, Frameworks and Guidance</u>

Not applicable: This is an Global initiative, hence applicable standards, frameworks and guidance exist only at Global Level.

3.4 DATA PROTECTION AND PRIVACY RIGHTS

3.4.1 General data protection and privacy

Cross-reference: For further information, see also 3.4.4 "Access to information and investigations".

<u>GLOBAL LEVEL – Laws, Regulations and Norms</u>

- United Nations "Universal Declaration of Human Rights" (10 December 1948).

<u>GLOBAL LEVEL – Standards, Frameworks and Guidance</u>

EU-US Data Protection Umbrella Agreement)

- European Commission C-131/12 ~Factsheet on the Right to be Forgotten ruling" (13 May 2014).
- EU-US Summit Joint Statement 8228/14, PRESSE 190 (26 March 2014) [14. Data protection and privacy].
- Communication COM(2013) 846 final on "Rebuilding Trust in EU-US Data Flows" (27 November 2013).
- Joint Press Statement following the EU-US-Justice and Home Affairs Ministerial Meeting in Washington (18 November 2013).

Binding Corporate Rules (BCRs)

- Article 29 Data Protection Working Party 1271-00-00/08/EN, WP 153 "Working Document setting up a table with the elements and principles to be found in Binding Corporate Rules" (24 June 2008).
- Article 29 Data Protection Working Party 1271-00-01/08/EN, WP 154 "Working Document setting up a framework for the structure of Binding Corporate Rules" (24 June 2008).
- Article 29 Data Protection Working Party 1271-04-02/08/EN, WP 155 rev.04 "Working Document on Frequently Asked Questions (FAQs) related to Binding Corporate Rules" (24 June 2008, As last Revised and adopted on 8 April 2009).
- Article 29 Data Protection Working Party WP133 "Recommendation 1/2007 on the Standard Application for Approval of Binding Corporate Rules for the Transfer of Personal Data" (10 January 2007).

- Article 29 Data Protection Working Party 05/EN, WP107 "Working Document Setting Forth a Co-Operation Procedure for Issuing Common Opinions on Adequate Safeguards Resulting From 'Binding Corporate Rules' " (14 April 2005).
- Article 29 Data Protection Working Party 05/EN, WP108 "Working Document Establishing a Model Checklist Application for Approval of Binding Corporate Rules" (14 April 2005).
- Article 29 Data Protection Working Party 11639/02/EN, WP 74 "Working Document: Transfers of personal data to third countries: Applying Article 26 (2) of the EU Data Protection Directive to Binding Corporate Rules for International Data Transfers" (3 June 2003).

ISO Privacy Standards

- ISO/IEC 15944-8:2012 "Information technology -- Business Operational View -- Part 8: Identification of privacy protection requirements as external constraints on business transactions".
- ISO/IEC 29101:2013 "Information technology -- Security techniques -- Privacy architecture framework".
- Chartered Accountants of Canada (CICA) and the American Institute of Certified Public Accountants (AICPA) - AICPA/CICA Privacy Task Force "Generally Accepted Privacy Principles (GAPP)".

EUROPEAN LEVEL – Laws, Regulations and Norms

Human Rights in the European Union

- Council of Europe "Convention for the Protection of Human Rights and Fundamental Freedoms as amended by Protocols No. 11 and No. 14" (Rome, 4.XI.1950), Protocol No. 14 (CETS No. 194) as from the date of its entry into force on 1 June 2010.
- Charter of Fundamental Rights of the European Union (2000/C 364/01) (Article 8 "Protection of personal data"), Solemn Proclamation by the European Parliament, the Council and the Commission (18 December 2000).
- Council of Europe "Convention for the Protection of Individuals with regard to Automatic Processing of Personal Data", Strasbourg (28 January 1981).
- Council of Europe, The European Convention on Human Rights "The European Convention on Human Rights and its Five Protocols", Rome (4 November 1950).
- Council of Europe, The European Convention on Human Rights "Convention for the Protection of Human Rights and Fundamental Freedoms", Rome (4 November 1950, last amendments on 1 June 2010).

Data Protection Directive/ Regulation

- European Parliament legislative resolution ((COM(2012)0011 – C7-0025/2012 – 2012/0011(COD)) on the proposal "on the protection of individuals with regard to the processing of personal data and on the free movement of such data (*General Data Protection Regulation*)" (12 March 2014).
- Proposal for a Regulation COM(2012) 11 final on "the protection of individuals with regard to the processing of personal data and on the free movement of such data (*General Data Protection Regulation*)" (25 January 2012).
  Note: This new General Data Protection Regulation is to come into force in 2016.
- Directive 97/66/EC on "processing of personal data and the protection of privacy in the telecommunications sector" (15 December 1997).
  - [UK] SI 1999/2093 – The Telecommunications (Data Protection and Privacy) Regulations 1999.
  - [UK] SI 1998/3170 – The Telecommunications (Data Protection and Privacy) (Direct Marketing) Regulations 1998.
  - [UK] SI 2000/2699 – Telecommunications (Lawful Business Practice) (Interception of Communications) Regulation 2000 [implementing ePrivacy Article 5.2].
- Directive 95/46/EC on "the protection of individuals with regard to the processing of personal data and on the free movement of such data" (*Data Protection Directive*) (24 October 1995).

Protection of personal data in relation to electronic communications networks and Data Retention

- Directive 2006/24/EC on "the retention of data generated or processed in connection with the provision of publicly available electronic communication services or of public communications networks amending Directive (2002/58/EC)" (*Data Retention Directive*) (15 March 2006).
- Directive 2002/58/EC on "processing of personal data and protection of privacy in the electronic communications sector" (*Privacy and electronic communications Directive*) (12 July 2002).

EUROPEAN LEVEL – Standards, Frameworks and Guidance

- Communication COM(2012) 9 final "Safeguarding Privacy in a Connected World – A European Data Protection Framework for the 21st Century" (25 January 2012).

Data Protection Working Party Guidance

Data Protection Working Party [established by Article 29 of Directive 95/46/EC as an independent EU Advisory Body on Data Protection and Privacy]:

- Article 29 Data Protection Working Party "Working Document on on-line authentication services (10054/03)" (29 January 2003).
- Article 29 Data Protection Working Party WP28 "Opinion 2/2000 concerning the general review of the telecommunications legal framework; presented by the Internet Task Force" (3 February 2000).
- Article 29 Data Protection Working Party WP28 "Opinion 1/2000 on certain data protection aspects of electronic commerce; presented by the Internet task force" (3 February 2000).
- Article 29 Data Protection Working Party WP25 "Recommendation 3/99 on the preservation of traffic data by Internet Service Providers for law enforcement purposes" (7 September 1999).

NATIONAL LEVEL (UK) – Laws, Regulations and Norms

- Freedom of Information Act 2000 c. 36.
- Data Protection Act 1998 c. 29 (eight key principles for European data protection in appendix).
  Secondary legislation:
  - SI 2015/312 — Data Protection Act 1998 (Commencement No 4) Order 2015.
  - SI 2006/2068 – Data Protection (Processing of Sensitive Personal Data) Order 2006.
  - SI 2009/1811 – Data Protection (Processing of Sensitive Personal Data) Order 2009.
  - SI 2000/417 – Data Protection (Processing of Sensitive Personal Data) Order 2000.
  - SI 2000/188 – Data Protection (Notification and Notification Fees) Regulations 2000.

NATIONAL LEVEL (UK) – Standards, Frameworks and Guidance

Cross-reference: For further information, see also 3.4.4 "Data protection and investigations".

ICO ([UK] Information Commissioners Office) Guidance).

ICO Data Protection

- ICO (25 February 2014) "Conducting privacy impact assessments code of practice".

- ICO Subject access code of practice/ checklist (August 2013) "How do I handle subject access requests? –Dealing with requests from individuals for personal information"
- ICO (20 December 2012) "Data Protection Act – Buying and selling customer databases".

Data Protection Employment Guidance
- ICO "(November 2011) Quick guide to the employment practices code: Ideal for the small business".
- ICO (November 2011) "The employment practices code".
- ICO (June 2005) "The Employment Practice Code: Supplementary Guidance".
- ICO (February 2014) "Subject access code of practice: Dealing with requests from individuals for personal information".

Processing personal data fairly and lawfully (Principle 1)
- ICO (20 December 1212) "Collecting information about your customers – small business checklist".

Retaining personal data (Principle 5)
- ICO (26 February 2014) "Deleting personal data".

The rights of individuals (Principle 6)
- ICO (24 October 213) "Direct marketing: Data Protection Act/ Privacy and Electronic Communications Regulations:"
- ICO (September 2013) "Direct marketing checklist".

Information security (Principle 7)
- Canon "A Practical Guide to Print Security Ideal for Businesses of All Sizes".
- Get Safe Online – Free expert Advice
  [Website: https://www.getsafeonline.org].

Various
- ICO (21 May 2015) "In the picture: A data protection code of practice for surveillance cameras and personal information".
- ICO (1 April 2014) "How we deal with complaints and concerns: A guide for data controllers".
- ICO (28 February 2012) "Assessing Adequacy International data transfer".
- ICO (28 February 2012) "Outsourcing: A guide for small and medium-sized businesses".
- ICO (20 November 2012) "Anonymisation: managing data protection risk code of practice summary".

ICO Freedom of Information

- ICO Good practice note "Advice on using the procedural codes of practice"
- ICO Good practice note "ICO policy on publication schemes"
- ICO Good practice note "Time constraints on considering the public interest"

3.4.2 Records management and data retention

<u>GLOBAL LEVEL – Laws, Regulations and Norms</u>

Not applicable: Binding laws, regulations and norms exist only at other Levels of governance.

<u>GLOBAL LEVEL – Standards, Frameworks and Guidance</u>

Information Management, Records Management and Data Retention

- ISO/IEC 24775-1:2014 "Information technology -- Storage management -- Part 1: Overview".
- ISO/TR 14873:2013 "Information and documentation -- Statistics and quality issues for web archiving".
- ISO 26324:2012 "Information and documentation -- Digital object identifier system".
- ISO 19005-3:2012 "Document management -- Electronic document file format for long-term preservation -- Part 3: Use of ISO 32000-1 with support for embedded files (PDF/A-3)".
- ISO/TR 23081-3:2011 "Information and documentation -- Managing metadata for records -- Part 3: Self-assessment method".
- ISO 30300:2011 "Information and documentation -- Management systems for records -- Fundamentals and vocabulary".
- ISO 19005-2:2011 "Document management -- Electronic document file format for long-term preservation -- Part 2: Use of ISO 32000-1 (PDF/A-2)".
- ISO 10789:2011 "Space systems -- Programme management -- Information and documentation management".
- ISO/TS 8000-150:2011 "Data quality -- Part 150: Master data: Quality management framework".
- ISO/TR 13028:2010 "Information and documentation - Implementation guidelines for digitization of records".
- ISO 10244:2010 "Document management -- Business process baselining and analysis".
- ISO 23081-2:2009 "Information and documentation -- Managing metadata for records -- Part 2: Conceptual and implementation issues".
- ISO/TR 22957:2009 "Document management -- Analysis, selection and implementation of electronic document management systems (EDMS)".
- ISO/TR 15801:2009 "Document management -- Information stored electronically -- Recommendations for trustworthiness and reliability".
- ISO/TR 10255:2009 "Document management applications -- Optical disk storage technology, management and standards ".

- ISO/TR 26122:2008 "Information and documentation -- Work process analysis for records".
- ISO 23081-1:2006 "Information and documentation -- Records management processes -- Metadata for records -- Part 1: Principles".
- ISO/TR 18492:2005 "Long-term preservation of electronic document-based information".
- ISO 19005-1:2005 "Document management -- Electronic document file format for long-term preservation -- Part 1: Use of PDF 1.4 (PDF/A-1)".
- ISO 15489-1:2001 "Information and documentation -- Records management -- Part 1: General".
- ISO/TR 15489-2:2001 "Information and documentation -- Records management -- Part 2: Guidelines".

EUROPEAN LEVEL – Laws, Regulations and Norms

- Directive 2006/24/EC on "the retention of data generated or processed in connection with the provision of publicly available electronic communications services or of public communications networks and amending Directive 2002/58/EC" (*Data Retention Directive*) (15 March 2006).
  - [UK] SI 2009/859 [draft] – The Data Retention (EC Directive) Regulations 2009.
  - [UK] SI 2007/2199 – Data Retention (EC) Regulation 2007.

NATIONAL LEVEL (UK) – Laws, Regulations and Norms

Cross-reference: No Act of Parliament is directly applicable. See applicable UK Statutory Instruments ("[UK] SI") implementing EU law in the corresponding European Level sub-section.

NATIONAL LEVEL (UK) – Standards, Frameworks and Guidance

Cross-reference: For further information, see also 3.4.1 "General data protection and privacy".

- BS 5454:2000 "Recommendations for the storage and exhibition of archival documents".
- BS ISO/IEC 10918-4:1999 "Information technology. Digital compression and coding of continuous-tone still images". [Registration of JPEG profiles, SPIFF profiles, SPIFF tags, SPIFF colour spaces, APPn markers, SPIFF compression types, and Registration Authorities (REGAUT)]
- PD 0006:1995 "Technical guide to JPEG. Digital compression of photographic images".
- HMG Infosec Standard 5 (IS5) on "data destruction".
- CESG (Communications-Electronics Security Group) IT Security Standards (Infosec Standard No. 1).

SUB-NATIONAL LEVEL (UK) – Standards, Frameworks and Guidance

Storage Devices/Interfaces

- Fibre Channel, Serial ATA (SATA), Serial Attached SCSI (SAS), parallel SCSI.
- DAS (Direct-Attached Storage) and FAS (Fabric-Attached Storage).
- Virtual Tape Libraries (VTL).

3.4.3 Pan-European data transfer

GLOBAL LEVEL – Laws, Regulations and Norms

Not applicable: This is an EU regulatory initiative, hence applicable laws, regulations and norms exist only at European Level and below.

GLOBAL LEVEL – Standards, Frameworks and Guidance

Not applicable: This is an EU regulatory initiative, hence applicable standards, frameworks and guidance exist only at European Level and below.

EUROPEAN LEVEL – Laws, Regulations and Norms

- Council Directive 2002/58/EC "concerning the processing of personal data and the protection of privacy in the electronic communications sector" (Directive on privacy and electronic communications) (12 July 2002).
  - [UK] SI 2003/2426 – The Privacy and Electronic Communications (EC Directive) Regulations 2003.

Protection from misuse of individuals' personal data by Community bodies

- Council Decision (2004/644/EC) adopting implementing rules concerning Regulation (EC) No 45/2001 on "the protection of individuals with regard to the processing of personal data by the Community institutions and bodies and on the free movement of such data" (13 September 2004).
- Regulation (EC) No 2001/45 on "the protection of individuals with regard to the processing of personal data by the institutions and bodies of the Community and on the free movement of such data" (18 December 2000).

Transmission of data to the Commission

- Commission Regulation 9 (EC) No 179/2005 amending Regulation (EC) No 1917/2000 with regard to the transmission of data to the Commission (2 February 2005).

Alternative set of standard contractual clauses for transfer of personal data to third countries

- Commission Decision (2004)915 "amending Decision (2001/497/EC) as regards the introduction of an alternative set of standard contractual clauses for the transfer of personal data to third countries" (27 December 2004).
- Commission Decision (2000)2441 "pursuant to Directive 95/46/EC of the European Parliament and of the Council on the adequacy of the protection provided by the safe harbour privacy principles and related frequently asked questions issued by the US Department of Commerce" (26 July 2000).

EUROPEAN LEVEL – Standards, Frameworks and Guidance

Cross-reference: For further information, see 3.4.1 "General data protection and privacy".

- Resolution (2000)0177 "European Parliament Resolution: Safe Harbour Privacy Principles", developed by the U.S. Department of Commerce in consultation with the European Commission (22 June 2000).

NATIONAL LEVEL (UK) – Laws, Regulations and Norms

Cross-reference: No Act of Parliament is directly applicable. See applicable UK Statutory Instruments ("[UK] SI") implementing EU law in the corresponding European Level sub-section.

NATIONAL LEVEL (UK) – Standards, Frameworks and Guidance

- ICO (29 April 2010) "Data Protection Act 1998: The eighth data protection principle and international data transfers".
- ICO (10 June 2013) "Binding Corporate Rules Authorisation".

3.4.4 Access to information and investigations

Cross-reference: For further information, see also 3.4.1 "General data protection and privacy".

GLOBAL LEVEL – Laws, Regulations and Norms

Cross-reference: For further information, see also 3.4.1 "General data protection and privacy".

GLOBAL LEVEL – Standards, Frameworks and Guidance

- U.S. Department of Commerce "Safe Harbour Privacy Principles" (21 July 2000).
- OECD Recommendation "Guidelines on the Protection of Privacy and Transborder Flows of Personal Data" (23 September 1980).

- OECD DSTI/ICCP/REG(98)12/FINAL, Working Party on Information Security and Privacy, "Inventory of Instruments and Mechanisms contributing to the Implementation and Enforcement of the OECD Privacy Guidelines on Global Networks" (11 July 1999).
- OECD DSTI/ICCP/REG(98)6/FINAL, Directorate for Science, Technology and Industry – Committee for Information, Computer and Communications Policy, "Practices to implement the OECD Privacy Guidelines on global networks" (23 December 1998).
- International Working Group on Data Protection in Telecommunications "Working Paper on data protection aspects of digital certificates and public-key infrastructures" (28 August 2001).

EUROPEAN LEVEL – Laws, Regulations and Norms

Transfer of air passenger name record data

- Council Decision 2007/551/CFSP/JHA on "the signing, on behalf of the European Union, of an Agreement between the European Union and the United States of America on the processing and transfer of Passenger Name Record (PNR) data by air carriers to the United States Department of Homeland Security (DHS) (2007 PNR Agreement)" (23 July 2007).
- Commission Decision 2006/253/EC on "the adequate protection of personal data contained in the Passenger Name Record of air passengers transferred to the Canada Border Service Agency" (6 September 2005).
- Data Protection Working Party Advisory Opinion 6/2004 on "the implementation of the Commission Decision of 14 May, 2004 and Council decision of 17 May, 2004 on the adequate protection of PNR of air passengers transferred to the United States Bureau of Customs and Border Protection and the Department of Homeland Security" (22 June 2004).
- Council Decision 2004/496/EC on "the conclusion of the Agreement between the EU and the USA on the processing and transfer of PNR data by Air Carriers to the US Department of Homeland Security" (17 May 2004), referring to COM/2004/0190final.
- Commission Decision 2004/535/EC on "the adequate protection of personal data contained in the PNR of air passengers transferred to the United States' Bureau of Customs" (14 May 2004).

EUROPEAN LEVEL – Standards, Frameworks and Guidance

Cross-reference: For further information, see also 3.4.1 "General data protection and privacy".

- Communication COM(2010) 747 "Green Paper –Less bureaucracy for citizens: promoting free movement of public documents and recognition of the effects of civil status records" (December 2010).

- Communication COM(2010) 492 final Communication from the Commisison on "the global approach to transfers of Passenger Name Record (PNR) data to third countries" (21 September 2010).
- Communication COM(2007) 185 "Green Paper: Public Access to Documents held by institutions of the European Community – A review" (18 April 2007).
- Communication COM(98) 585 "Public sector information: a key resource for Europe – Green Paper on public sector information in the information society" (20 January 1999).
- European Commission/ Migration and Home affairs website on Bilateral agreements at http://ec.europa.eu/dgs/home-affairs/what-we-do/policies/police-cooperation/passenger-name-record/bilateral-agreements/index_en.htm.

Card fraud protection databases

- Guidelines by the EU Committee of Data Protection Authorities on "the collection and processing of data on merchants whose contracts to accept payment cards have been terminated" (2 March 2005).

NATIONAL LEVEL (UK) – Laws, Regulations and Norms

Cross-reference: For further information, see also 3.4.1 "General data protection and privacy" and 1.3.1 "Financial Crime: Anti-Money, sanctions Laundering and Terrorism".

- Protection of Freedoms Act 2012 c. 9.
- Coroners and Justice Act 2009 c. 25, Part 8.
- Children Act 2004 c. 31, esp. § 63.
- [Electronic] Communications Act 2003 c. 21.
  Secondary legislation:
  - SI 2011/1208 – The Privacy and Electronic Communications (EC Directive) (Amendment) Regulations 2011.
  - SI 2004/2426 – The Privacy and Electronic Communications (EC Directive) Regulations 2003.
- Freedom of Information Act 2000 c. 36.
- Regulation of Investigatory Powers Act 2000 c. 23 (RIPA)
  - Part 1 (communications, ePrivacy in Article 5.1 [Interception with a warrant])
  - Part 2 (surveillance and covert human intelligence sources)
  - Part 3 (disclosure of information)
- Public Interest Disclosure Act 1998 c. 23.
- Data Protection Act 1998 c. 29, incl. Schedule 1 "The Data Protection Principles".
- Human Rights Act (HRA) 1998 c. 42, Article 8 [Right to respect for private and family life].

- Directive 2003/4/EC on "public access to environmental information and repealing Council Directive 90/313/EEC" (28 January 2003).
  - SI 2002/3391 – The Environmental Information Regulations 2004.
- Council Directive 90/313/EEC on "the freedom of access to information on the environment" (7 June 1990).
  - SI 1998/1447 – Environmental Information (Amendment) Regulations 1998.
  - SI 1992/3240 – Environmental Information Regulations 1992.
- Public Records Act 1958 c. 51.

NATIONAL LEVEL (UK) – Standards, Frameworks and Guidance

UK Information Commissioners Office (ICO)

- ICO (October 2005) "Data Protection Technical Guidance – Subject access requests and legal proceedings".
- ICO "Employment Practices Code" (November 2011).
- ICO "CCTV Code of practice" (January 2008).
- ICO "Guidance for marketers on the Privacy and Electronic Communications (EC Directive) Regulations 2003" (2007).
- ICO "A strategy for data protection regulatory action" (November 2005).
- ICO "Employment Practices Code, Supplementary Guidance" (June 2005).
- ICO "Data Protection Audit Manual" (June 2001).

Ofcom

- Oftel Code of Practice on "Telecommunications Directory Information Covering the Fair Processing of Personal Data" (21 December 1998).

UK-specific Information Management Standards (examples)

- BIP 10008 "Evidential weight and legal admissibility of information stored electronically" (CoLa).
- BIP 0008-1 "Legal Admissibility of stored information".
- BIP 0008-2 "Legal Admissibility of communicated information".
- BIP 0008-3 "Legal Admissibility of electronic identity".

Business associations

- Intellect UK (2010) "Data Protection and Data Security Guidelines for Offshoring and Outsourcing"

3.5 INTELLECTUAL PROPERTY RIGHTS

3.5.1 General

GLOBAL LEVEL – Laws, Regulations and Norms

- Decision of the EEA Joint Committee (No 110/2004) amending Annex XVII (intellectual property) to the EEA Agreement (9 July 2004).
- World Intellectual Property Organization, (WIPO) "Washington Treaty on Intellectual Property in Respect of Integrated Circuits" (Done at Washington, D.C., on May 26, 1989).
- World Intellectual Property Organization, (WIPO) "Convention establishing the World Intellectual Property Organization" (Signed at Stockholm on July 14, 1967 and as amended on September 28, 1979).

GLOBAL LEVEL – Standards, Frameworks and Guidance

- WIPO, Cornell University and INSEAD (2014) "Global Innovation Index 2014 – The Human Factor in Innovation".
- World Intellectual Property Organization (WIPO) (2013) "World Intellectual Property Report 2013: Brands – Reputation and Image in the Global Marketplace".
- WIPO (2012) "The Enforcement of Intellectual Property Rights: A Case Book", 3rd edition.
- WIPO and UN High Commissioner for Human Rights (November 1998) "Intellectual Property and Human Rights".
- WIPO "Intellectual Property and Small and Medium-Sized Enterprises".
- WIPO "Intellectual Property Audit Tool", IP Assets Management Series.
- World Intellectual Property Organization (WIPO) Global Brand Database [Website: http://www.wipo.int/reference/en/branddb/].

EUROPEAN LEVEL – Laws, Regulations and Norms

- Directive 2004/48/EC on "the enforcement of intellectual property rights" (29 April 2004).

EUROPEAN LEVEL – Standards, Frameworks and Guidance

- Communication COM(2012) 372 on "collective management of copyright and related rights and multi-territorial licensing of rights in musical works for online uses in the internal market" (11 July 2012).
- Intellectual Property Rights Helpdesk (2012) "Fact Sheet: How to deal with IP-related issues in transnational negotiations".

- Statement by the Commission 2005/295/EC "concerning Article 2 of Directive 2004/48/EC of the European Parliament and of the Council on "the enforcement of intellectual property rights" (13 April 2005).
- Recommendation 2005/737/EC on "collective cross-border management of copyright and related rights for legitimate online music services" (18 May 2005).
- European Charter for the Development and the Take-up of Film Online, agreed on 23 May 2006 at the Europe Day of the 59th Cannes Film Festival.
- The European Commission's Intellectual Property Rights (IPR) Helpdesk [Website: https://www.iprhelpdesk.eu/].

NATIONAL LEVEL (UK) – Laws, Regulations and Norms

- Intellectual Property Act 2014 c.18.
  Secondary legislation:
  - SI 2014/2330 – The Intellectual Property Act 2014 (Commencement No. 3 and Transitional Provisions) Order 2014.

NATIONAL LEVEL (UK) – Standards, Frameworks and Guidance

- Intellectual Property Office (IPO) – Patents, trade marks, copyright and designs [Website: https://www.gov.uk/government/organisations/intellectual-property-office/].
- Intellectual Property Office (IPO) (21 October 2014) "Intellectual Property for business".
- Intellectual Property Office (IPO) "Patents, Trade Marks, Copyright and Designs"

SUB-NATIONAL LEVEL (UK) – Laws, Regulations and Norms

- Intellectual Property Policy

3.5.2 Copyright

GLOBAL LEVEL – Laws, Regulations and Norms

- World Intellectual Property Organization, (WIPO) "Marrakesh Treaty to Facilitate Access to Published Works for Persons Who Are Blind, Visually Impaired or Otherwise Print Disabled" (adopted by the Diplomatic Conference to Conclude a Treaty to Facilitate Access to Published Works by Visually Impaired Persons and Persons with Print Disabilities in Marrakesh, on June 27, 2013).
- World Intellectual Property Organization, (WIPO) "Beijing Treaty on Audiovisual Performances" (adopted by the Diplomatic Conference on the Protection of Audiovisual Performances in Beijing, on June 24, 2012).

- World Intellectual Property Organization, (WIPO) "WIPO Copyright Treaty" (adopted in Geneva on December 20, 1996).
- World Intellectual Property Organization, (WIPO) "WIPO Performances and Phonograms Treaty" (adopted in Geneva on December 20, 1996).
- World Intellectual Property Organization, (WIPO) "Rome Convention for the Protection of Performers, Producers of Phonograms and Broadcasting Organizations" (Done at Rome on October 26, 1961).
- World Intellectual Property Organization (WIPO) "Berne Convention for the Protection of Literary and Artistic Works" (of September 9, 1886; completed at PARIS on May 4, 1896; revised at BERLIN on November 13, 1908; completed at BERNE on March 20, 1914; revised at ROME on June 2, 1928; at BRUSSELS on June 26, 1948; at STOCKHOLM on July 14, 1967; and at PARIS on July 24, 1971; and amended on September 28, 1979.
    - [UK] International Copyright Act 1886 c.33.
- World Intellectual Property Organization, (WIPO) "Paris Convention for the Protection of Industrial Property" of March 20, 1883; as revised at Brussels on December 14, 1900; at Washington on June 2, 1911; at The Hague on November 6, 1925; at London on June 2, 1934; at Lisbon on October 31, 1958; and at Stockholm on July 14, 1967; and as amended on September 28, 1979.

GLOBAL LEVEL – Standards, Frameworks and Guidance

- World Intellectual Property Organization, (WIPO) "Agreed Statements concerning the WIPO Copyright Treaty" (adopted by the Diplomatic Conference on December 20, 1996).

EUROPEAN LEVEL – Laws, Regulations and Norms

- Directive 2006/115/EC on "rental right and lending right and on certain rights related to copyright in the field of intellectual property" (12 December 2006).
- Directive 2001/84/EC on "the resale right for the benefit of the author of an original work" (27 September 2001).
- Directive 2001/29/EC on "the harmonisation of certain aspects of copyright and related rights in the information society" (22 June 2001).
- Directive 93/83/EEC on "the coordination of certain rules concerning copyright and rights related to copyright applicable to satellite broadcasting and cable retransmission" (27 September 1993).

EUROPEAN LEVEL – Standards, Frameworks and Guidance

- Intellectual Property Rights (IRP) Helpdesk (2012) "Fact Sheet: How to deal with IP-related issues in transnational negotiations".

- European Commission Intellectual Property Rights (IPR) Helpdesk provides guidance, a Helpline and training on European IP [Website: https://www.iprhelpdesk. eu/].
- Communication COM(2008) 466 "Green Paper: Copyright in the Knowledge Economy" (16 July 2008).
- Communication COM(98) 569 "Green Paper: Combating counterfeiting and piracy in the Single Market" (15 October 1998).
- Communication COM(95) 382 "Green Paper: Copyright and Related Rights in the Information Society" (27 July 1995).
- Communication COM(88) 172 "Green Paper on copyright and the challenge of technology – Copyright issues requiring immediate action" (7 June 1988).

NATIONAL LEVEL (UK) – Laws, Regulations and Norms

- Legal Deposit Libraries Act 2003 c. 28.
- Copyright (Visually Impaired Persons) Act 2002 c. 33.
- Copyright, etc. and Trade Marks (Offences and Enforcement) Act 2002 c. 25.
- Copyright, Design and Patents Act 1988 c. 48.
- Patents, Designs, Copyright and Trade Marks (Emergency) Act 1939 c. 107.

NATIONAL LEVEL (UK) – Standards, Frameworks and Guidance

- Intellectual Property Office (IPO) – Patents, trade marks, copyright and designs [Website: https://www.gov.uk/government/organisations/intellectual-property-office/].

3.5.3 Patents

GLOBAL LEVEL – Laws, Regulations and Norms

- World Intellectual Property Organization, (WIPO) "Patent Law Treaty" (adopted at Geneva on June 1, 2000).
- World Intellectual Property Organization, (WIPO) "Vienna Agreement Establishing an International Classification of the Figurative Elements of Marks" (Done at Vienna on June 12, 1973; as amended on October 1, 1985).
- World Intellectual Property Organization, (WIPO) "Strasbourg Agreement Concerning the International Patent Classification" (of March 24, 1971; as amended on September 28, 1979).
- World Intellectual Property Organization, (WIPO) "Patent Cooperation Treaty"(Done at Washington on June 19, 1970; amended on September 28, 1979; modified on February 3, 1984, and on October 3, 2001).

GLOBAL LEVEL – Standards, Frameworks and Guidance

- World Intellectual Property Organization, (WIPO) "Regulations under the Patent Cooperation Treaty" (as in force from July 1, 2014).
- World Intellectual Property Organization, (WIPO) "Administrative Instructions under the Patent Cooperation Treaty" (as in force from September 16, 2012).

EUROPEAN LEVEL – Laws, Regulations and Norms

- Directive 2009/24/EC on "the legal protection of computer programmes" (23 April 2009).

EUROPEAN LEVEL – Standards, Frameworks and Guidance

- Communication COM(97) 314 "Green Paper: Promoting Innovation Through Patents – Green Paper on the Community patent and the patent system in Europe" (24 June 1997).
- The European Commission's Intellectual Property Rights (IPR) Helpdesk [Website: https://www.iprhelpdesk.eu/].

NATIONAL LEVEL (UK) – Laws, Regulations and Norms

- Patents Act 2004 c. 16.
- Copyright, Design and Patents Act 1988 c. 48.
- Patents Act 1977 c. 37.
- Patents, Designs, Copyright and Trade Marks (Emergency) Act 1939 c. 107.

NATIONAL LEVEL (UK) – Standards, Frameworks and Guidance

- Intellectual Property Office (IPO) – Patents, trade marks, copyright and designs [Website: https://www.gov.uk/government/organisations/intellectual-property-office/].

3.5.4 Trade marks and designs

GLOBAL LEVEL – Laws, Regulations and Norms

- World Intellectual Property Organization, (WIPO) "Trademark Law Treaty" (adopted at Geneva on October 27, 1994).
- World Intellectual Property Organization, (WIPO) "Lisbon Agreement for the Protection of Appellations of Origin and their International Registration" (of October 31, 1958; as revised at Stockholm on July 14, 1967; and as amended on September 28, 1979).
- World Intellectual Property Organization, (WIPO) "Locarno Agreement Establishing an International Classification for Industrial Designs" (Signed at Locarno on October 8, 1968; as amended on September 28, 1979).

- World Intellectual Property Organization, (WIPO) "Nice Agreement Concerning the International Classification of Goods and Services for the Purposes of the Registration of Marks" (of June 15, 1957; as revised at Stockholm on July 14, 1967; and at Geneva on May 13, 1977; and amended on September 28, 1979).
- World Intellectual Property Organization, (WIPO) "Hague Agreement Concerning the International Registration of Industrial Designs" (1925).
- World Intellectual Property Organization, (WIPO) "Madrid Agreement Concerning the International Registration of Marks" (of April 14, 1891; as revised at Brussels on December 14, 1900; at Washington on June 2, 1911; at The Hague on November 6, 1925; at London on June 2, 1934; at Nice on June 15, 1957; and at Stockholm on July 14, 1967; and as amended on September 28, 1979).
- United Nations World Trade Organisation (WTO) (2003) "3.5 GATT 1994".
- World Trade Organisation (WTO) "Annex 1C: Agreement on Trade-Related Aspects of Intellectual Property Rights (TRIPs)".

GLOBAL LEVEL – Standards, Frameworks and Guidance

- World Intellectual Property Organization (WIPO) Guidance [Website: http://www.wipo.int/].
- World Intellectual Property Organization, (WIPO) "Protocol Relating to the Madrid Agreement Concerning the International Registration of Marks" (adopted at Madrid on June 27, 1989; as amended on October 3, 2006; and on November 12, 2007).

EUROPEAN LEVEL – Laws, Regulations and Norms

Trade Marks

- Regulation (EC) No 355/2009 "amending Regulation (EC) No 2869/95 on the fees payable to the Office for Harmonization in the Internal Market (Trade Marks and Designs) and Regulation (EC) No 2868/95 implementing Council Regulation (EC) No 40/94 on the Community trade mark" (31 March 2009).
- Council Regulation (EC) No 207/2009 "on the Community trade mark" (26 February 2009).
- Directive 2008/95/EC "to approximate the laws of the Member States relating to trade marks" (22 October 2008).
- Regulation (EC) No 1687/2005 "amending Regulation (EC) No 2869/95 on the fees payable to the Office for Harmonization in the Internal Market (Trade Marks and Designs) with regard to adapting certain fees" (14 October 2005).
- Decision 2003/793/EC "approving the accession of the European Community to the Protocol relating to the Madrid Agreement concerning the international registration of marks" (27 October 2003).

- Regulation (EC) No 2869/95 on the fees payable to the Office for Harmonization in the Internal Market (Trade Marks and Designs) (13 December 1995).
- Regulation (EC) No 40/94 on "the Community trade mark" (20 December 1993).
- Directive 89/104/EEC for "the harmonisation of the substantive law of validity and infringement of trade marks" (21 December 1988).

Designs

- Council Regulation (EC) No. 6/2002 "on Community designs" (12 December 2001).
  Amendments:
  - Regulation No 1891/2006 "amending Regulations (EC) No 6/2002 and (EC) No 40/94 to give effect to the accession of the European Community to the Geneva Act of the Hague Agreement concerning the international registration of industrial designs" (18 December 2006).
- Directive 1998/71/EC on "the legal protection of design" (13 October 1998).

EUROPEAN LEVEL – Standards, Frameworks and Guidance

- The European Commission's Intellectual Property Rights (IPR) Helpdesk [Website: https://www.iprhelpdesk.eu/].
- Office for Harmonisation in the Internal Market (OHIM) – Trade Marks and Design [Website: https://oami.europa.eu/ohimportal/en/trade-marks].

NATIONAL LEVEL (UK) – Laws, Regulations and Norms

- Copyright, etc. and Trade Marks (Offences and Enforcement) Act 2002 c. 25.
- Trade Marks Act 1994 c. 26.
- Copyright, Design and Patents Act 1988 c. 48.
- Patents, Designs, Copyright and Trade Marks (Emergency) Act 1939 c. 107.

NATIONAL LEVEL (UK) – Standards, Frameworks and Guidance

- Intellectual Property Office (IPO) – Patents, trade marks, copyright and designs [Website: https://www.gov.uk/government/organisations/intellectual-property-office/].

- IPO website – Search for a trade mark [Website: https://www.gov.uk/search-for-trademark].

- IPO website – Check the trade marks journal [Website: https://www.gov.uk/check-trade-marks-journal].

- IPO Guidance (21 January 2015) "Trade mark forms and fees".

3.5.5 Legal protection of hardware

EUROPEAN LEVEL – Laws, Regulations and Norms

Note: This is an EU regulatory initiative, hence applicable laws, regulations and norms exist only at European Level and below.

Semiconductors

- Council Decision 96/644/EC on "the extension of the legal protection of topographies of semiconductor products to persons from the Isle of Man" (11 November 1996).
- Council Decision 94/824/EC on "the extension of the legal protection of topographies of semiconductor products to persons from a Member of the World Trade Organization" (22 December 1994).
- Decision 1994/828/EC on "the extension of the legal protection of topographies of semiconductor products to persons from certain territories" (19 December 1994).
- Council Decision 94/700/EC on "the extension of the legal protection of topographies of semiconductor products to persons from Canada" (24 October 1994).
- Council Decision 93/520/EEC "amending Decision 93/16/EEC on the extension of the legal protection of topographies of semiconductor products to persons from the United States of America and certain territories" (27 September 1993).
- Council Decision 93/16/EEC on "the extension of the legal protection of topographies of semiconductor products to persons from the United States of America and certain territories" (21 December 1992).
- Council Directive 87/54/EEC on "the legal protection of topographies of semiconductor products" (16 December 1986).

3.5.6 Legal protection of software

EUROPEAN LEVEL – Laws, Regulations and Norms

Note: This is an EU regulatory initiative, hence applicable laws, regulations and norms exist only at European Level and below.

Databases

- Directive 96/9/EC on "the legal protection of databases" (11 March 1996).

3.5.7 Domain names

GLOBAL LEVEL – Laws, Regulations and Norms

- US Department of Commerce (June 1998) US Policy Statement on "Management of Internet Names and Addresses.

GLOBAL LEVEL – Standards, Frameworks and Guidance

- ICANN Guide "Beginner's Guide to Domain Names".
- ICANN (Internet Corporation for Assigned Names and Numbers) guidance. [Website: https://www.icann.org/]

EUROPEAN LEVEL – Laws, Regulations and Norms

- Regulation (EC) No 874/2004 "laying down public policy rules concerning the implementation and functions of the .eu Top Level Domain and the principles governing registration" (28 April 2004).
- Regulation (EC) No 733/2002 on "the Implementation of the Internet Top Level Domain .eu" (22 April 2002).

EUROPEAN LEVEL – Standards, Frameworks and Guidance

Various technical standards are available from the following organisations:

- ICANN (Internet Corporation for Assigned Names and Numbers) standards. [Website: https://www.icann.org/]

- EURid (European Registry of Internet Domain Names) guidance. [Website: http://www.eurid.eu/]

- Nominet-DRS (Register of all .UK domain names) guidance. [Website: http://www.nominet.org.uk/].

- Verisign Global Registry Services. [Website: http://www.verisigninc.com/].

- Technical guidance by Internet Engineering Task Force (IETF) and the Internet Architecture Board. [Website: https://www.ietf.org/]

3.6 ELECTRONIC COMMERCE

3.6.1 e-Commerce regulation for applications and services

Cross-reference: For further information, see 3.3 "Information Security" and other relevant domains in this Matrix.

GLOBAL LEVEL – Laws, Regulations and Norms

- OECD (16.11.2005) "Task Force on Spam background paper: Anti-Spam Regulation", DSTI/CP/ICCP/SPAM(2005)10/Final.
- OECD (26.05.2005) "Anti-Spam Law Enforcement Report", DSTI/CP/ICCP/SPAM(2004)3/Final.
- OECD (26.05.2005) "SPAM issues in developing countries", DSTI/CP/ICCP/SPAM(2005)6/Final.
- OECD (25.7.2002) "OECD Guidelines for Information Security on Information Systems and Networks: Towards a Culture of Security".

GLOBAL LEVEL – Standards, Frameworks and Guidance

OECD Guidance

- OECD DSTI/CP(2000)7/Final "First Report: Government and Private Sector Initiatives to Promote and Implement the OECD Guidelines for Consumer Protection in the Context of Electronic Commerce" (5 March 2001).
- OECD (December 1999) "OECD Guidelines for Consumer Protection in Electronic Commerce".
- OECD (16.11.2005) "Task Force on Spam background paper: Anti-Spam Regulation", DSTI/CP/ICCP/SPAM(2005)10/Final.
- OECD (25.7.2002) "OECD Guidelines for Information Security on Information Systems and Networks: Towards a Culture of Security".

ISO (electronic Commerce)

- ISO 10008:2013 "Quality management – Customer satisfaction – Guidelines for business-to-consumer electronic commerce transactions".
- ISO/IEC 15944-7:2009 "Information technology – Business Operational View – Part 7: eBusiness vocabulary".

ISO (Software Development/ Software engineering)

- ISO/IEC 90003:2014 "Software engineering – Guidelines for the application of ISO 9001:2008 to computer software".

- ISO/IEC 25001:2014 "Systems and software engineering – Systems and software Quality Requirements and Evaluation (SQuaRE) – Planning and management".
- ISO/IEC/IEEE 26511:2011 "Systems and software engineering – Requirements for managers of user documentation".
- ISO/IEC 26555:2013 "Software and systems engineering – Tools and methods for product line technical management".
- ISO/IEC 26513:2009 "Systems and software engineering – Requirements for testers and reviewers of user documentation".
- ISO/IEC 14764:2006 "Software Engineering – Software Life Cycle Processes – Maintenance".
- ISO/IEC 29155-1:2011 "Systems and software engineering – Information technology project performance benchmarking framework – Part 1: Concepts and definitions".
- ISO/IEC/IEEE 24765:2010 "Systems and software engineering – Vocabulary".
- ISO/TR 10013:2001 "Guidelines for quality management system documentation".
- ISO/IEC 15445:2000 "Information technology – Document description and processing languages – HyperText Markup Language (HTML)".

EUROPEAN LEVEL – Laws, Regulations and Norms

e-Commerce regulation

Electronic Commerce regulation is covered in other thematic sections of this Matrix, including "Consumer protection and employment law" (section 3.2) "Information security" (sections 3.3) and "Data protection and privacy rights" (section 3.4). This section lists only regulations that define the scope of the EU jurisdiction over e-Commerce.

- Directive 2009/110/EC on "the taking up, pursuit and prudential supervision of the business of electronic money institutions amending Directives 2005/60/EC and 2006/48/EC and repealing Directive 2000/46/EC" (*the Electronic Money Directive*) (16 September 2009).
  - [UK] SI 2011/99 – The Electronic Money Regulation 2011.
- Directive 2000/31/EC on "certain legal aspects of information society services, in particular electronic commerce in the Internal Market Directive on electronic commerce" (*Electronic Commerce Directive*) (8 June 2000).
  - [UK] SI 2015/852 — Electronic Commerce Directive (Financial Services and Markets) (Amendment) Order 2015.
  - [UK] SI 2004/3378 – Electronic Commerce Directive (Financial Services and Markets) (Amendment) Regulations 2004.
  - [UK] SI 2002/2013 – Electronic Commerce (EC Directive) Regulations 2002.

EUROPEAN LEVEL – Standards, Frameworks and Guidance

Cross-reference: For further information, see 3.3 "Information Security" and other relevant domains in this Matrix.

EU Regulation is purposely standard-neutral. Standards are developed by standards institutes, industry associations or/and often innovative or market dominant market players.

NATIONAL LEVEL (UK) – Laws, Regulations and Norms

Cross-reference: No Act of Parliament is directly applicable. See applicable UK Statutory Instruments ("[UK] SI") implementing EU law in the corresponding European Level sub-section.

NATIONAL LEVEL (UK) – Standards, Frameworks and Guidance

Cross-reference: For further information, see 3.3 "Information Security" and other relevant domains in this Matrix.

SUB-NATIONAL LEVEL – Laws, Regulations and Norms

Organisations have implemented a number of policies and processes, such as:

- Social media in employment and developments in "bring your own device" (BYOD)
- Internet Usage Policy
- Information Security Policy

SUB-NATIONAL LEVEL – Standards, Frameworks and Guidance

Software standards for documents, images, video and music (examples)

- Documents: MS Windows (.doc), MS-DOS Text (.txt), Adobe Acrobat (.pdf), Word Macintosh (.mcw), Word Perfect (.doc).
- Images: TIFF (.tif), JPEG (.jpg, .jpe), photoshop (.eps), Bitmap (.bmp), Macromedia Flash.
- Video: Real Player, Windows Media Player.
- Music: MP3 (MPEG-1 Audio Layer 3, more commonly referred to as MP3).

Internet Software and Web Technology (examples)

- JavaTM – Java Scripts, Java Enterprise Edition (JEE), Java Management extension (JMX), Joram (Java Open Reliable Asynchronous Messaging), J2EE Development, MIDP 2.0, CLDC (Connected Limited Device Configuration (J2ME)), Ajax (Asynchronous Javascript and XML).

- Google browser technology (incl. Google Apps Premier Edition web-based office suite).
- HTML 4.0 etc, HTTP.
- WAP 2.0 XHTML/HTML multimode browser (Wireless Application Protocol).

Operating Systems/ Server Architecture (examples)

- Microsoft OS: Windows DOS/95/97/98/2000/NT/XP/Vista (previously Longhorn)/ Office 2007, .NET Framework, Internet Explorer, Exchange Server 2007; Microsoft Communication Protocol Program (MCPP).
- Windows Mobil OS (v. 6.0, using MS SharePoint collaboration server).
- UNIX and AIX (advanced Interactive Execution).
- Apple Macintosh.

Database/ Enterprise Resource Planning (ERP) standards (examples)

providing multiple application modules for business in the areas of Financial Management, Logistics, Manufacturing, Human Resources and extended supply chain operations; *e.g.*:

- SAP Enterprise Resource Planning (ERP)/ Service Oriented Architecture (SOA) system: SAP NetWeaver, MySAP ERP, SAP xApp Composite Applications, SAPDB.
- Oracle Database/ Management System/ Financials(Procedural language (SL) and Structured query language (SQL), MySQL, relational databases).
- PeopleSoft
- Hyperion Enterprise.
- JD Edwards.

Electronic Communications – Internet and email (examples)

- Simple Mail Transfer Protocol (SMTP, defined in RFC 821 (STD 10) as amended by RFC 1123 (STD 3) chapter 5).
- Local Area Networks (LANs): IEEE802 LAN standards, Ethernet 802.3, Switched LANs.
- Wide Area Networks (WANs): T1/CEPT-30(E1), Fractional T1, SONET/8DH, Transparent LAN service.

3.6.2 e-Government

eGovernment regulation is covered in other thematic sections of this Matrix, including consumer regulation, information security and VAT taxation.

<u>GLOBAL LEVEL – Laws, Regulations and Norms</u>

Not applicable: This is an EU regulatory initiative, hence applicable laws, regulations and norms exist only at European Level and below.

<u>GLOBAL LEVEL – Standards, Frameworks and Guidance</u>

- United Nations (2014) "E-Government Survey 2014: E-Government for the future we want".
- United Nations Public administration Network (13 January 2010) "A General Framework for E-Government: Definition - Maturity Challenges, Opportunities, and Success".
- United Nations Public administration Network, Department of Economic and Social Affairs (2006-2013) "Knowledge Base of Innovative: Compendium of Innovative E-Government Practice (Volume I - V)".

<u>EUROPEAN LEVEL – Laws, Regulations and Norms</u>

eGovernment legal and regulatory framework

- Directive 2004/18/EC "on the coordination of procedures for the award of public works contracts, public supply contracts and public service contracts" (*European Procurement Directive*) (31 March 2004), Article 33 on eProcurement.
- Directive 2003/98/EC on "the re-use of public data regulating the possibility of usage of public data" (17 November 2003).
- Directive 2000/31/EC "on certain legal aspects of information society services, in particular electronic commerce, in the Internal Market (Directive on electronic commerce)" (*E-Commerce Directive (ECD)*)) (8 June 2003).
- Directive 1999/93/EC on "a Community Framework for Electronic Signatures" (13 December 1999).
- Directive 95/46/EC on "the protection of individuals with regard to the processing of personal data and on the free movement of such data" (*Data Protection Directive*) (24 October 1995).
- Directive 2002/58/EC "concerning the processing of personal data and the protection of privacy in the electronic communications sector (Directive on privacy and electronic communications)" (Privacy and Electronic Communications Directive) (12 July 2002).
- Five directives constituting the new EU regulatory framework for the liberalisation of the European telecommunications markets:
  1. Framework Directive (Directive 2002/21/EC)
  2. Access Directive (Directive 2002/19/EC)
  3. Authorisation Directive (Directive 2002/20/EC)

4. Universal Services Directive (Directive 2002/22/EC)
5. ePrivacy Directive (Directive 2002/58/EC)

EUROPEAN LEVEL – Standards, Frameworks and Guidance

- European Commission Communication COM(2010) 744 final "Towards interoperability for European public services" (16 December 2010).
- European Commission Communication COM(2010) 743 final "The European eGovernment Action Plan 2011-2015 – Harnessing ICT to promote smart, sustainable & innovative Government" 15 December 2010.
- European Commission Communication COM(2006) 173 final "i2010 eGovernment Action Plan – Accelerating eGovernment in Europe for the Benefit of All" (of 25 April 2006).
- Ministerial Declaration on eGovernment approved unanimously in Malmö, Sweden on 18 November 2009 (Malmö Declaration).
- Ministerial Declaration on the European Digital Agenda agreed in Granada, Spain on 19 April 2010 (Granada Declaration).
- Study on "eGovernment and the Reduction of Administrative Burden. A study prepared for the European Commission, DG Communications Networks, Content & Technology" (Contract number: 30-CE-0532668/00-38; SMART number: 2012/0061).
- "A vision for public services", draft version dated 13 June 2013, European Commission, Directorate General for Communications Networks, Content and Technology.
- Consultation on "Directions for ICT-driven public sector innovation at European Union level" (Research and innovation in Horizon 2020).
- Study on Cloud and Service Oriented Architectures for eGovernment. A study prepared for the European Commission, Directorate General for Information, Society and Media (Contract number: DI/06691-00) (5 December 2011).
- European Interoperability Framework (EIF) for Pan-European eGovernment Services, Version 1.0 (2004).

NATIONAL LEVEL (UK) – Laws, Regulations and Norms

eGovernment legal and regulatory framework:

- Freedom of Information Act 2000 c. 36.
- Data Protection Act 1998 c. 29.
- Electronic Communications Act 2000 c. 7.
- SI 2002/2013 – Electronic Commerce (EC Directive) Regulations 2002.
- SI 2002/318 – Electronic Signatures Regulations 2002.
- SI 2005/1515 – The Re-use of public sector information regulations 2005.

NATIONAL LEVEL (UK) – Standards, Frameworks and Guidance

- UK eGovernment portal [Website: http://www.gov.uk].
- Public Services Network (PSN) [Website: http://psngb.org/public-services-network/].
- Portal to public service information from the UK Government [Website: https://www.gov.uk/]

BIBLIOGRAPHY

In addition, the following literature was consulted in compiling this publication and the Regulatory Compliance Matrix:

Anonymous (2001) *Lobbying in the European Union: Explanatory guide and contacts*, 2nd edition (Euroconfidential S.A.: Genval/Belgium).

Anonymous (2000) *The Europa Directory of International Organizations*, 2nd edition (European Publications Ltd.: London).

Astbury Marsden (2014) "Report 013 Compensation – Life Working Series 2014/5".

CEC (2001) *EURO-GUIDE: Yearbook of the institutions of the European Union and the other European organisations*, 18th edition (Editions Delta: Brussels).

EBA/Op/2014/10 (15 October 2014) "Opinion of the European Banking Authority on the application of Directive 2013/36/EU (Capital Requirements Directive) regarding the principles on remuneration policies of credit institutions and investment firms and the use of allowances." (European Banking Authority, London)

English, Stacey; Hammond, Susannah (2014) "The rising costs of non-compliance: From the end of a career to the end of a firm" (Thomson Reuters Accelus).

FCA (July 2014) "Annual Report 2013/14 Appendix 1: Skilled persons' reports" (Financial Conduct Authority, London).

Financial Times (27 October 2013) "Salaries surge for scarce compliance staff".

Financial Times (6 January 2015) "PPI complaints forecast to continue for years".

Financial Stability Board (18 November 2013) "Principles for an effective risk appetite framework".

McKinsey & Company (2002) "Comparative Assessment of the Licensing Regimes for 3G Mobile Communications in the European Union and their Impact on the Mobile Communications Sector", Report for European Commission/DG Information Society and Media, June 2002 (European Commission: Brussels/Luxembourg).

McGregor, Richard; Stanley, Aaron (25 March 2014) "Banks pay out $100bn in US fines" (Financial Times, Washington).

Philip, Alan Butt; Gray, Oliver (1996) *Directory of Pressure Groups in the EU*, 2nd edition (Catermill Publishing: London).

Reinke, Guido (2012) "Industry Governance and Regulatory Compliance: A Theoretical and Practical Guide to European ICT Policy" GOLD RUSH Publishing, London).

Schiavone, Guiseppe (1997) *International Organizations: A Directory*, 4th edition (Macmillian Direct, Basingstoke, UK).

Seingry, Georges-Francais (1998) *Euro-Lobbying: Directory of the pressure groups in the EU, Vol. I: trade and professional associations*, 6th edition (Editions Delta, Brussels).

The Telegraph (22 January 2015) "Banks fined £2.7bn after currency rigging investigation".

Index

Please note that this index lists regulatory categories and key regulations, and not every single entry of the Regulatory Compliance Matrix. Please see the Table of Contents, and review the relevant (regulatory) domains and this index if you are searching for a specific law, regulation, norm, standard, framework or guidance.

Printed in Great Britain
by Amazon

40645532R00169